THE NEW SERFDOM

ANGELA EAGLE AND IMRAN AHMED

THE NEW SERFDOM

THE TRIUMPH OF CONSERVATIVE
IDEAS AND HOW TO DEFEAT THEM

Biteback Publishing

First published in Great Britain in 2018 by
Biteback Publishing Ltd
Westminster Tower
3 Albert Embankment
London SE1 7SP
Copyright © Angela Eagle and Imran Ahmed 2018

ISBN 978-1-78590-313-7

10 9 8 7 6 5 4 3 2 1

A CIP catalogue record for this book is available from the British Library.

Set in Adobe Caslon Pro and Futura

Printed and bound in Great Britain by
CPI Group (UK) Ltd, Croydon CR0 4YY

CONTENTS

Foreword *by Helen Clark*   vii

Acknowledgements   xi

Introduction   xv

Part 1: Two Ideas

Chapter One   Market Fundamentalism   3

Chapter Two   Democratic Socialism   17

Part 2: The State of Our Nation

Chapter Three   Want   25

Chapter Four   Idleness   41

Chapter Five   Ignorance   57

Chapter Six   Squalor   71

Chapter Seven   Disease   89

Chapter Eight   Loneliness   107

Chapter Nine   Mental Health and Illness   121

Chapter Ten   Bigotry and Intolerance   137

Part 3: Democratic Socialism in the Twenty-First Century

Chapter Eleven   The History and Future   161
     of Democratic Socialism

Chapter Twelve   Austerity in the UK   205

Chapter Thirteen   The Second Machine Age   215

Chapter Fourteen   An Ethical Economy   237

Chapter Fifteen   An Active, Empowering State   247
Chapter Sixteen   Taxation in an Ethical Economy   257
Chapter Seventeen   The Labour Market   283
                      and Fairness at Work
Chapter Eighteen   A Modern Industrial Strategy   303
Chapter Nineteen   Enlightenment 2.0   333
Chapter Twenty   A New Collective National Mission   351

Endnotes   361
Index   367

FOREWORD

This book targets the market fundamentalism which has done so much to undermine social solidarity, cohesion and equity wherever it has held sway.

While the authors' focus is on the United Kingdom, 12,000 miles away in New Zealand similar forces were at work for a number of years and led to similar results.

Both our societies have seen rising inequality, and for many a loss of hope that they could have decent work, a place they could call home, safety in their community, and access to the services they need for themselves and their children.

There has to be a better way – and there is. This book explores what that might be. A return to the core values on which democratic socialist parties were founded and finding a better balance between market and society are central to that. We have much to learn from those societies of northern Europe which found and kept that balance, and thereby maintained their economic dynamism and social solidarity.

Now, the new global sustainable development agenda, Agenda 2030, urges all countries to leave no one behind in development. It specifically urges sustained income growth for the bottom 40 per cent of the population at a rate higher than the national average, and the adoption of fiscal, wage and social protection policies which progressively achieve greater equality.

Reaching those targets requires building higher-value

economies which generate decent work for all, and which can fund the levels of social protection that ensure that no one is left behind because of age, illness, disability, size of family or any other factor. Comprehensive social security which encompasses cash transfers, public pensions and affordable housing is required.

In these times of growing inequality which cry out for transformational change, democratic socialist parties must be seen as the standard bearers of inclusive societies which recognise the human dignity of all. Populists of the political right have often proved adept at appealing to those who have every right to be aggrieved about their circumstances. Yet they don't offer solutions which would change individual or national circumstances for the better – indeed, they generally make them worse.

The biblical phrase 'to every thing there is a season' may be relevant here. As market fundamentalism and years of austerity transparently fail to deliver a better life to most, and as populist solutions are exposed as charades, their time of influence will end. Progressive parties of the centre-left must work for that to materialise, and, when it does, be ready to launch and implement policies which will rebuild social cohesion and economic strength. A sense of urgency and national purpose around that needs to be communicated.

In New Zealand, the political wheel has already turned. Now, a broadly based coalition government led by Labour is in power, and is determined to fight poverty, inequality and homelessness. Nine years of underinvestment on all fronts and *laissez-faire* policy settings across sectors have created huge challenges for the new government. But there are solutions.

This book is an appeal to reason – a call for ethical and proactive governance which can facilitate both economic and social revival. All societies which have been traumatised by market fundamentalism can benefit from applying its insights into how to build the more equitable and inclusive communities which enable individuals, families and nations to thrive.

Helen Clark

HELEN CLARK
Prime Minister of New Zealand 1999–2008
Administrator of the United Nations Development
Programme 2009–2017

ACKNOWLEDGEMENTS

ANGELA EAGLE MP

I was born in Bridlington, one of twins, in 1961. It was the dawn of the age of the Beatles. Britain was about to emerge from a long period of Conservative misrule and change was in the air. *That Was The Week That Was* was busy inventing a new form of political satire that rang the final death knell for deference to authority. My parents were both from working-class families in Sheffield, clever, but denied access to post-fifteen education. Instead they were channelled inexorably to the work assigned to 'their sort' – in the factory. Both were adamant that the same fate would not befall their children. Their determination formed the background to my childhood and kindled my motivation to tread where the class system had prevented them from going.

Due to their support and the opportunities created by Labour governments, my twin sister Maria and I both won places to study at Oxford, the first in our family ever to go to university. Both of us joined the Labour Party at sixteen and both became MPs. I won Wallasey from the Tories for Labour in 1992, spending eight years as a government minister, eleven years on Labour's National Executive Committee, which I was proud to chair, and four years as chair of the party's National Policy Forum. I have worked in male-dominated environments ever since I took up chess and attended my first competitive tournament aged eight, only to be told by my terrified opponent (a boy) that girls couldn't play chess. After beating him and winning the title, I realised I was a feminist. I was a fiercely competitive chess player, winning national titles and representing England. Committed to equality, I was in the thick of battles to open up the male-dominated trade union movement and Parliament to women's participation. I championed Labour's move to women-only shortlists and still support positive action to include all under-represented groups. When I came out in 1998, I was the first out lesbian ever to serve as a minister in any government, contributing to a Labour administration which transformed LGBT rights in our country. In coming out, I could not have wished for more support from those around me: from the Prime Minister, Tony Blair; from John Prescott, my then boss; from my local party; and, most important of all, from my constituents in Wallasey.

Throughout my forty-one years of active Labour membership I have always believed that the values of democratic socialism are the best foundation upon which to build the society we need, which is what this book is about. Writing comes after conversation and contemplation. I would like to thank all those whose observations have helped shape it, especially my colleagues in the PLP, the party and the trade unions. My loyal office staff, Bridget Frear, Matt Daniel and Tim Gallagher. My friends, especially Lois Quam and Anni Hogan, whose encouragement kept me going. And especially to my family: my mum and dad for giving me my values, my brother Andrew and sister Maria and, last but never least, my erudite and wonderful partner Maria Exall.

In memory of my late mother Shirley, who I think about every day.

Angela Eagle MP
March 2018

IMRAN AHMED

I was born in 1978, the year before Margaret Thatcher won her first election as Conservative Party leader. My family were poor and had to make tough decisions about how to survive. I was lucky to have six siblings, so life never lacked love or fun. The welfare system kept us alive. As a sickly child, the NHS saved my life several times. I remember the clinicians and my fellow patients on the children's wards with great clarity and affection.

Neither of my parents had the privilege of a full education, but I received one, paid for by the state. My grandfather, a first-generation immigrant, would never fail to remind me that this was thanks to taxpayers from all over the country. It is humbling to think that my fellow citizens, many on modest incomes, collectively contributed to give me such opportunities in life.

Some years later, I became the first in my family to go to university. Again, this was thanks to taxpayers. I received a grant and a student loan. And when I went to work I was protected against discrimination by Labour's equality laws.

These drivers of opportunity in my life were products of Labour governments. That is why I owe my eternal thanks to the Labour Party I went on to serve and my colleagues there, past and present, who turned our ambitious dreams into reality.

I have served the Labour Party and its MPs through five elections and referendums, under three leaders, in constituencies around the country as well as in Parliament. As is true for all the hard-working parliamentarians and councillors that inspired and encouraged me, I believe there is no higher calling than to seek to improve our nation for the good of all. I am also convinced that the route to betterment comes from getting your hands dirty and mucking in. A lot of people think politics is about talking. It's not. It's about action.

So, this book is dedicated to the people who gave me the chance to act and who supported me in those endeavours.

To those who let me serve: Andy Slaughter, Willy Bach, Hilary Benn, Alan Johnson and Angela Eagle.

To my family: my parents, grandparents and siblings, Riaz, Fayaz, Aisha, Salma and Farheen.

And to the friends who encouraged me: Tom, Joanne, Felicity, Kate, John, Blakey, Mo and, most of all, Gabrielle.

Imran Ahmed
March 2018

INTRODUCTION

People are angry. Britain is divided and resentful. As our society has become more unequal and insecure, our politics has polarised between intractable and potentially irreconcilable world views. Understanding and empathy between people is losing ground to blame and resentment, especially against 'outsiders'. Fear and insecurity have replaced solidarity and sympathy. And, feeding off this insecurity, the extreme right is on the march once more. Trump, Brexit and the growing success of populist parties across Europe are alarming symptoms of a far greater malaise that must not be ignored. The warning lights are flashing red.

The truth is, people are right to be angry. Over decades, our society has been slowly and inexorably changed by a set of forces that have acted unseen against the public interest. Selfish values have been prioritised over the desire for mutualism and equality, and the greed and self-interest of the few have been prioritised above the prosperity and welfare of the many. The promise that the further enrichment of the already-wealthy represented an advancement of the interests of all, that wealth and prosperity would 'trickle down', was an empty one. But now many of the victims of this con are awake to it. If you think our societies and economies aren't working the way they are meant to, you're right. We must act. Cherished values of democracy and liberty are at stake if we do not change the way our country works.

Ideas affect politics. Ideologies attract followers and get translated into reality, but not always in plain sight. In this book we consider the effect of two such ideologies. The first is called market fundamentalism, and it has been dominant for the past forty years. It is the belief that all value can be expressed by a price, and market mechanisms are the best way to distribute everything; that human agency outside of market choice is inferior to the price signals that make markets work. And so only by making markets 'free' can we prosper. In contrast, democratic socialism – which outside of that brief window between 1997 and 2010 has been on the back foot in the past four decades – is the belief that we human beings are motivated by collective as well as individual values, and that we prosper most by living in a fairer and more equal society that incorporates human needs not expressed by a price mechanism. This protects our true liberty and creates opportunities for all to thrive through compassion, care and co-operation.

So how did market fundamentalism become the dominant idea in the political arena? It all started with a man named Friedrich Hayek, a prophet extolling the divine properties of free markets. Hayek was an Austrian economist and political theorist who, amidst the smoke and chaos of the Second World War, wrote a book that provocatively sought to discredit socialism as akin to Nazism. He ludicrously claimed that any collective instinct, however small, would extinguish his very narrow definition of 'freedom' and therefore constituted the 'road to serfdom'. Hayek was ridiculed for these extreme views, especially by the then Labour leader, Clement Attlee. In Britain, during the Second World War, the benefits of democracy, state planning, national solidarity and international co-operation were there for all to see. It is ironic that amidst one of the greatest triumphs of central planning, the seeds of its subsequent destruction had been planted by Friedrich Hayek.

Forty years ago, Margaret Thatcher came to power in Great Britain and set about ripping up the economic and political consensus that had prevailed since the Second World War. That post-war consensus was a mixed economy, combining a vibrant, regulated and managed private sector and a large and redistributionist public sector that sought to ensure people had a set of protections if they experienced tough times in their lives – for their health, housing and social security. Mrs Thatcher looked at the world through Hayek-tinted spectacles. She expected people to look after themselves and she wanted the government out of the market. The Conservative government she ushered in ruled Britain from 1979 until the Labour Party, led by Tony Blair, decisively defeated it eighteen long years later in 1997. Mrs Thatcher was a devoted disciple of Hayek, like her close friend, American President Ronald Reagan. Mrs Thatcher and President Reagan relentlessly promoted Hayek's ideas and legislated to change our societies to work in accordance with his reactionary and extreme beliefs – that people should look after themselves and the government should not interfere with 'free' markets. Their successors – people like Donald Trump and David Cameron – have gone further still.

At the heart of Hayek's philosophy were three big lies: that the free market is the only way to make any decision while preserving freedom; that only when human beings act out of selfishness and greed will the best solution be found; and that inequality drives personal achievement and is therefore a good thing. Despite their dubious morality and their downright untruthfulness, belief in these three falsehoods still forms the background to much decision-making today.

The first lie is that the 'free market' is the best proxy for all decisions and so human agency is not valid outside of the price signal and the market mechanisms which price animates. In short, the belief is that the market is correct, infallible and superior to any other choice mechanism.

This forty-year-long uncritical veneration of markets, of the private enterprise that competes via markets, and the actors within those markets, has led to the infiltration of marketisation into all sorts of spheres of public life and even into our language. Universities 'produce' graduates rather than educate and enrich the intellectual and emotional capacities of their students. Civil servants, working in government departments re-defined as 'service providers', are urged to focus on efficiency, rather than other desirable social outcomes such as improving equity or empowering citizens. As individuals, we are encouraged to package ourselves as products – our CVs become part of our personal brand; our relationships with other people recast as strategic means of self-progression. We are in a 'global race' with other countries, as George Osborne put it, in which each person is forever locked in competition with their neighbour. We are meant to celebrate the 'self-made' person; forgetting that there are myriad individuals and institutions that, without exception, have contributed to that 'individual' success. Are we meant to ignore the innumerable people that contribute to each of our lives? It is a depressingly narrow and desiccated view of humanity and one that has contributed to the steady erosion of social solidarity. It has obliterated our community life and left many alone and friendless. Which was, of course, the point. Because without solidarity and the democratic socialism that springs from it, the strongest take the most and the weakest are left behind, blaming themselves for their inadequacies as social mobility stalls. How very convenient for those who are already privileged. The failure of the system is cruelly recast as an individual's own personal failing. The victims are blamed for their plight while the system itself goes unscrutinised. This also leads to the erosion of trust in institutions and expertise because they cease to deliver for the majority.

Even a moment's deliberation proves that the price mechanism should not be regarded as sacrosanct. It gives a person without the means to 'buy' no say or influence on the outcome. Thus, it disenfranchises the already vulnerable and supports the already privileged. It denies the possibility of any other valid decision-making mechanism, such as voting, having an influence greater than that delivered by the 'free market', rendering democracy a sideshow. It begins with an astonishing but convenient presumption that the market is always, and everywhere, 'perfect'. The thing is, markets aren't perfect. Just look at the evidence. From the Dutch tulip mania in the seventeenth century, to the madness of the dot-com boom at the turn of the twenty-first, to the most recent enormous global failure with sub-prime loans in the unregulated American housing market and the collateralised debt obligations sold worldwide, it is not possible to argue that markets are even rational. Markets are amoral, often illogical, prone to herd behaviour and, as we can now see, left free and unsupervised, have driven rapaciousness and inequality in the industrialised world to extreme levels.

The second lie is that markets perform best when those who operate within them display 'self-regarding materialism', which is a posh way of saying 'greed'. Turning conventional ethics on its head, what was once a deadly sin has been transformed into a virtue – one that will not only be rewarded, but is conveniently proclaimed to be essential to the proper functioning of the free-market system.

In the past forty years, a toxic culture of venerating those who have succeeded in becoming fabulously wealthy has emerged in our societies. The notion that CEOs are uniquely responsible for the success of their companies and therefore need to be obscenely compensated has led to huge and growing inequalities of income and wealth between the top 1 per cent and the rest. According to research by the Chartered Institute of Personnel and Development, the CEOs of the biggest companies in our economy – the FTSE 100 – now take home in one year what an average UK full-time worker would take 160 years to earn. We know, however, that the success of any company depends on every part of the organisation, not just those at the very top. Like a Swiss watch, a company comprises myriad components that all need to work well and in sync for it to succeed. Comprehensive surveys show time and again that performance-related pay is a flawed concept, because pay is not a motivator. Research shows that we do better when we co-operate and are unified around shared goals rather than motivated by self-interest, as the manager of any sporting team would tell you. None of us could possibly get by on our own; we are better when we are together. Pay and reward should reflect that basic human truth much more than it now does.

The third big lie is that inequality incentivises those with less to work harder, and is therefore a good thing. It follows from this that 'progressive' taxation and redistribution – taking from those who have more and redistributing to those who have less – reduces incentives for the less well-off to work harder, leading to economically suboptimal outcomes.

Taken together, these three lies have seen the wealth and opportunity afforded to the 1 per cent race ahead of the 99 per cent. With the slowing of social mobility in Britain, how much we have at the start of our lives, not how hard we work or how well we lead our lives, is today the best predictor of what we end our lives with. This is a substantial part of the reason for the emergence of nihilistic, 'tear-down-the-system' populisms, from Trump to the animating forces behind Brexit.

As democratic socialists, we are not arguing that everyone should receive exactly the same outputs for their work. Most British people believe some range of unequal income is acceptable, but it is clear that the range between the top 1 per cent and the rest is currently far too wide – and it is getting worse. The majority accept that doctors should earn a good wage, for example. But the majority are also likely to be angered at the stupendous rewards given to investment bankers responsible for tanking our economy or the CEOs of companies that aggressively avoid tax and under-pay their workers. According to study after study, it is the *unfairness* of our system that rankles most with people. It damages social solidarity and our mental health and actually holds our economy back.

It's time for us to ditch these three big lies and the market fundamentalist philosophy that goes with them.

In the first part of this book, we will begin by looking more closely at democratic socialism and market fundamentalism, the two most influential political philosophies to have shaped our country in the past seventy years.

In the second part of the book, we will assess where we are now. Before Clement Attlee's transformative post-war Labour government and before the 1997 New Labour government, two reports assessed the state of our nation and laid the foundation for major reform. The first, published at the height of the war in 1942, was the Beveridge Report, which proposed major changes to the system of social insurance in Britain. The second, published in 1994, the Report of the Commission on Social Justice, formed the basis of much of the social policy pursued by Tony Blair's New Labour government.

The Beveridge Report aimed to tackle five 'Giant Evils' of society: want; idleness; ignorance; squalor and disease. The Commission on Social Justice added racial discrimination as a sixth. Twenty-four years later, we have extended that sixth 'Evil' to all forms of bigotry and intolerance. We have also added two new 'Evils', which have grown in seriousness in our era of Hayek-induced hyper-individualism: loneliness and mental illness.

After assessing the current state of our nation, the third part of this book looks at what a Labour government, pursuing a reinvigorated democratic socialism, might do to remake our economy and our society in a complex and rapidly changing world. This begins with examining how a new ethical approach to our economy and our society would improve outcomes. It considers the case for creating an empowering state which actively intervenes to improve on market-based outcomes and ensure greater opportunities for all. We observe that the most pressing concerns facing us today, from the threat of global climate change to trading in a post-Brexit future, require not isolationism and selfishness, but engagement and co-operation with the wider world. We believe that we will do better if we create a fairer and more equal society where we maximise the chances for all to be included and play their part. And we observe that these values are central to the beliefs of democratic socialists the world over.

Before we begin, it's perhaps worth explaining why we felt we should write this book together. Like so many Labour friendships, ours started as two colleagues spending time together and discovering their similarities. We accept this may sound quite odd, because on the face of it we may not seem to have that much in common. Imran is six foot tall, Lancashire-born and of Muslim Pashtun origin; Angela is five foot three, a Yorkshire-woman and adopted Merseysider who made history as the first out lesbian government minister. But in spite of this, we soon discovered incredible similarities in the roots of our political convictions. One morning we were talking and discovered that when we were kids, both of us would regularly be woken in the middle of the night by the sound of our seamstress mums working on their sewing machines to keep the food on the table. Our common northern working-class roots and sensibilities made this book remarkably smooth to write. We agree on the analysis of what is going wrong in Britain, in particular the loss of social mobility and the terrible impact that has had on working-class people. We were both aspiring working-class kids given great opportunities to fulfil our potential and we fiercely believe everyone should get the same. Angela's experience over twenty-six years representing her constituency of Wallasey, on the Wirral, and dealing with thousands of people's problems during that time in her MP's surgery, has given her countless real-life cases to draw upon in forming that analysis. We have no compunction in recommending a fundamental shake-up of our economy; one that will finally rebalance it after four decades of a politics that has been toxic to working people, who are expected to work harder for less and are more stressed, atomised and lonely than ever before. We believe there is another way and we both feel that it is the Labour Party, the greatest, most important force for liberation and social progress in British history, which is best placed to accomplish this historic shift. This book, we hope, will be part of our ongoing service to that great endeavour. We hope that you will agree with us and join the fight to create a better society.

PART 1

TWO IDEAS

CHAPTER ONE

MARKET FUNDAMENTALISM

Vienna in the early years of the twentieth century was a seething ferment of art, science, modernism, political thought and debate. The perfect milieu in which to foment radical political thought, a number of people who would go on to shape the politics of the twentieth century resided there around this time, including the Communists Joseph Stalin and Leon Trotsky; a young painter named Adolf Hitler, who was inspired by the populist, anti-Semitic politics of the city's mayor, Karl Lueger; and the father of political Zionism, Theodor Herzl. Living in Vienna too was another, perhaps less-known figure: Friedrich August von Hayek. Born in Vienna, the capital of the mighty Austro-Hungarian Empire, in 1899, Hayek's father, August, was a medical doctor and lecturer, while his mother, Felicitas, was an aristocrat and heiress, related to the philosopher Ludwig Wittgenstein. There could have been no better place than Vienna for young Friedrich to hone his analytical, economic and philosophical skills. Hayek was bright and took full advantage of opportunities to gain knowledge and develop his opinions. However, the First World War interrupted his studies, and he served in an artillery regiment in the Austro-Hungarian Army. That brutal, murderous war left an indelible mark on him. What on earth could have caused such madness, he asked himself, and how could we stop it from happening again?

Although Hayek had initially flirted with democratic

socialism, he eventually settled on economic liberalism as the answer to his 'burning question' of how to build a more just society. Individual liberty, he believed, was key to peace. Hayek's career as an economist was glittering. He joined the London School of Economics in 1931, where he developed important and influential economic theories, and some decades later he would win a Nobel Prize for Economics.

In 1939, however, war broke out once again in Europe, this time a result of the totalitarian fascism and expansionism of Adolf Hitler. Between 1940 and 1943, Hayek wrote *The Road to Serfdom*, his most politically influential work and the purest statement of his political and economic philosophy. It was a deeply personal work – indeed, it was one of his least technical and most polemical texts – written in defence of capitalism at a time when many believed that fascism was in fact a capitalist reaction to socialism.

In the book, Hayek provocatively argued that socialism was the root cause of national socialism. He warned that a centralising state which sought the exclusive right to plan economic and social activity would require ever more intrusion and power. He warned that such a state would need to centrally aggregate a lot of information that is dispersed among the populace and private enterprise. In its zeal to make better-informed decisions, that information would be interpreted by an ever more powerful cadre of civil servants. And then, if the state had the courage of its convictions, he argued, it would demand the right to decide on how individuals conduct their lives to such an extent that it would squash their right to make decisions for themselves. In so doing, it would restrict their individual freedom, eventually making the citizen a mere serf: a cog in a vast machine that would continue to demand more control and greater servility and punish deviation from what has been planned from the centre. He claimed that the Nazis had succeeded in suborning the German people to their tyrannical programme because socialism had already done so much of the work in de-individualising citizens and persuading them to submit to state direction and authority in the name of their own security and welfare. Similar dubious arguments can still be heard today on the Conservative back benches.

The Road to Serfdom was released to considerable controversy. George Orwell, a great opponent of tyranny, wrote in one of the more balanced reviews of Hayek's book:

> In the negative part of Professor Hayek's thesis there is a great deal of truth. It cannot be said too often – at any rate, it is not being said nearly often enough – that collectivism is not inherently democratic, but, on the contrary, gives to a tyrannical minority such powers as the Spanish Inquisitors never dreamed of.

He also stated, however, that

> [Hayek] does not see, or will not admit, that a return to 'free' competition means for the great mass of people a tyranny probably worse, because more irresponsible, than that of the State. The trouble with competitions is that somebody wins them. Professor Hayek denies that free capitalism necessarily leads to monopoly, but in practice that is where it has led, and since the vast majority of people would far rather have State regimentation than slumps and unemployment, the drift towards collectivism is bound to continue if popular opinion has any say in the matter.

Other economists and philosophers were much less balanced in their criticism. This should have come as no surprise. Hayek's thesis was deliberately provocative at a time when millions had met their deaths in a war against a fascist regime that represented the ultimate evil. Ascribing this evil's success to the desire by socialists to make their societies fairer, more equal and more efficient was – in modern parlance – an epic troll.

The Road to Serfdom received an approving reception from many Conservative and Liberal politicians to an extent that is forgotten now. In particular, it had both an immediate and enduring impact in the United Kingdom on the Conservative Party. Shortly after the book's publication, then Tory Party Chairman Ralph Assheton was delighted to discover Hayek's arguments. In 1942, Assheton had chaired the Conservative Party policy committee dealing with the Beveridge Report. Formed in response to Conservative concern at the widespread popular enthusiasm for the report, the committee concluded that universal state entitlements funded by increases in taxes would discourage hard work and act as a 'sofa rather than a springboard'. His argument is still familiar to us today as one used by Conservative politicians and pundits when talking about social security – that the poor will only be incentivised to work if they experience hardship rather than kindness. They argue that if worklessness is rewarded by 'handouts', that punishes the economically successful and undermines the forces that drive growth, productivity and economic success.

In Hayek, Assheton found a corpus of useful intellectual arguments, framed against the resonant and contemporary backdrop of the war, to justify the Conservatives' instinctive, class-driven rejection of tax-funded state intervention and redistribution. He relayed its central arguments to the Prime Minister, Winston Churchill, and advised election agents and candidates to read the book. Assheton was so taken with it that he wanted an abridged version to be used as campaign literature. He went on to use some of Hayek's core arguments in writing the initial outline for Churchill's infamous 1945 'Gestapo' speech, in which Churchill argued that a 'socialist government' run by Labour would need 'some form of Gestapo' to empower the 'supreme party' and its 'vast bureaucracies'. The conflation of a larger state with a more dangerous and brutal one was a typically Hayekian flourish.

Clement Attlee, then Labour Party leader, ruthlessly mocked Churchill's speech for its hyperbole. Identifying Hayek as the source of Churchill's arguments, he noted that the freedoms Churchill wanted to protect included employers' rights to work children for sixteen hours a day, underpay women and neglect health and safety. It was in fact 'freedom for the rich and slavery for the poor', Attlee said, going on to argue:

> Make no mistake, it has only been through the power of the state, given to it by Parliament, that the general public has been protected against the greed of ruthless profit-makers and property-owners … [The Conservative Party] represents today, as in the past, the forces of property and privilege. The Labour Party is, in fact, the one party which most nearly reflects in its representation and composition all the main streams which flow into the great river of our national life.

These arguments sound very familiar to us today. They represent the two most compelling ideological arguments of the twentieth century and, indeed, this century too. On one side, the desire of capital – to free itself to profit and keep those profits. On the other, the desire of the majority of workers – to enjoy lives that allow them their rightful share of health, opportunity and prosperity. This war between labour and capital continues to rage today, even if it is not played out in the more overt, class-based language that was once used.

In 1945, millions of returning soldiers demanded better lives after having successfully defended their homeland and the world itself from fascism. The working classes, the middle classes and the Labour Party were united in their desire for change. They were determined to avoid the mistakes made after the end of the First World War, when Lloyd George's 'land fit for heroes' turned into poverty, mass hardship and slump in the iron grip of the prevailing *laissez-faire*, pre-Keynesian economic orthodoxy.

The Conservatives made a terrible mistake in likening Labour's plans for a National Health Service and for social security based on national insurance for those returning war heroes to the need for a British Gestapo. It is a classic example of how engaging in hyperbole can overwhelm the point you're trying to make. The Conservatives would go on to more successfully and more subtly use these Hayekian themes in the 1950 and 1951 general elections, which they ran under the slogan 'Set the People Free'. Accepting that the NHS and welfare state were extremely popular and would be difficult to reverse, Churchill argued in 1948 in a well-received speech that 'the socialist planners have miscalculated and mismanaged everything they have touched. They have tried to substitute government control and direction for individual enterprise and skill. By their restrictions they make scarcity; and when scarcity comes they call for more restrictions to cure it.'

In the 1950 election, Labour managed to hold on to a slim majority. By this time, most of Labour's towering figures had been in government throughout the war years and were increasingly ill and exhausted from the effort of winning the war and building the peace. In 1951, just six years after winning their first election and bringing about the NHS and welfare state, the Labour Party would cede the next thirteen years to Conservative rule.

Over the following decades, the battle continued to rage but it was not until thirty years later that Hayek's and capital's most ideologically convinced proponent appeared, in the form of Margaret Thatcher. She had read Hayek at Oxford University, aged eighteen. It would have a profound effect on her beliefs – although, she claimed, not immediately. She was not particularly political at Oxford, despite being a member of the University's Conservative Association. In fact, at university, Mrs Thatcher, an occasional Methodist lay preacher, was more religious than political. By the time Margaret Hilda Roberts had met and married her husband, Denis Thatcher, however, going on to become the MP for Finchley, and then – in February 1975 – Conservative Party leader, no one would doubt the importance of Hayek and his brand of anti-socialism to her politics. Thatcher was much taken by Hayek's arguments that conservatives cannot compromise with any brand or variant of socialism because the core logic of all socialisms inexorably lead to totalitarian outcomes. She scorned her colleagues who had some sympathy with social democratic politics or outcomes, labelling such compromisers 'wets' who needed to be belittled and defeated.

A moment that perhaps sums up Thatcher's relationship to Hayek's philosophies came on a visit to the Conservative Research Department in the summer of 1975. Listening to an official explain why the Tories should take the 'middle path' in their policy platform, so as to avoid the extremes of left and right, Thatcher snapped and thwacked one of Hayek's books onto the table. 'This is what we believe,' she imperiously announced. She would go on to repeatedly reference Hayek in public, and even corresponded with him while in government. One of her most important economic advisers, Keith Joseph, was as taken by Hayek as was Mrs Thatcher, and corresponded with him frequently. Joseph may well have been preferred to Mrs Thatcher as the right-wing standard-bearer in the Conservative leadership contest had he not been forced to resign in disgrace a few months earlier after suggesting poor people should stop having children, to keep their DNA out of the British gene pool and thus restore 'the balance of the human stock'. Thus was Mrs Thatcher catapulted into pole position as the next best leadership choice for the right-wing of the Conservative Party.

Mrs Thatcher's own contribution to making real Hayek's philosophy came when she reframed the argument against paying for better services through higher taxes by making it all about balancing the budget, using the idiom of household budgets.

In 1976, three years before she became Prime Minister, she argued:

> I think you're tackling public expenditure from the wrong end, if I might say so. Why don't you look at it as any housewife has to look at it? She has to look at her expenditure every week or every month, according to what she can afford to spend, and if she overspends one week or month, she's got to economise the next.
>
> Now governments really ought to look at it from the viewpoint of 'What can we afford to spend?' They've already put up taxes, and yet the taxes they collect are not enough for the tremendous amount they're spending. They're having to borrow to a greater extent than ever before, and future generations will have to repay.

Now, this was, objectively speaking, ingenious political rhetoric, and it worked.

Misleading? Absolutely. It is preposterous to compare household finances to a country's economy. Not least because by borrowing money to invest wisely in skills and capacity in the economy the state can put rocket-boosters on growth, covering the cost of borrowing and then some.

Cynical? Again, absolutely. Mrs Thatcher knew that her words were misleading. She understood the above argument. But she also understood how well the false analogy to balancing a household budget communicated an idea to voters.

Effective? Unfortunately, for the great mass of citizens who suffered under Thatcher's rule, absolutely. So effective, indeed, that a reinterpreted version was used to great effect by David Cameron and George Osborne in 2010. Cameron and Osborne knew they couldn't use her precise example because neither of them were housewives and because no one believed that either of them had to worry too much about balancing their own household budgets. Instead, they repeatedly told Britain that we couldn't keep spending on public services on the nation's credit card, an argument that had painful emotional resonance for those who recognised the pleasure of splurging on something expensive, and the corollary pain of having to tighten one's belt over following months.

Hayek was still an active participant in academia and politics as Thatcher came to power, and he did not refrain from excitedly writing to her key advisers and sending letters to newspapers, urging her to bring his ideas to fruition. Every philosopher needs political advocates to turn their ideas into policy and statute. And when Mrs Thatcher faced opposition to her philosophy, to her uncompromising opposition to socialism and in particular to the trade unions movement within her own party, Hayek supported her enthusiastically. In 1978, Hayek wrote in a letter to *The Times*:

The majority of the prospective Tory candidates are naturally and understandably primarily concerned about winning a seat in the coming election and feel that their chances may be reduced by what I have seen described as Mrs. Thatcher's 'extremism' ... A statesman and patriot should prefer being defeated in the election to being charged with a task in which he has not the support of the public ... I still hope that the British people will honour Mrs. Thatcher for putting the long run interests of the nation above the short run prospects of her party.

The country will not be saved by the Tories being elected, but it may be saved by what they can do, but not a party dependent on the trade union leaders who owe their power to the very privileges which the law has granted them but which must be revoked.

Mrs Thatcher's all-out war on the trade union movement and workers would delight Hayek, and over the years of her premiership the closeness and intensity of their relationship and their mutual admiration and affection deepened. In 1984, he sent her a gift of a leather-bound edition of *The Road to Serfdom*. She wrote back, in a personal note in her own handwriting: 'It means so much to me. I remember well the days when I first read it.'

By the time she left Downing Street in tears, felled by a revolt in her own party, she had fundamentally recast the relationship between capital and labour, giving the whip hand to capital. So, Hayek's legacy was confirmed. The philosopher had found the politician that could translate his beliefs into economic and social reality. It is not unfair or hyperbolic to identify Hayek as the intellectual father of much of the suffering that the poor and working people have endured since under successive Conservative administrations.

We have tried to present Hayek's ideas fairly but we do not agree with them. We believe Hayekian conservatism is short-sighted, selfish and just plain wrong. *The Road to Serfdom* was a classic straw man argument, in which Hayek built up and then smashed down a caricature of socialism. He then claimed democratic socialism – a different type of political philosophy to revolutionary socialism or communism – was identical for the purposes of his argument. In pursuit of an extreme and distorted version of 'freedom' Hayek sacrifices any form of co-operation or collectivism. The effect of his philosophy on our politics and on our society has been devastating. His ideas have led Britain into a cul-de-sac of inequality, poverty and a lack of opportunity that resemble the very serfdom that Hayek claimed socialism would bring about. Indeed, the weakening of the bargaining power of trade unions and the 'freedoms' granted to capitalists to take advantage of workers were given dubious moral force by Hayek's notion that socialism was not just wrong but evil. This corrosive idea has led directly to the low-paid exploitive segments of the labour market we examine below.

We hold these opinions so forcefully because we are politicians, not philosophers. Politics is the realm of *praxis* – that is, practical action. Our first instinct is to look not at ideology but at material reality; the sphere in which we seek to exert influence. That is why we state with confidence that the practical effects of Hayekism have been a disaster for many. Indeed, we are not the only ones to say so. In recent months, even Conservatives, from Theresa May's first speech as Prime Minister opining about the 'just about managing', to Ruth Davidson in the wake of the disastrous 2017 general election, to journalists such as Matthew D'Ancona and Matthew Parris, have criticised how opportunity and outcomes have been devastated by decades of unbridled market fundamentalism. The plain truth of this is obvious to those who look.

Hayek was not just an economist but sought political ends. He delighted in being the philosopher king behind Mrs Thatcher's throne. He and his great opponent, Marx, are examples of philosophers whose aims and legacies involved huge political change. Ideas always affect politics, since they can fundamentally change how we perceive and interpret reality. For example, if we believed regulation was stifling economic productivity, we would seek to avoid it. Conversely, if we see regulation as an economic good because it ensures workers remain healthy, happy, effective and productive, and that products have minimum standards of safety so that consumers can have confidence when purchasing, we would welcome it. Ideas become the lens through which we interpret the world around us and seek to act. Hayek's philosophies, advocated by the Conservatives over decades, helped to shape Britain's understanding of socialism, of trade unions, of taxation and of freedom. This contributed fundamentally to Margaret Thatcher's ability to win, for the first time in over a century and a half, three consecutive Conservative terms in office. Her brand of conservatism wasn't somehow innately popular to British citizens; it required decades of ideological argument and conditioning for her policies to be interpreted as a good thing by people for whom, quite often, they would be highly detrimental.

Fundamentally, Hayekian conservatism is populist at its heart. Its most compelling promise is that anyone can become very rich and then retain that wealth without state interference or the obligation to support others. Wealth is deeply attractive. The wealthy can clad themselves in fine clothes, live in luxurious surroundings, spend more leisure time and own goods that others envy. Today, gossip magazines, Instagram and the right-hand bar on the *Daily Mail*'s website feature photographs of an endless array of ingénues wearing designer clothing, driving in sports cars from enormous gilt-clad mansions to private clubs populated solely by other expensively dressed people. The message is simple: all you have to do to have the same things is to win the lottery of life and join the wealthy elite. Through a multiplicity of deceits, such propaganda tells people that all it takes is hard work and playing by the rules. This, we know, is profoundly untrue. The rules were always there to protect capital, not to grant the dispossessed access to its privileged environs. But this shimmering dream is even more untrue now in the Britain shaped by Hayek's market fundamentalism and delivered by Mrs Thatcher's ideological devotion. The possibilities of becoming rich have narrowed, not widened.

In Part 2, as we look at the state of our nation, we will identify the changes Hayek's ideas have wrought upon Britain. We will identify the victims of Hayekian/Thatcherite politics – the socially isolated and marginalised, those starved of opportunities, that feel 'left behind' by the other Britain that is wealthier, healthier and more secure. We will argue that it is this philosophy that has caused the growing inequality and insecurity of so many. And we will show that only an empowering state implementing democratic socialist policies can rebalance the woefully lopsided relations between labour and capital and restore a healthier and happier society.

It is social democracy that created the sustainable, effective, civilised British institutions of the NHS and welfare state which have saved and enhanced millions of British lives. It is social democratic policies on education – from free pre-infant intellectual enrichment classes like SureStart, to the comprehensive education system, to the expansion of university education – that have in the past empowered so many.

We recognise that democratic socialism, too, is in crisis and has been since the fall of the Berlin Wall. In Europe, it is losing ground to populist parties of the right and left. The extent to which the Hayekian/Thatcherite programme of anti-socialism has permeated our laws, our policies and our political discourse means that a party that sought to right this balance would need to have the same confidence in re-writing the fundamental rules governing the relationship between labour and capital as Mrs Thatcher had when she followed Hayek's blueprint.

Our goal is to reinterpret social democratic values for the twenty-first century because we believe our values are crucial to re-establishing a healthy and sustainable society. The world is changing and this change brings dangers as well as opportunities. Digitisation, automation and our growing understanding of the building blocks of life and the universe mean that the world of tomorrow will be quite different to that of today. We still, profoundly, believe that it is only through a combination of democracy and democratic socialism – the rational, intelligently combined efforts of all people – that we can deal with the challenges of tomorrow to create a stable, prosperous and happy society.

CHAPTER TWO

DEMOCRATIC SOCIALISM

L abour is a democratic socialist party. Labour's core values are an enduring signpost to the better society we strive to create together. While the methods by which we achieve this must evolve as the context we find ourselves in continues to transform, the values we seek to live by never change. Here, we set them out.

EQUALITY

We believe that everyone is created equal in dignity and worth, regardless of talent and ability.

As democratic socialists, we wish to see social chances and economic opportunities more fairly distributed. Our aim is to organise our society so that crucial needs are met and individuals have fair access to resources to help them reach their potential and live happy and fulfilling lives in dignity and respect.

In doing so, we should seek to end the dominance in our society of inherited privilege, income and wealth. And we should strive to end all forms of discrimination and bigotry, because it stunts individual human potential and unfairly narrows opportunity.

While individual progress is important, we recognise that we are social beings that exist and prosper best in a nurturing and respectful society. There is a collective as well as an individual wellbeing.

As democratic socialists, we have a vision of how a society could be more equal and liberated through collective action. Thus, we have collective duties to each other and our communities as well as the capacity to express ourselves as individuals and pursue our own individual goals. This balance between the individual and the collective is crucial to our understanding of the world. Our communities are important building blocks in a fairer society. Human flourishing requires us to be aware of our social bonds and the duties of empathy, social solidarity and selflessness. We have responsibilities and duties to others as well as enjoying for ourselves the human rights our democracy confers on us. Therefore success is by definition not based solely on the acquisition of individual income and wealth.

LIBERTY

We believe in a positive vision of a pluralistic, diverse society, where universal rights are upheld and respect for others is paramount. To flourish, liberty demands respect for the truth and for facts.

The Labour Party has always been about providing freedom from insecurity and fear, liberating working people and their communities from servitude, exploitation and poverty.

To emphasise this point, the original Labour Party badge displayed the symbol of liberty, the flaming torch of knowledge, alongside a crossed quill pen and a shovel, representing the workers by hand and by brain. Labour always regarded liberty as an essential precondition to social and economic progress. It is what our pioneers dreamed about: freedom from the arbitrary control of exploitation at work; freedom to make your own choices, both social and economic; freedom *from* as well as freedom *to*.

Liberty and equality are not at odds. The defence of individual human rights and the recognition of universal human values go hand in hand with campaigning for greater social and economic equality in a society which is fairer for all.

DEMOCRACY

We believe in government *by* the people, *for* the people. The UK Labour Party has always been committed to making progress by democratic means. Democracy is key to the spirit of social equality, which is central to the creation of a fairer society and what it is to be a citizen. It is also what confers legitimacy upon collective decision-making about the direction we wish to see our society as a whole take.

Labour developed out of a desire for the majority of working people to control their own destiny through direct parliamentary representation, rather than indirect lobbying of other political parties. The battle to win the modern democratic franchise predates the Labour Party, but it was at the centre of the struggle. From the Levellers and the Chartists to the early trade unions and our first leader, Keir Hardie, our pioneers enthusiastically joined the battle for women's suffrage and a universal franchise. This inclusive and progressive democracy is part of Labour's proud heritage.

We believe that this democratic approach should extend far beyond the right to vote in national and local elections, important though that is as a prerequisite for further progress. Labour has always been focused on the workplace and the importance of a productive economy, where working people enjoy the fruits of their labour and are allowed to develop to their full potential. Economic democracy, industrial democracy – a voice at work – are crucial, as is the right to collective representation. Living in a democratic political system but being subject to autocracy at work shows that the ideal of participation and having an input needs to be developed and deepened in all walks of life throughout the UK and be present and accessible throughout life. Participatory democracy is thus a principle that deepens the democratic spirit animating all healthy societies.

CO-OPERATION

We believe in the values of community and social solidarity. Consequently, we believe in the power of co-operation. We believe that people working together achieve more than people existing in solipsistic isolation or dog-eat-dog competition, where morality is based on what succeeds and the only measure of success is the size of your personal bank balance.

To quote the party constitution's current Clause IV, which set out Labour's aims and values after 1995:

> The Labour Party is a democratic socialist party. It believes that by the strength of our common endeavour, we achieve more than we achieve alone so as to create for each of us the means to realise our true potential and for all of us a community in which power, wealth and opportunity are in the hands of the many not the few, where the rights we enjoy reflect the duties we owe, and where we live together, freely, in a spirit of solidarity, tolerance and respect.

The earliest pioneers of socialism in Britain, such as Robert Owen, experimented with communities based on the co-operative principle. They understood that we are social beings living an interconnected life. Modern technology will only increase this connection, so our society and our community remain important. As such, they need to be nurtured, supported and strengthened.

INTERNATIONALISM

We believe that the true emancipation of human beings from injustice and exploitation can only be achieved by international co-operation. Just as capital is global, it is important that the interests of labour can be co-ordinated across national borders too. Throughout its history, the Labour Party has forged alliances and campaigned internationally for social and economic justice. From its support of the battle for self-determination in the colonies of the British Empire to the campaign against the evils of apartheid in South Africa, Labour has sought to project its values around the world. Labour's backing in the fight against fascism was crucial in defeating the policy of appeasement that led to it joining the wartime coalition headed by Winston Churchill. In the aftermath of the war, Labour's support for the creation of the United Nations and the adoption of the Universal Declaration of Human Rights neatly encompass the value of internationalism in action. As the world becomes more interdependent, the need for international co-operation will only grow stronger. The battle against catastrophic climate change is only the most important example of this.

CONCLUSION: WHAT LABOUR BELIEVES

Labour was born to create a better society for all. It came into existence in an era of rapid economic and social transformation which was changing Britain out of all recognition. Its appearance on the political scene was the culmination of the work and dreams of many generations. It embodied the aspirations of millions for a better chance at life and the pursuit of prosperity and happiness for all. Fighting for a fairer society was its core task. And that is the basic task which now needs to be accomplished once more in another era of rapid change and transformation, where inequality is rising sharply and life chances are once more correlated with the social class of one's parents.

Labour was focused primarily on the empowerment of the working classes as the lever for change and it certainly ensured that those who came from the working class were represented in the ranks of those seeking to govern for the first time in our country's history. But Labour also attracted plenty of idealists and activists from the middle and professional classes, too, who were horrified by the poverty they witnessed and saw the need for a fairer, more equal society, in which all human beings were afforded the dignity and opportunity to live a good and rewarding life.

Labour came into existence to rebalance the rewards flowing to those who work for a wage (labour) relative to those who own the means of production (capital). Prior to its emergence, it was clear that there was a gross imbalance between the forces of capital and labour which needed to be addressed in our politics. This task is as relevant today as it was then.

It is now vital that we consider how democratic socialism should once more evolve to answer the challenges facing Britain in the twenty-first century. These have been made infinitely more difficult by Brexit. There are signposts to be found in the insights of earlier thinkers who wrestled with these questions in their own time, but we must find our own answers for our own generation.

PART 2

THE STATE OF OUR NATION

CHAPTER THREE

WANT

We humans are an ingenious species. We've reached the moon, plumbed the depths of our seas, split the atom and eradicated some of our most dangerous diseases. But we have never managed to create a society that hasn't experienced the evil of want: poverty and the attendant ills that go with it, such as hunger, homelessness and mental ill-health.

Poverty is stressful, humiliating and degrading to self-worth. If there was something we as human beings should put our minds to, it would be eliminating this wasteful and unnecessary evil.

Britain's most famous chronicler of the lives of the poor was Charles Dickens. Dickens wrote with huge moral force about the iniquities of a time in which children starved on our streets and slaved away in brutal workhouses. In part thanks to him, a series of laws were passed in the nineteenth century and early twentieth century to alleviate the suffering of the poorest in British society.

By the time William Beveridge first wrote about the 'evil' of want, Britain had already legislated for a basic safety net and many of the horrors of Dickens's times had been eradicated. The poverty Beveridge sought to fix was one of worklessness, and so getting people into jobs was central to his plan. In the aftermath of the mass unemployment of the inter-war period, which had done so much to turbo-charge the rise of fascism,

Beveridge broke sharply from previous political practice in Britain by making his aim to reduce unemployment as much as possible, if necessary by having the state create jobs. The work of J. M. Keynes had established how economic policy could be used to accomplish this goal. Clement Attlee's government went on to nationalise part of the British economy, and helped our industries become globally competitive by investing to improve productivity. If demand for labour went down, Keynesian economics had shown how the government could intervene to give it a kick-start. This approach to managing our economy endured until the 1970s, when rising unemployment and inflation (so-called stagflation) caused the political consensus to break down. During this time it became fashionable to recast unemployment as a problem of employability – the attractiveness of individuals to prospective employers, aka the 'supply side' of the labour market – rather than being associated with fluctuations in demand. The focus of the government switched to helping businesses to create jobs by making life easier for them. Cutting down on regulations and the demands on private enterprise, they claimed, would keep Britain prosperous.

Apart from a brief period after the financial crisis, this approach has persisted. In its purest, most ruthless form, under Margaret Thatcher's government, it led to soaring unemployment of up to 12 per cent – over 3 million people. Beveridge would have turned in his grave. No post-war politician before Mrs Thatcher would have been prepared to countenance unemployment rates so high. The Conservative government had allowed poverty to become a problem again, blaming it on individuals for not being employable while making life easier for the rich owners of large companies.

There are two types of modern poverty. One is the kind that is gleefully depicted on shows such as *Shameless* and the exploitative, disgusting 'poverty porn' of *Benefits Street*. This portrayal of poverty is the subject of fulminating editorials about the 'feckless poor' in right-wing tabloids. They present it as the result of individual problems such as a lack of education, alcohol or drug dependency, or criminality, and often portray it as intergenerational and persistent. As it happens, Britain has one of the lowest 'persistent poverty' rates in the world and the fifth lowest in the EU – around 7.3 per cent of our population have been in poverty for two of the last three years.

Despite these figures, the evil of want is much more pervasive than we might think. Britain has quite a high poverty rate – around 16.7 per cent of the population – because a lot of people are on low wages, are underemployed or not able to get the hours they need to get by. This is the other kind of poverty – the type that is caused by the structure and nature of our economy, which cannot plausibly be blamed on individual failings, even for the purposes of right-wing Hayekian propaganda.

On top of those figures, around 30 per cent of people are at risk of poverty. This means a really significant proportion of our fellow citizens are always teetering on the edge of not being able to fulfil their basic needs. The insecurity and fear that this sort of precariousness causes is inherently stressful and causes a constant strain on rising numbers of people. And this is all happening at the same time as we have record low unemployment.

This structural poverty is a result of the Hayekian revolution of market fundamentalism and the Thatcherite policies that put them into effect. The Conservatives stripped back the state and our safety nets because they perceived them as dangerous socialist ideas. They strengthened the power of owners over workers by going to war with trade unions and making it fundamentally harder for workers to exert their collective power to ensure that pay and conditions were improved and not eroded.

They celebrated the extraordinary accrual of wealth by those who already have capital, claiming it was all OK because it would eventually 'trickle down' to everyone else.

As a recent report on the state of the British economy, *Time for Change: A New Vision for the British Economy* by the Institute for Public Policy Research's Commission on Economic Justice, asserts:

> The UK's high employment rate has been accompanied by an increasingly insecure and 'casualised' labour market. Fifteen per cent of the workforce are now self-employed, with an increasing proportion in 'enforced self-employment' driven by businesses seeking to avoid employer responsibilities. Six per cent are on short-term contracts, and almost 3 per cent are on zero-hours contracts. More workers are on low pay than ten years ago. Insecure and low-paid employment is increasing physical and mental ill-health.

Is it any surprise that so many people are only just about managing?

All of this is even more difficult to stomach when there appear to be so many people, sometimes perceived as undeservingly so, like the bankers who caused the latest financial crash and Britain's endless supply of Z-list celebrities, who are living life so large.

The creation of this economy, which is characterised by precariousness, actual inequality and growing perceptions of inequality, has played a big part in driving the political anger and volatility that has been such a feature of elections over the past few years, not just in the UK but in comparable countries like the US and in some European countries.

All this is not to say that the United Kingdom has not made

enormous strides in improving living standards over the past decades and centuries. We have more material possessions than before, because the costs of those goods has been inexorably driven down. Think of the cost of clothing, of household goods like televisions, washing machines and dishwashers. That fall in price has been a result of our particular globalised form of capitalism. It has driven down the costs of consumer goods and widened choice and availability.

However, it's also true that there is a decline in how many people own their own homes in which to put these goods. The real-term costs (i.e. once you adjust for inflation) of some of our basic needs – housing and utilities in particular – have gone up over the past few decades. Both housing and gas – since 1996 – and electricity – since 1998 – are now primarily provided by the private sector, which means by companies whose first directive is to create profit for their owners. But given housing and fuel are captive markets, providing basic necessities you cannot live without, the providers are under no pressure to lower the price or increase quality. All they care about is that they make a profit.

In short, our current system is quite good at providing cheap consumer goods and quite bad at providing affordable basic needs.

The psychologist Abraham Maslow wrote in the 1940s about people's 'hierarchy of needs'. It was an evolution of other think- ers' theories of human nature, wants and needs, including that of Karl Marx. Maslow argued that only by satisfying our most basic physiological and security needs – which he identified as belonging, self-esteem and self-actualisation – can we be freed to satisfy our higher wants. His pyramid of needs, shown below, has had a profound influence on a number of fields, so how might we use it to look at the extent to which our basic needs and our higher wants are being satisfied by what our modern economy actually delivers?

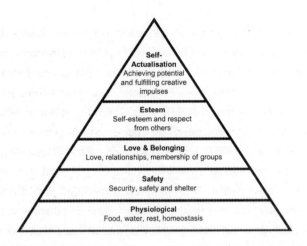

Capitalism has proven itself to be brilliant at producing cheap consumer goods and services. We have more 'stuff', more access to information and to a richer array of entertainment than ever before, so our higher wants have never been so satisfied. But profit-driven private markets are remarkably bad when it comes to providing for our most basic needs. In Britain, we have thus far decided that some of our most basic needs should be out of the hands of the market. Our National Health Service, our emergency services and our social security safety net are administered by the state, despite the market fundamentalists continuing to argue for marketisation of this provision, and their continuing efforts to encroach around the edges of it. We know from other countries that when you do privatise services like healthcare, the outcomes are terrible. In America, millions are without coverage and yet the US spends more as a percentage of its national income on healthcare than any other developed country. Most British people would understand that this is because healthcare is a basic need; profit-driven healthcare providers would by their very nature exploit the captive market of people that need their services to maximise their own profits.

But before we get too smug at identifying the idiocy that has lain at the heart of US healthcare policy for decades, let's just remember that that's pretty much the situation our housing market is in. And our utilities markets, which were privatised by Mrs Thatcher in the 1980s. Substantial swathes of our transport network, too, went the same way and are now largely owned by foreign states seeking to maximise their profit at our expense. Even our broadband network, an increasingly indispensable utility in modern Britain, is privately owned and provided for. It is precisely the injection of market fundamentalism into the provision of services and goods that we all need that has allowed those who provide these services to get richer and richer while the public pays through the nose for the utilities that are essential to life. This is why Labour's calls for nationalisation of certain national utilities and the transport network has gone down so well. Other EU countries efficiently and effectively run these necessary services on a public basis; there is absolutely no reason beyond the blind dogma of market fundamentalism and its abhorrence of state action why we shouldn't do so too.

It is an irony that right-wing newspapers love to fulminate about poor people in council houses owning large televisions and spending money on clothes, since it's the trickle-down system for which they have advocated – on behalf of their plutocrat owners – that has allowed this anomaly to emerge. It is the offshored production of consumer goods from Britain to locations with much lower labour costs and weaker regulatory regimes that has brought down the cost of 50-inch televisions and jeans and dishwashers and party dresses to a level at which they can be bought by poorer people. But, of course, it is the shedding of the jobs producing those goods, the evisceration of our manufacturing and industrial base, the failure to invest into lifetime education, the deliberate weakening of the trade unions, that has kept people poor and income distribution so skewed. The impoverishment of British people was done at the behest of plutocrats, and then they have the temerity to slam those very same people – many of whom work one or more jobs to earn their thin gruel – for being able to buy the cheap goods that were, apparently, the upside of the market fundamentalist economic experiment. For shame.

At the same time as we are having to work harder and harder to fulfil basic needs because of real-term rises in the prices of necessities, inequality, which declined for forty years after the Second World War, has been rising in Britain for thirty years.

This trend was exacerbated by the financial crisis, which has led to stagnating wages and living standards for most Britons in the past decade, whereas the richest have recovered to the status quo ante. A 2017 study by the Resolution Foundation showed that households with incomes of £275,000 or more – the top 1 per cent – had seen their share of national income return to its pre-crisis levels. However, the other 99 per cent of UK households continued to struggle to regain their financial power.

The Office for National Statistics' figures on average wages in Britain show that we have had ten years of stagnation in real terms. Families on low and middle incomes have seen their living standards rise by just 3 per cent since 2002/03. Once housing costs had been taken into account, they were no better off than they were fifteen years ago. One way of looking at how much families have to spend and how confident they are about parting with it is to look at household spending data, which the Office for National Statistics collates. There has been a *decline* in real-term spending by British families over the past decade, a remarkable reversal of what had been a soaring trend in spending power.

It means that families are finding it harder to pay for what they need and more frequently find it impossible to pay for what they want.

This affects everyone's future prospects, but it hits the youngest generation hardest. The age at which young people buy their first house in Britain is rapidly rising. The time taken to save for a deposit for low- to middle-income households has increased from less than five years in 1997 to more than twenty years today. At the same time, rents are going up and up. The Office for National Statistics reported in its August 2017 bulletin that 'between January 2011 and August 2017, private rental prices in Great Britain increased by 15.1 per cent'. And all this means we are saving far less than ever before, leaving people far less resilient to sudden shock, like loss of employment or a bereavement, which can drive them into acute destitution.

In the past, analyses of want have tended to focus on either poverty or inequality. But that is insufficient to understand what is happening today. There are more and more people just getting by; more and more who graft every day but find themselves going backwards. For them, no matter how hard they work, the standard of living they once had or expect is increasingly out of reach. This is not a perception issue, but one of hard economics. If wages are stagnating and basic needs are getting more expensive to acquire while wage growth isn't keeping up with inflation, there can be no doubt that for the first time in decades, we have had a sustained period in which things are not getting better for British people. They are getting worse.

Not to mention that, while all of this is happening, the FTSE 100 Stock Index, a measure of the value of British companies, has reached an all-time high on the back of soaring corporate profits.

It doesn't quite seem fair, does it?

In the post-war years, until the 1970s, Britain was overall a poorer but much more equal country than it is today. Since then, inequality in Britain, by any measure, has increased.

There are lots of different ways to understand and quantify inequality, but what is true is that the UK has a very high level of income inequality compared to other developed countries.

In Britain today, the poorest 10 per cent receive, on average, an income of £4,436, while the top 10 per cent receive twenty-four times more: an average of £107,937. After you take into account taxes and redistribution, things get a little better, but the situation is still pretty dire. Households in the bottom 10 per cent of the population have on average a disposable (or net) income of £9,644 (this includes wages and cash benefits, and is after direct taxes like income tax and council tax, but not indirect taxes like VAT). The top 10 per cent have net incomes almost nine times that (£83,875).

It gets worse if you look at the most rich of all. The top 1 per cent have incomes substantially higher than the rest of those in the top 10 per cent. In 2012, the top 1 per cent had an average income of £253,927 and the top 0.1 per cent had an average income of £919,882.

All of this has happened in the past forty years. The rise in inequality in Britain started under Thatcher, continued under John Major, and, to our regret, was held static but not reversed under New Labour. Meanwhile, the top 1 per cent soared further away from the rest. One measure of inequality is something called the Gini coefficient, which is a measure of the dispersion of income distribution among the population. This radically increased after 1979 and has remained at the high it reached under Thatcher since then.

So how was this allowed to happen? Politics is, at one level, about telling stories to explain complex phenomena like the economy. Stories and ideas matter, and in this instance it was the story that inequality creates an incentive for people to work harder and that redistributing income actually disincentivises hard work.

As Gordon Gekko, the main character in the 1980s Oliver Stone movie *Wall Street*, would say: 'Greed, for lack of a better word, is good ... Greed clarifies, cuts through, and captures the essence of the evolutionary spirit. Greed, in all of its forms – greed for life, for money, for love, knowledge – has marked the upward surge of mankind.'

This social Darwinian mantra is part of the core Hayekian creed. It was the bedrock of Conservative economic and political ideologies in the 1980s and 1990s both in Britain and around the world. This explained why it was right in their minds to cut the welfare state and allow the concentration of Britain's wealth into fewer and even more lavishly wealthy hands. It was selfishness recast as kindness; greed cast as virtue; poverty cast as wrongdoing.

It turned out, however, that they were wrong. In 2009, two epidemiologists – people who study the spread, incidence and solutions to disease and ill-health – started looking at what happened as societies become more unequal. The results of Richard Wilkinson and Kate Pickett's analysis, detailed in their book *The Spirit Level*, was startlingly clear. They identified the 'pernicious effects that inequality has on societies: eroding trust, increasing anxiety and illness, (and) encouraging excessive consumption'. Their work showed that for eleven different health and social problems – physical illness, mental illness, drug abuse, poor education, imprisonment, obesity, social immobility, lack of trust and community life, violence, teenage pregnancies, and low child wellbeing – outcomes are significantly worse in more unequal rich countries.

As they went on to say:

> human beings have deep-seated psychological responses to
> inequality and social hierarchy. The tendency to equate out-
> ward wealth with inner worth means that inequality colours
> our social perceptions. It invokes feelings of superiority and
> inferiority, dominance and subordination – which affect the
> way we relate to and treat each other ... Research has shown
> that greater inequality leads to shorter spells of economic ex-
> pansion and more frequent and severe boom-and-bust cycles
> that make economies more vulnerable to crisis.

The book's serendipitous timing, shortly after the financial
crash, meant it had a huge impact. At a time when around 80
per cent of Britons now think the income gap is too large, world
leaders cannot help but listen. Barack Obama has said income
inequality is the 'defining challenge of our times', while Pope
Francis states that 'inequality is the root of social ills'. Even the
IMF has now decided that inequality is pernicious and needs
mitigating.

Further research showed a link between inequality and economic growth. The Organisation for Economic Co-operation
and Development released a study in 2014 which argued that
reducing inequality was crucial to kick-starting growth. Their
analysis of countries around the world showed that rising
inequality slowed down growth. Unveiling the report, the organisation's Secretary-General, Angel Gurría, said: 'This compelling
evidence proves that addressing high and growing inequality is
critical to promote strong and sustained growth and needs to
be at the centre of the policy debate ... Countries that promote
equal opportunity for all from an early age are those that will
grow and prosper.'

This overdue reformation against the greed gospel of Hayek's acolytes is something that we found, in talking to people around the country, was deeply felt. Countless people have told us: 'It just really gets me angry that I'm busting a gut to survive and yet so many people are making money for doing nothing really or actually causing all these financial crises.' It's this perception of inequality that has really exploded, powered in part by the enormous expansion of our access to news and information, to see people doing very, very well, while most people feel that they are just as decent and hard-working, if not more, but simply aren't getting by.

When so many feel their basic needs and wants are being denied, it's not hard to see where the inchoate, latent anger that is driving our political volatility comes from. When people feel the rich have lived it too large and left so little for their fellow citizens, there comes a time of political revolution.

We've spoken about those just managing to get by, but what about the very poorest in our society?

Britain has established an enormous infrastructure to support our country's post-war determination to eliminate destitution. This comprises the collection of taxes and the disbursement of tens of billions of pounds a year to support those with little income and capital. Unfortunately, thanks to relentless propaganda, there is little popular understanding of what the money is actually spent on. The truth is that most of the 'benefits' budget goes on pensions, and comparatively little on unemployment benefits. One of the biggest growth areas in our benefits bill is actually housing benefit. This might be more accurately called 'landlord benefit', because it is of course paid by the state overwhelmingly to landlords and, increasingly, to private landlords. It's another shocking and disgraceful example of the housing crisis in Britain. Instead of building new houses, we're giving money to private landlords to subsidise private rents, which are rising because of the subsidy.

The social security system has been under severe pressure to reduce the amount of benefits and eligibility for quite some time, however. The truth is that the distribution of unemployment benefits has never been a popular cause to advocate. The British Social Attitudes Survey shows that support for greater spending on unemployment benefits was highest in 1996 – after seventeen years of a Conservative assault on the poorest. But even then, only one third of people supported higher spending. In the most recent survey, in 2016, only 16 per cent of people supported an increase.

Polls are just a snapshot. As more people become aware of the scale of suffering of the poorest in Austerity Britain, attitudes will change. But it is never easy to champion the rights of the poor and it does not always make you popular. That doesn't mean that politicians, in particular those from the Labour tradition, can't always be there to protect those that are struggling. Many MPs would agree that in recent years, since the financial crisis, there has been an increase in the number of people coming to their advice surgeries that are in acute crisis – destitution. That's when someone can't afford to buy the essentials to eat, keep clean and stay warm and dry.

The Joseph Rowntree Foundation, one of the biggest charities focused on poverty in Britain, estimated that 1,252,000 people, including 312,000 children, were in this situation in the UK in 2015. Their report states that the key triggers pushing people into poverty include debt repayments, benefit delays and sanctions, high living costs and, for some migrants, extremely low levels of benefits and lack of access to the UK labour market. Disability and ill-health were important factors. Seventy-six per cent of these people – our fellow citizens – said they had had to go without food. Seventy-one per cent didn't have clothing and/or shoes suitable for the weather.

It is the case that many of those classified as destitute in Britain today are there as a result of the cuts to benefits and the introduction of a punitive sanctions regime that means people can be punished with a complete loss of their safety net in a variety of sometimes Orwellian circumstances.

The Conservatives have always tried to portray those who are destitute as individually responsible for the difficulties in which they find themselves. They believe that you have to punish people and give them tough love to shock them back into economic sufficiency. In 2011, when launching a scheme intended to help, David Cameron identified some of these people as 'troubled families'. It's worth rereading his words:

> I want to talk about troubled families. Let me be clear what I mean by this phrase. Officialdom might call them 'families with multiple disadvantages'. Some in the press might call them 'neighbours from hell'.
>
> Whatever you call them, we've known for years that a relatively small number of families are the source of a large proportion of the problems in society. Drug addiction. Alcohol abuse. Crime. A culture of disruption and irresponsibility that cascades through generations … Now there are some who say: 'Yes, this is terrible, but this *Shameless* culture is now a fact of modern British life, and there's nothing we can do.' They're the same people who believe that poverty and failure, like death and taxes, will always be with us. But I am an optimist about human nature. I don't believe in writing people off. I don't think people are pre-programmed to fail because of where they come from. And I hate the idea that we should just expect to pay ever-larger amounts in welfare

to an ever-larger chunk of society and never expect the recipients to change their lives.

He ploughed half a billion pounds into the scheme and issued an endless slew of press releases and newspaper briefings on its success. But, as the National Audit Office later revealed, of the 120,000 families targeted, only 12,000 ended up with one person back in work. That means the scheme cost roughly £40,000 per job. They could have paid them a year's wage for less than that. Instead, the underpinning rationale behind the scheme was persuading Britain that 'troubled families' were all about individual fecklessness, rather than an economy that wasn't working.

And therein lies the problem. We have an economy that is delivering fewer of the well-paying jobs than people want. We have an accrual of capital by those that already have capital. We have a system that delivers lots of goods we want but is terrible at delivering some of the basic necessities of life – such as affordable housing and utilities. As state spending is relentlessly stripped back, we are robbing people of opportunities to improve their lot in life. People are more financially insecure and vulnerable to a sudden shock in their life circumstances than ever before because they have less saved for when they go through a shock, like losing their job or bereavement. People are more in debt and personal indebtedness is rising rapidly. Moreover, it is a system in which workers have very little voice, as forty years of assaults against the trade unions has left them with fewer members, present in fewer workplaces and incapable of pushing back against these worrying trends. All this has combined to create an unfair economic system that rewards the few while punishing the many.

CHAPTER FOUR

IDLENESS

Labour. It's the name of our party and it also represents our historic mission: to help people to work and thus contribute to society, and to improve the conditions, wages and security of those workers. William Beveridge saw work as the primary route out of poverty, and for the post-war Labour government, full employment was its central economic goal.

This has not been uncontroversial. Some people – we would argue unfairly – claim that Labour's obsession with work has made it blind to the needs of those that cannot work. Some people on the right claim that Labour panders to the workless. The truth is that we have always tried to balance the two: self-reliance balanced with care for those that find themselves vulnerable for whatever reason.

It is worth addressing why Labour believes that work is so important. This question is at the heart of some of the most ferocious debates about politics and economics. The Conservatives, after all, claim they are the party of 'hard-working people', and there has been a long tradition of people on the political left who are at best ambivalent about the importance of work, from Paul Lafargue, a nineteenth-century Marxist who extolled the virtues of laziness, to some who extol the virtues of fully automated luxury communism.

So why do we work? Let's start by looking at two perspectives. Adam Smith, the eighteenth-century British economist, is regarded as one of the fathers of modern capitalism. His most famous contribution was his description of 'the invisible hand' of the market. But something that 21st-century market fundamentalists would prefer to ignore is the fact that Smith was very interested in alleviating poverty. In *The Wealth of Nations*, he writes:

> No society can surely be flourishing and happy, of which the far greater part of the members are poor and miserable. It is but equity, besides, that they who feed, clothe, and lodge the whole body of the people, should have such a share of the produce of their own labour as to be themselves tolerably well fed, clothed, and lodged.

Smith recognised the power of inequality and the envy it invokes. In *The Theory of Moral Sentiments*, Smith wrote of the 'poor man':

> To obtain the conveniences which [wealth] afford[s], he submits in the first year, nay in the first month of his application, to more fatigue of body and more uneasiness of mind than he could have suffered through the whole of his life from the want of them. He studies to distinguish himself in some laborious profession. With the most unrelenting industry he labours night and day to acquire talents superior to all his competitors. He endeavours next to bring those talents into public view, and with equal assiduity solicits every opportunity of employment. For this purpose he makes his court to all mankind; he serves those whom he hates, and is obsequious to those whom he despises.

'Tranquillity', in Smith's view, is to not have to work. But to achieve this, we must bust a gut in a laborious profession that we might hate and seek to continually improve ourselves faster than our competitors. In short, our reward for unrelenting toil, fatigue and uneasiness of mind is the ability to have tranquillity in our life outside work.

In contrast, there is the perspective of Karl Marx, the nineteenth-century philosopher, economist and author of *The Communist Manifesto*.

In his work, *Grundrisse*, Marx mocks Smith's view of work as a punishment; instead seeing work as a means of internal liberation.

> In the sweat of thy brow shalt thou labour! was Jehovah's curse on Adam. And this is labour for Smith, a curse. 'Tranquillity' appears as the adequate state, as identical with 'freedom' and 'happiness.' It seems quite far from Smith's mind that the individual, 'in his normal state of health, strength, activity, skill, facility,' also needs a normal portion of work, and of the suspension of tranquillity. Certainly, labour obtains its measure from the outside, through the aim to be attained and the obstacles to be overcome in attaining it. But Smith has no inkling whatever that the overcoming of obstacles is in itself a liberating activity – and that, further, the external aims become stripped of the semblance of merely external natural urgencies, and become posited as aims which the individual himself posits – hence as self-realisation, objectification of the subject, hence real freedom, whose action is, precisely, labour.

Marx had a really keen sense of human nature. He believed humans are fundamentally productive beings. Work is the means by which we live in the natural world, making ourselves feel part of it. Work allows us to satisfy our own wants and needs and defines our role within a community. Social solidarity is strengthened when each of us contributes to the collective needs of society, which is why access to work is so important. Marx, however, was writing at a time when industrialisation had created factories in which workers were merely cogs in machines, and often treated as such. He differentiated between work that he said 'alienated' people from their labour and emancipatory work. In *Das Kapital*, Marx wrote:

> A spider conducts operations that resemble those of a weaver, and a bee puts to shame many an architect in the construction of her cells. But what distinguishes the worst architect from the best of bees is this, that the architect raises his structure in imagination before he erects it in reality. At the end of every labour-process, we get a result that already existed in the imagination of the labourer at its commencement. He not only effects a change of form in the material on which he works, but he also realises a purpose of his own that gives the law to his modus operandi, and to which he must subordinate his will.

There's a really lovely idea in there, and one that cuts to the heart of the Labour movement. Work has the potential to be truly fulfilling and liberating – if what we are producing is something that we *want* to produce or providing a service which we know is needed and appreciated then work adds to the purpose of our lives. That's why the Labour movement has always fought to make conditions at work safe and aimed to ensure that work was worthwhile and fulfilling. It's also why the Labour movement encourages co-operation at work so that each worker feels their ideas are listened to and feels valued and personally invested in their work. Gaining a fair share of the reward from work for all is a key part of what the labour and trade union movement came into existence to achieve.

So firstly, what does work look like in the twenty-first century?

Ten years after the financial crisis, in which unemployment reached 8 per cent of the population (over 2.5 million people), the ONS unemployment rate today in Britain is at a 42-year record low of 4.3 per cent. That is, around 1.4 million people are seeking and are available for work but haven't got a job. It has been a remarkable and welcome turnaround. There are 32.1 million people in work, which is – again – a historic high. Some have claimed that unemployment figures may mask the actual inactivity rate – those people between the ages of sixteen and sixty-four who are economically inactive. But, again, this is at a record low of 21.4 per cent – around 8.8 million people.

This is a marked contrast to the conditions recorded by Beveridge and the Commission on Social Justice. In 1942 and 1992, there was much more economic inactivity. Labour governments in both instances eventually helped to drive down inactivity and to increase employment, in the first instance by creating jobs and in the second by encouraging the creation of new jobs in the private sector through prudent management of the economy as well as investment. It would be remiss of any Labour Party to fail to welcome the improvements in the headline figures on employment. However, there is a more complex picture emerging from these figures than may at first be apparent. The labour market is becoming increasingly fragmented into 'lovely' and 'lousy' jobs. The quality rather than the quantity of jobs is increasingly important as the levels of underemployment and fragmented work patterns on low pay rates rise. We will consider the implications of this later.

Second, how happy are we in work?

Here, again, there is evidence that things are getting better for some. The British Social Attitudes Survey is conducted annually by the National Centre for Social Research. Since 1983, it has asked a representative sample of citizens questions on their feelings about a huge array of topics, from crime to benefits, immigration to work. The survey's most recent analysis of citizens' feelings about work demonstrates this improvement for some. It found that 71 per cent of workers feel they 'have a "good" job (one with at least four positive attributes such as being interesting, helping others and/or society, and offering chances for advancement), compared with 62 per cent in 2005 and 57 per cent in 1989.' They also found that '62 per cent of respondents say they would enjoy having a job even if they didn't need the money, up from 49 per cent in 2005.' When asked what they thought was most important about a job, the three most popular responses were that it was secure, interesting and offered opportunities for advancement. These answers reinforce our belief that British people perceive work is important to them and that they want and are willing to work hard and get on.

If all this is true though, then what explanation can we give for the political anger that we see and the frustration with the current government? After all, we know that wages have stagnated, but one would expect those in work as well as their dependents and friends and families to be delighted that so many people have been able to find gainful employment.

The truth is that while the government likes to cite these headline figures, in part because they are genuinely worth celebrating, they hide deep areas of concern – for example, when you look at specific groups of people, such as the young, the low-skilled and those from the working class. The areas of concern are actually quite clear once you drill beneath the surface of the statistics, and it is beyond our comprehension as to why the government has failed to take seriously trends in which opportunity has disappeared and discontent has grown for many people. They directly led to the growth in anxiety and anger among younger Britons that expressed itself at the ballot box in 2017. The labour market is segmenting and, at the 'lousy' end, it is getting worse.

Take the employment rate, which the government assures us is at its healthiest ever. When we look at the ONS employment rate by age group, some concerns emerge. Whereas there has been a marked uptick in the employment rate for older people, the employment rate for young people has not recovered to pre-crisis levels. This means that young people today are less able to build experience, a CV, as well as contributions to their social security and pension. Pathways to careers appear to be closing off and jobs are being hoarded by those who already have experience. The older people who have benefited from the jobs recovery will already have had work experience before the crisis and, as such, a real competitive advantage over those younger people. But discrimination in the labour market is not only seen between young and old. The fact is that women, black and ethnic minorities and the young all find themselves facing discrimination and a lack of good job opportunities.

Another criticism that is levied at the government over employment is that the increase in jobs has been in part-time work and in self-employment. There is some truth in this. If we look at what has happened over the past few years, the percentage of self-employed people in the workforce has increased from 12.9 per cent before the crash to 15.1 per cent now. That is around 1 million more self-employed people. This statistic will include people who have set up legitimate businesses for themselves, but it will also include those forced into 'fake self-employment'. This is where full-time employees are told to go 'freelance' but retain their current job on a sub-contractual basis. This shifts all of the risk onto individual workers while depriving them of the rights they would enjoy if they were directly employed. It reduces the cost *and* the tax bill for the 'employer' too. This is unfair and must stop.

We can also see that there has been an increase of 1.2 million in the proportion of the workforce working part-time. Some do so because they don't want full-time work. Students, for example, enjoy the ability to work part-time. New parents who aren't ready to re-enter the workforce and older people wanting to keep active may also want part-time work. But many are forced to accept part-time work when they want to work full-time. Luckily, the ONS records the percentage of those part-time workers who say they have had to take part-time work despite wanting full-time work. In 2006, there were around 650,000 people in that situation. Today there are around 1,050,000 stuck in part-time work and wanting full-time work. If they then suffer arbitrary cuts in hours at the whim of the employer they can suddenly find themselves unable to make ends meet.

Any jobs recovery claimed by the government has therefore been patchy and incomplete. There are signs of problems and we would argue that the most dangerous is the youth employment rate, the effects of which will ripple through society over time. Those who have been lucky enough to get into work young will have a serious advantage over those who have not. There must also be a concern that if there are fewer young people getting into work, those from more advantaged backgrounds, who are more likely to have access to familial social networks, will get these jobs over those from less-advantaged backgrounds.

This is exactly what Alan Milburn has been looking at for

the government in his independent Social Mobility and Child Poverty Commission (though he has since resigned in frustration at the lack of government action on his reports). His research has shown a strong correlation between people's social origins and their ability to get decent work. This is driving real despair among young people, and though it has always been a feature of the class-based system in the UK, as Alan has shown in his reports on social mobility, the situation is getting worse not better.

The Commission has found that nearly half of people (48 per cent) say that where you end up in society is largely determined by who your parents are – compared with a third (32 per cent) who say that everyone has a fair chance to get on regardless of their background.

It is the younger generation who feel more acutely that background determines where you end up, with around half (51 per cent) of 18–24-year-olds agreeing with this statement compared with 40 per cent of those aged sixty-five and over.

In addition, half of young people think the situation is getting worse, with only 30 per cent of 18–24-year-olds believing it is becoming easier to move up in British society.

For both authors, this is a deeply worrying finding. We both know the difficulties of being people of working-class origin trying to get on in life, and that was in better times than today's young people enjoy. Today, only 4 per cent of doctors, 6 per cent of barristers and 11 per cent of journalists are from working-class origins, according to recent research by the London School of Economics using Labour Force Survey data. The government has failed to ensure the recovery was managed so that opportunities were distributed fairly. Whereas we both eventually found work after university, that might not be true for us if we were to be in the same position today. Chasing a dwindling number of jobs available to people with no experience, young people from working-class families will slip behind those from more advantaged backgrounds. In five or ten years' time, that will mean an entire generation for whom social origin will play a big part in defining what job they do, how much experience they can accrue and, as a result, how much they get paid. It will deepen inequality and has worrying implications for social solidarity.

Internships are a particular bugbear. When your authors graduated, they were eventually able to access graduate jobs. These provided vital preparation for the workplace while allowing us to have an adequate standard of living in the cities we moved to. That is no longer true for so many young people. A survey by Prospects, an employment agency, found in 2017 that 48 per cent of 16–25-year-olds had undertaken unpaid internships. Only 17 per cent had been paid for their work experience. This, of course, is a driver of inequality. Moving to London, for example, or any other big city, with high housing costs and overall cost of living, is beyond the means of many young people without parental assistance. Employers love to tell us the story of the young person who did an internship while working two other jobs and sleeping on a friend's sofa and was eventually rewarded for their pluck, but the truth is that these opportunities mainly go to those with parents who can support them. That puts a significant – and often unmanageable – burden on parents with lower incomes and especially children from single-parent families, and means many young people from less-wealthy backgrounds end up having to save up to take a job. There is also an increasing trend for 'training periods', which can last months, to be unpaid. This should be made illegal. The notion is repellent – even more so when you see internships being auctioned off by rich donors at Conservative

Party black-tie balls. In 2011, the Conservatives auctioned off five lucrative City internships for £14,000. Is there any clearer example of how our labour market has been perverted?

If we go back to the British Social Attitudes Survey, concerns emerge when we look at those factors that we said British workers perceive as being important: job security, that their job is interesting and that their job permits advancement. On all three, fewer people rate their job as having those attributes than perceive those attributes as important. And when it comes to a good income, less than 30 per cent of people feel their job is well-remunerated, while over 60 per cent feel that's an important aspect of work.

This is not just perception. The Resolution Foundation's 'A steady job?' report, published in July 2015, found a rising trend over the past twenty years in the proportion of 18–29-year-olds who find themselves in an insecure job, particularly young men. They also discovered that younger people are less likely to be in a job categorised as privileged, which means they are highly secure, whereas that has been rising slightly for older people. The weakening of trade union rights and the fall in trade union membership, especially in the private sector – a deliberate result of Conservative policies in government – has weakened the protections for all. Conservative governments' neglect of the enforcement of employment protection has helped this trend to develop virtually unchecked.

Insecurity has risen to such an extent that even the Bank of England's chief economist, Andy Haldane, has highlighted the problems caused by a shift of power to employers – precisely the problem we highlighted that Hayekism had caused. In a speech delivered in August 2017, Mr Haldane explicitly linked insecurity and a squeeze on wages to the shift in power that turned the relationship between labour and capital into one not seen since before the Industrial Revolution. He highlighted the rise in self-employment, which is usually associated with lower incomes, and the steep decline in trade union membership over recent decades. When workers lack power within the economy and capital has the whip hand, and when there is a glut of available workers, this gives employers the ability to set people against one another and squeeze hours, security and wages.

This is especially true for those who have the least power – young people. Many young people say that when they do find a job, it is because they've had to deliberately aim low to get that job. The 2017 UK University Graduate Employment Study by Accenture Strategy found that almost three quarters of recent graduates believe they are underemployed. Young people aren't to blame for the plight they find themselves in: 83 per cent in that survey were happy to move across the country for work and 90 per cent took into account job availability before selecting a course. This also explains the greater prevalence of systems like internships and long 'probationary' periods in contracts.

We realise that much of the evidence that is emerging is about young people. There may be some who say: 'Good, young people need to learn that life is tough!' This, however, would be myopic. The effects of the shift in power dynamics between labour and capital ripple throughout the jobs market, and this has manifested itself in the intensity, stressfulness and enjoyment of work for the majority of workers.

Despite wages stagnating, a Smith Institute study in 2016 showed more than two thirds of employees say they are working longer hours than two years ago. Ironically, more than a quarter of staff in the Smith Institute study said their productivity had declined as a result and only one in ten thought it had increased.

The Mental Health Foundation discovered that 13 per cent of UK workers are clocking over forty-nine hours of work a week – the EU 'working time directive' states that, in the UK, the maximum number of hours a worker should put in is forty-eight, unless that worker opts out.

A study for TotallyMoney.com in 2017 showed that British overtime has hit a record high, with employees working sixty-eight hours – a week and half's work – more each year than they are contracted to, usually for no additional pay. There is a gender-balance issue here too: 43 per cent of men get paid for overtime while that's only true for 30 per cent of women. The Trades Union Congress provided figures showing that the number of employees working longer hours than contracted had grown by 15 per cent in the past five years.

Fewer and fewer people have control over their work hours. The British Social Attitudes Survey found that in 2015, 57 per cent of semi-routine and routine workers (i.e. those not in managerial or professional occupations) had no control over their hours or how their work is organised. Ten years ago, that was only 42 per cent. Work is becoming more regimented and workers have less input and control over their work environment. The converse is true of those in managerial and professional occupations, though, with 86 per cent saying they have some or complete control over how they organise their day in 2015, a little bit more than the 81 per cent ten years ago. Voice and agency in the workplace are really important to the well-being of individuals and their capacity to enjoy their work and be productive. The deterioration in this area is a huge problem.

Smith's cynicism about the realities of work appears to be prevailing over Marx's aspirations. It is a Pyrrhic victory though.

Stress at work is increasing. The British Social Attitudes Survey found that in 2015, 37 per cent said they always or often find their work stressful. This is a rise on both 1997 and 2005, when only 32 per cent said the same, and compared with 1989 when the equivalent figure was 28 per cent. Forty per cent of those in professional or managerial occupations said they found work stressful always or often. There is a peak in people between thirty-five and forty-four years old.

More of us work, more of us work harder and more of us are suffering noticeable increases in stress as a result, which, to make matters even worse, is having a negative effect on our health. A study published in the *International Journal of Epidemiology* by researchers at Manchester University followed people returning to work after the recession. They took blood tests, asked questions and had health practitioners assess the health of the workers. The study found that people moving into low-pay, low-autonomy and low-security work had the highest levels of chronic stress – more so than those who remained unemployed. This stress manifests physically as well as mentally. Their long-term glucose levels were worse, their 'bad fat' levels were worse, and proteins in the bloodstream related to illness were higher. In short, bad work is making us ill – more so even than unemployment.

This is a startling indictment of work in Britain today. And it's affecting us all. More of us are working, we're doing so harder and longer, pay is stagnating, and yet our work is becoming less pleasurable. Work isn't giving us the security, satisfaction and pride that it should. And despite employers squeezing employees until their pips squeak, there is no evidence at all that it is improving productivity. In fact, British productivity is way behind our European neighbours. In the time a British worker makes £1 of value, a German worker makes £1.35, according to the ONS. We're behind the US, France and Italy too.

Part of the problem, as most people who work will recognise, is that in a system that necessarily privileges employers over employees, capital over labour, certain dynamics emerge. First, as we have said, labour is squeezed to work harder in the hope this will increase productivity, which only serves to increase stress levels, unhappiness and physical illness. An alienated worker works less efficiently, less passionately and therefore less effectively than a motivated and mentally positive worker. A further damaging effect of this misalignment is that workers are treated more like subordinates and less like partners in the workplace, which again damages productivity.

In Germany, workers and employers have much more effective relations. The German practice of *Mitbestimmung* sees workers' representatives on company boards, allowing them to have a voice on important issues, including human resources and corporate strategy. That means they have better industrial relations, with few strikes. This underpins the high-productivity, high-innovation culture there. If you want to make a quality product, you listen to your workers. You respect experience forged through practice. You increase institutional knowledge retention by having happy, motivated workers. That leads to more efficiency and more innovation.

Or, of course, you can do it Hayek's way and end up with a workforce that is squeezed for short-term gain and now – overworked, stressed and alienated – is falling further and further behind the rest of the world.

CHAPTER FIVE

IGNORANCE

By the time William Beveridge published *Social Insurance and Allied Services* in 1942, successive governments had already made considerable movement towards a coherent, universal educational system. A series of Acts of Parliament, starting in the mid-nineteenth century, had raised the school leaving age and extended both the provision and funding of schools. Victorian educationalists started to develop recognisable theories of pedagogy and the purpose of education.

The historian G. A. N. Lowndes, in his 1937 book, *The Silent Social Revolution*, which examined the changes in the education system over the previous few decades, stated:

> The contribution which a sound and universal system of public education can make to the sobriety, orderliness and stability of a population is perhaps the most patent of its benefits. What other gains can be placed to its credit? ... Can it be claimed that the widening of educational opportunity in the long run repays that cost to the community by a commensurate increase in the national wealth and prosperity? Or can it be claimed that it is making the population happier, better able to utilise its leisure, more adaptable?
>
> Anyone who knows how the schools have come to life in the past decade, anyone who is in a position to take a wide view of the social condition of the people and compare conditions

to-day with those forty years ago, will have no hesitation in answering these questions in the affirmative.

Similarly, William Beveridge saw education as an essential part of the means by which we preserve the order, integrity and success of our nation, especially by comparison with the totalitarian states with whom we were at war. In his 1944 book, *Full Employment in a Free Society*, he pointedly noted: 'Ignorance is an evil weed, which dictators may cultivate among their dupes, but which no democracy can afford among its citizens.' His book melded Fabian democratic socialist statism with Keynesian economics, arguing that government must both create demand for goods and services (as it had during the war) and ease unemployment by bringing industry to places where there was spare labour and also by making it as easy as possible for unemployed people to find labour. Education played a huge role, then, in maximising employment and ensuring the labour force's skills married up with the nation's needs. But Beveridge did take a more expansive view of education. In notes for his addresses to incoming students for 1924–26 at the London School of Economics, where he was the director, he wrote:

> The School … is not a place of technical education fitting you for one and only one profession. It makes you better for every occupation, it does help you get on in life … But you will lose most of the value of the School if you regard it solely as a means of getting on in life. Regard it as a means of learning, to advance science and civilisation.

By the time Beveridge had published *Full Employment in a Free Society*, the wartime coalition government had already promulgated the 1944 Education Act, the basis for our modern universal education system. Richard Austen 'Rab' Butler was the Conservative politician who created the post-war education system, working with politicians from all parties. The Act guaranteed free education for every child in England and Wales, divided schools into primaries and secondaries and set the aim of increasing the school leaving age from fourteen to sixteen. The 1944 Act created the Tripartite System, which consisted of three types of secondary school: grammar schools, secondary technical schools and secondary modern schools. While little-known now, the Act also created comprehensive schools and direct grant schools, which allowed independent schools to receive state funding in exchange for 'free places' for some students. It also introduced the eleven-plus exam, which streamed children to schools deemed appropriate to their skills, and it provided free milk for children.

Since then, the specific provisions of the 1944 Education Act have been replaced or repealed. A series of Acts of Parliament by hyperactive governments changed the implementation and funding of the education system repeatedly over the following decades but it never eliminated the educational segregation which was such a feature of the 1944 Act, even though its final formal provisions were repealed in 1996. Famously, Margaret Thatcher, 'the Milk Snatcher', took away free milk for children between seven and eleven. The pace of change has been such that few in politics ever really remember when things changed and why. One of the most common complaints, for example, of the Tory right is that Labour turned the polytechnics into universities, which they claim 'dumbed them down'. In fact, this change was carried out in the Tories' Further and Higher Education Act of 1992.

The reason for the hyperactivity around education is perhaps explained by the economic motives for ensuring the wider spread of knowledge and skills. Knowledge is recognised as the key driver of productivity and economic growth in Western countries, which is why we have focused so much as a nation on the role of information, technology and learning in economic performance. That was just as true when we were leading the world in industrial productivity as it is today in the digital economy.

Britain's education system comprises four parts. The first is the formal schooling of children. The second is higher education in universities. The third is further education, which is any study after secondary education that is not part of higher education (i.e. part of a degree). And the fourth is apprenticeships, which combine on-the-job training with accompanying study. In theory, all four should combine seamlessly to provide each individual with a cogent pathway to enlightenment and equip them with the skills they need and want to fulfil their aspirations in life. However, a combination of insufficiency of provision and barriers to access, like fees, means that isn't true for many British people.

If we start with schools – the one experience all British people share – generally speaking the thing that politicians and policy-makers use to assess progress is league tables that gauge pupil performance. There is a lot of excitement, for example, around the publication of the OECD's PISA rankings (Programme for International Student Assessment). This triennial survey assesses education systems based on international tests taken by a sample of fifteen-year-olds in maths, reading and science. The UK is generally a mid-table performer, with Asian education systems ranking at the top. Perhaps more useful than the relative rankings (which delight journalists, who love breathless but useless headlines on how we have fallen behind [insert relatively poor country] in [insert subject]) are the scores. Our scores were stable despite all the changes in the structure of our educational system in the past two or three decades. However, they did decline between 2012 and 2015 (the last tranche). This is almost certainly a reflection of the decline in the number of teachers. The BBC reported:

> The OECD education chief highlighted concerns about the impact of teacher shortages – saying that an education system could never exceed the quality of its teachers.
>
> 'There is clearly a perceived shortage,' he said, warning that head teachers saw a teacher shortage as 'a major bottleneck' to raising standards.

Similarly, the National Union of Teachers said the survey showed that 'the government is failing in one of its key responsibilities – to ensure that there are enough teachers in the system.' This failure underlies findings by the Joseph Rowntree Foundation (JRF) that a significantly growing number of young people have been leaving school under this government with the lowest levels of literacy and numeracy. Not just that, but unlike almost every other developed country, older people in Britain have higher literacy and numeracy scores than young people: a shocking symptom of a failure to drive improvement across the entire system of which we should be deeply ashamed. The JRF explained the kind of social exclusion this can cause:

> It means [the 5 million adults lacking basic reading, writing and numeracy skills] may struggle to carry out a number of basic tasks, ranging from writing short messages, using a cashpoint to withdraw money, being able to understand price labels on food or pay household bills.

A further 12.6 million adults lack basic digital skills – meaning they struggle to carry out tasks such as sending emails or filling out online job application forms.

A good school education requires three things: high-quality school leadership; high-quality teaching; and engaged and supportive parents. And, as with almost every public service, you get what you pay for. Singapore, the top-ranked country in PISA tables, invested heavily in the quality of its teachers. They focused on the prestige and status of teaching, recruiting its teachers from the top 5 per cent of graduates. In addition, all teachers are trained in the National Institute of Education (admittedly only possible in a city-state like Singapore). Finland, another very highly rated education system, also treats teaching as a high-status profession, and they also give teachers extensive training. All teachers take a five-year master's degree in which they are given the chance to test their skills in classrooms which act as laboratories – almost like university teaching hospitals for medical students, after which they are given huge autonomy – liberated from the inspection, testing and government control that bedevils teaching in the UK. Here, the Conservative government allowed non-qualified teachers to teach in free schools and academies, letting them compete for jobs with fully qualified teachers. As Tristram Hunt, then shadow Education Secretary, told Michael Gove when this change was first introduced in 2013: 'You need more qualifications to get a job in a burger bar than you do to teach in an English school.'

For all teachers, however, their one overriding aim is to improve the life chances of the children under their care, and to bring out their potential. In researching this book, we heard testimony from teachers – near tears – describing how they were simply incapable in the time available to provide the support required. In September 2017, 4,000 headteachers across England wrote to parents to warn that budgets face a real-terms cut of 4.6 per cent by 2020. According to the teaching unions, a typical primary school will be worse off annually by £52,546 and a typical secondary school will have lost £178,000 each year since 2015. Added to this are deep regional inequalities in the funding provided to schools. The Social Market Foundation explained in 2016 that

> how much money a child's parents earn, which region they live in and their ethnicity are all very significant factors in how successful they are at school. Where someone comes from can still matter much more in determining where they end up in life than their talents or efforts. This is the reality that should be weighed against political discussions of Britain as a meritocracy.

London had the highest spend by school per pupil in Department for Education figures published in 2014/15. In inner London, an average of nearly £6,000 was spent on each student. Unsurprisingly, therefore, over 70 per cent of students in London got five or more A*–C grades in their GCSEs that year. Compare that to Yorkshire and the Humber, where spending was £4,198 in that year, and only 63 per cent of students reached the same grades. Family income has long been recognised as a key influence of academic outcome. The reason for this is multi-factorial but predictable: parents who are working longer hours to compensate for low wages can give less time to their children for additional learning, helping with homework, etc. According to Ofcom figures for 2017, roughly 20 per cent of UK adults – one fifth of the country – don't have broadband access at home. Unsurprisingly, poorer households are less likely to have broadband than richer households. All this compounds the disadvantages suffered by poorer children.

A combination of hyperactive policy-making, systematic and regional underfunding and the inevitable consequences of economic inequality mean that we are simply not doing right by our children. Policy-making needs to be evidence-driven; not motivated by ideological programmes such as grammar schools, which are superficial at best, atavistic and counter-productive at worst. The Sutton Trust, for example, has identified the sorts of changes that would work for the better:

The two factors with the strongest evidence of improving pupil attainment are:

- Teachers' content knowledge, including their ability to understand how students think about a subject and identify common misconceptions;
- Quality of instruction, which includes using strategies like effective questioning and the use of assessment.

Specific practices which have good evidence of improving attainment include:

- Challenging students to identify the reason why an activity is taking place in the lesson;
- Asking a large number of questions and checking the responses of all students;
- Spacing out study or practice on a given topic, with gaps in between for forgetting;
- Making students take tests or generate answers, even before they have been taught the material.

Common practices which are not supported by evidence include:

- Using praise lavishly;
- Allowing learners to discover key ideas by themselves;
- Grouping students by ability;
- Presenting information to students based on their 'preferred learning style'.

Michael Gove used to boast that the pace of his change was 'fast' and the reaction of teachers 'furious' – as if that was something to be proud of. What he actually did was introduce an avalanche of ideological structural changes to the education system at the same time as stripping back one of the most important of the last Labour government's educational policies: SureStart, which was designed to bring help where it would be most effective – the early years. It's worth considering this for a moment. Before coming to power in 1997, Labour had considered a raft of research showing that one of the best ways to improve educational outcomes was to give kids access to pre-infant intellectual enrichment classes and activities. Hence, the introduction of SureStart, which also had the knock-on effect of bringing mums and dads together to listen to and share advice on parenting. The Tory government cut the budgets to local authorities, who administered SureStart, and then blamed the inevitable cuts to SureStart provision – resisted at first and then acceded to as inevitable in the worst-hit authorities – on the councils themselves. It was such an abrogation of duty by a government that claimed to care about education.

When it comes to universities, the media and some politicians often make the same mistake we do with schools in obsessing over rankings – domestic and international. Both writers were the first in their families to go to university: Angela to Oxford; Imran to Cambridge. University can be the most extraordinary experience for a young person. It is terrifying, thrilling, occasionally turgid and truly life-changing. Yes, employability and future earnings are important for students, but higher education should be valued for those reasons Beveridge once described. Education equips young people with skills in advanced critical thinking to help them navigate a complicated world; it gives them the technical skills to contribute to society; and it also exposes them to people they might never have met otherwise. University teaches you how to live, not just make a living.

The marketisation of higher education is, then, in those terms, a historic mistake. Angela campaigned against the introduction of tuition fees for that very reason. It was only when she, in co-operation with others, secured the introduction of a means-tested maintenance grant for the poorest pupils, no interest charges on repayments, the creation of the Office for Fair Access and a commitment that the fees would be capped for ten years at a maximum of £3,000 that, with much reluctance, she agreed to support the legislation. At least, she thought, the extra money raised actually went to universities, without any cuts in government funding. Then, however, the coalition and Tory governments abolished the £3,000 cap and tripled fees to £9,000, introduced interest on student loans, abolished maintenance grants for poorer pupils and, finally, completely cut government funding to universities, effectively marketising the entire system.

The truth is that our universities are genuinely world-class. Oxford and Cambridge dominate international league tables, sure, but thirty-one of our universities were in the top 200 in the respected Times Higher Education World University

Rankings 2018. Almost one in ten of the top 1,000 universities in the world were British. The reason for this is that we have a long-standing veneration of education. We were one of the first countries in the world to treat pedagogy with the importance it deserves. Our young people are taught to look at society, the world and our universe with wonder and the desire to both understand and make it better. That has always held Britain in good stead in competing internationally.

There is a legitimate debate to be had on how best to fund our universities. If we look at universities solely as mechanisms by which to improve the marketability of individuals – the Hayekian view – then tuition fees make complete sense. But if we look at them as the means by which we enrich our own society, then it is easier to see them as a price that should be borne by all of society. The solution will inevitably be found somewhere in between – whereby funding is be shared by the individual, the state and business. There is an argument to be made that because our tax system is progressive and that graduates tend to earn more, they already pay more towards our education system. It is also clear that if we are to succeed in the knowledge-driven economies that will manifest after the Fourth Industrial Revolution – in which automation, artificial intelligence and algorithms will replace substantial numbers of human jobs – we will need to prioritise the intellectual development of our citizens. Collective funding of the drivers of our economic success is not a transfer of wealth from all to the richest; it is an investment in our own prosperity.

Where our system breaks down, however, is in the options for those who don't want to go down the path of a university education. Britain has very low levels of apprenticeships and people in further education than in comparable economies worldwide. Lord David Sainsbury – a former Labour science minister – was tasked with looking at the further education and apprenticeships system in the UK in 2017. He found that Britain had just over a quarter of the number of apprentices per total number of employees of Germany – a country with a far more successful manufacturing sector. The disparity is not circumstantial; if we are to have a coherent industrial strategy, we will need not only highly skilled conceptual specialists but also highly skilled operational and technical specialists. That will require a mix of three things: (1) companies investing into workforce education; and formal training and – most importantly as our technological development accelerates – retraining opportunities provided by the government through (2) apprenticeships and (3) further education. All of this is vital to kick-start wage growth in Britain, which has flatlined for a decade since the financial crisis. Productivity growth and wage growth go hand-in-hand, so it is vital we invest in our skills.

The problem is that when it comes to all three goals, we're doing poorly. Generally speaking, Britain has left skills and training to the market for some time now. The Hayekian mindset would tell us that lots of individual decisions on training by companies would create a coherent whole that is best for Britain. But it just isn't true. The Institute for Public Policy Research, a left-wing think tank, has shown that British employers spend half as much as the EU average on vocational training and that investment fell in real terms in the past decade. The IPPR also found that one in three employees in the UK feel they are over-qualified for their jobs, which is the highest level in the EU. That means we have low demand for and low provision of skills training, which combine to devastating effect. It is clear that this is a space in which the state should intervene, to shape the outcomes we desire. But a Conservative Party held hostage by Hayekian hostility to the notion of government 'interference' will never take the actions required to encourage companies to utilise the skills of its workers and incentivise further investment in worker skills. They have masked their inaction behind the euphemism of 'employer-led training' and cut off any attempt to do so at the knees before it can get going.

When it comes to apprenticeships and further education, the Conservative government has boasted that it has vastly increased the number of apprentices in the country. While this is true, there is considerable evidence that in doing so they have sacrificed quality for quantity. The 60 per cent fall in apprenticeships offered after legislation mandated the standards of training expected to be included in an apprenticeship demonstrates this fact. Furthermore, the overall participation in government-funded adult further education, including apprenticeships, has declined drastically. The participation rate dropped from just under 4 million in 2005/06 to 2.25 million in 2016/17. The IPPR reported in 2017 that 'the vast majority of apprenticeships and further education courses are delivered at low level, many don't lead on to further study and much of existing vocational provision has poor labour market returns for adults.' They go on to explain that the government's laconic attitude to skills and stubborn reticence in intervening means that 'adults who could most benefit from participation in learning – including those who left school early and those with lower levels of qualification – are least likely currently to be taking part.' This is a cruel irony and one that simply holds back our economy. If we are not bringing out the potential in everyone, we are failing in our duty and we are putting our economic prosperity at risk too.

One of Labour's greatest achievements in higher and further education was the Open University. It was founded by Harold Wilson's government in 1969 but the bulk of the work to conceptualise it was done by the formidable Minister of State for

Education, Jennie Lee. Wilson and Lee saw the Open University as a means to enhance social mobility, give opportunities to those who may have been failed by the school system and enhance Britain's international competitiveness. It was a truly innovative solution to the question of how to both drive social mobility and meet the needs of our economy. In 2015/16, there were just under 175,000 enrolled students. In our technologically advanced society, there can be no barriers to expanding the provision of education to a broader range of society. It is dispiriting that most universities do not broadcast their lectures or have not sought ways to expand access to their research and insight. This is almost certainly a result of the marketisation of education, making it a privilege rather than a right.

Perhaps, then, our age's new Jennie Lee is Angela Rayner, a colleague on the Labour benches today. She proposes a National Education Service that would provide education from cradle to grave. As our industrial cycles shorten and the pace of technological innovation accelerates, we will need to ensure every citizen is given the chance to contribute to society in the way they feel is most appropriate. We will need to rediscover the spirit of Beveridge: to bring work closer to people, which is easier with the rise in remote working in fields as disparate as engineering to management consultancy to clinical surgery; and to ensure people are able to develop the knowledge, understanding and skillsets they need to prosper in the twenty-first century.

CHAPTER SIX

SQUALOR

On the morning of 14 June 2017, Britain awoke to one of the most horrific sights of recent years: the smouldering husk of Grenfell Tower. The news of dozens of deaths of men, women and children; of dozens more in hospital; images of firefighters blackened from soot, slumped on the grass outside with the thousand-yard stare of those who've experienced unbelievable horror. To some, the fire was viewed as an accident. For many, however, that blackened, ravaged shell was a terrible symbol of the austerity project. Kensington and Chelsea council, which was responsible for Grenfell Tower, was part of a gang of right-wing authorities in London, alongside others such as Westminster, Wandsworth, and Hammersmith and Fulham (pre-2014), which seemed to revel in cutting services and so-called 'red tape' while giving tax rebates to wealthy homeowners. These councils were the beating heart of Hayek's conservatism in modern Britain: cut taxes, cut services, cut regulations, ignore poor communities and privatise to diminish the power of trade unions in the public sector.

HOUSING

The problems of housing today in Britain are not limited to social housing or estates. In fact, Labour's Decent Homes

Standard was instrumental in increasing the quality of social housing for millions of people. Politicians, who spend a significant amount of time knocking on doors, could see with their own eyes the rapid and quite extraordinary transformation over the Blair and Brown governments. In 1997, 69 per cent of the social housing in the Wirral, which contains Angela's constituency of Wallasey, was classified as unfit. By the time the Labour government left office in 2010, this had fallen to 5 per cent. Today, the most appalling standards in housing are in fact most often found in homes rented privately by landlords (the private rented sector). Government figures show that 28.5 per cent of private rented homes did not meet the Decent Homes Standard in 2015, compared to 13 per cent of social homes.

Beyond the specific issue of standards, all political parties agree that we have a housing crisis today. Quite simply, for a long time we've been building fewer houses than we need to match demand. As a result, young people and families are priced out of the market and those seeking to upgrade to larger homes to accommodate growing families are also stuck in smaller, increasingly cramped dwellings. There are those that would tell us that, to solve this housing crisis, all we need to do is stop migration. This is plainly untrue. The major components of growth in housing demand are (1) people living for longer and therefore not handing down homes to the next generation; (2) the increase in family breakdown leading to the creation of new households; and (3) population growth, including, in part, migration. If we cut migration to zero tomorrow, we'd still have a serious mismatch between supply and demand for new homes. Not all the problems we've seen in our housing market were visible in the 1990s and the first few years of the new millennium. Under Labour, house-building continued at a steady pace; it was the crash of 2008 that exposed the huge structural problems at the heart of housing in Britain today.

The coalition government's response when they first exploited widespread anger over the financial crisis to win power in 2010 was to cut the affordable housing budget while relaxing planning rules that private housing developers had to build affordable housing and community facilities in each development. The government has, by almost every measure of outcome, failed to meet its ambitious stated aims. Housing has continued to become more unaffordable and young people are increasingly locked out of the housing market. Meanwhile, those who own have continued to benefit from a purely technical bounce in the value of their housing.

It's impossible to overstate the extent to which housing has influenced politics and policies in recent decades. One of the most politically potent housing policies was Margaret Thatcher's Right to Buy, which Labour initially welcomed. It was popular, ensuring that those who took part had a valuable asset, until its sheer success resulted in a diminishing social housing stock for those who could not afford to buy their own home. Those who own houses have done well out of them: since 1980, the ONS has found that, on average, house prices have increased by 7 per cent per year, far beyond the rate of inflation or wage growth. That has meant that houses are less and less affordable for new buyers but also that maintaining house-price growth has been a clear aim for Conservatives: any drops would be met, they fear, with a catastrophic decline in their vote. The ONS found that the unaffordability of housing has led to a decline in mortgage approvals. From the 1980s until the early 2000s, there were typically between 400,000 and 600,000 loans to first-time buyers each year. That went down to under 200,000 in the housing crash. This has led to a change in the composition of who owns houses in Britain. In 1991, 67 per cent of those aged 25–34 were homeowners. By the financial year ending 2014, this figure was down to 36 per cent. For the 16–24 age group, homeownership declined from 36 per cent in 1991 to 9 per cent in 2015. Meanwhile, for those aged over 65, the proportion of homeowners leapt from under 50 per cent to over 75 per cent.

This has profound implications for the distribution of wealth in Britain. Lloyds Bank estimated that total British household wealth at the end of 2016 was £10.5 trillion (£10,500 billion). Of that, real estate company Savills estimated that the total value of all housing in the UK was £6.8 trillion. That means 68 per cent of all household wealth is held in homes – a classic asset bubble. Analysis by the *Financial Times* showed that 'as well as rising sharply in nominal terms, housing wealth has grown in relation to the size of the economy: it was equivalent to 1.6 times Britain's gross domestic product in 2001, rising to 3.3 times in 2007 and 3.7 times in 2016.' Furthermore, when it comes to regional disparities, the *FT* found that

> the value of homes in London and south-east England has topped £3tn ... meaning almost half the total is accounted for by a quarter of UK dwellings. This concentration of wealth is most evident in the richest London boroughs, Westminster and Kensington & Chelsea, where housing stock adds up to £232bn, more than all of the homes in Wales.

Given this wealth is concentrated in older hands and will be passed on to their children and grandchildren, it shows how the vast majority of British capital is being concentrated into fewer and fewer hands and propagated not by any system of natural justice but by kinship. It is becoming more likely that you will own a home in your lifetime if your parents owned a home. And if you are poor, it is becoming more likely that you will be paying rent to a landlord who is further building their assets as well as enjoying generous tax advantages.

The biggest issue with house-building is that there simply hasn't been sufficient political will invested into changing the dynamics of this market. Over recent decades, the number of small- and medium-sized builders has dropped, and so we are over-reliant on large companies who have disproportionate power when dealing with councils and communities. We also have a serious problem in our planning system. Councils and residents refuse to authorise planning applications for local development in part because of NIMBYism ('Not In My Back Yard'), in part because developers come up with unacceptable schemes that prioritise their profits over residents' demands. One of the most remarkable and frustrating statistics around housing was that polling showed that a majority of respondents expressed worry about whether their children would be able to buy houses, but also said they didn't want more house-building locally. This, accompanied with the fear that if house-building increased dramatically it might cause prices to go down and thus put a dent in the asset values of older voters, has led to a lack of political will to deal with this serious social problem. It is the imbalance between the rights of owners and those that don't own – once again between capital and labour – that has seen our young citizens cramped in homes with multiple occupants, a resurgence of Rachmanite slum landlordism and, alongside policies like the bedroom tax, a profound redistribution in wealth from those who have little money to those who own property. While those with homes have seen massive, unearned increases in their wealth over recent decades,[1] indebtedness is greater than it's ever been, including unsecured debt, which is now at a higher level than it was before the financial crisis.

Labour conducted a serious review of housing in 2014. Commissioned by the then shadow Secretary of State for Communities and Local Government, Hilary Benn, and conducted by Sir Michael Lyons, it explicitly pointed blame at a dysfunctional land market that lacks transparency and has been used for speculative gain. Furthermore, because local communities do not trust developers to work hand-in-hand with them but rather in pursuit of their own interests and profits, many people feel they cannot get houses built where they think they should be built, such as on brownfield land or areas of low aesthetic or environmental value. Finally, in order to build good homes with the infrastructure – like schools, health facilities, green spaces, leisure facilities and transport – that turns a housing development into a community, we need a better system of planning and executing medium- and large-scale development. If Labour had won in 2015, the policies in its manifesto, which under the Salisbury Convention could not be refused outright by Conservative peers in the House of Lords, would undoubtedly have caused a major expansion of house-building. This government has never shown an iota of ambition on housing, despite endless pronouncements, initiatives and press releases. This one issue alone is a case for electing a Labour government right now.

Bad housing damages the health of residents. Mould and damp are particular problems, and these have been getting worse since 2010. Labour had brought the number of houses with damp down from 2.6 million to just over 1 million by 2011. But this declining trend slowed and has now reversed as of 2015, according to the government's own published figures. Children in bad, cramped housing have worse educational outcomes because they simply cannot find the space to study peacefully. It leads to family discord and there is compelling evidence about the connection between bad housing and mental health problems, which is a good reminder of the connection that quite different areas of government policy can have with each other. A House of Commons Library paper in 2011 stated that 'poor housing conditions have a detrimental impact on health, costing the NHS at least £600 million per year'. That is a good reason for spending money on improving housing – a fixed investment now – to make big savings in the future.

The problem of homelessness – an acute symptom of the underlying disjunction in our housing market – is illustrative of the overall patterns of the past twenty years. Labour targeted homelessness as a policy priority. Under Labour, statutory homelessness acceptances by local authorities reached their peak in 2003, having increased since 1997 before being relentlessly driven down to historic lows by the end of the Brown government. Since then, the independent fact-checking organisation Full Fact report that 'around 58,000 households were accepted by councils as entitled to be housed in 2015/16. This number has been rising since 2009/10, and is up by a third since 2010/11.' But when it comes to temporary accommodation, the figures are not as positive. By the end of the Brown government, virtually no progress had been made on the numbers of people in temporary housing. That is because, while the Blair government had made the statutory accommodation available to more people, they were languishing for long periods in temporary housing until appropriate accommodation was sought. These waiting times were a reflection of the scarcity of homes. It is to Britain's credit that we do so much to ensure those that are homeless are provided with accommodation. But it is shameful that the broken housing market keeps people in inappropriate accommodation for so long, including an estimated 120,000 children.

ENVIRONMENT AND POLLUTION

The second component of squalor is our environment and pollution; something that affects everyone, whether rich or poor. There are two very distinct elements to this: first, climate change on a global level; and second, the quality of our environment in Britain.

On the dangers of global climate change, neither author has any time for climate change deniers, who reject the bulk of evidence indicating its existence, cherry-pick data to support their own agenda and make strange assertions that, since we can't control non-anthropogenic (non-human-induced) climate change, we shouldn't deal with our own mess. It is a matter of pride that Britain has been one of the world's leading nations when it comes to dealing with climate change. As recently as 2015, the UK ranked behind only Denmark in the Climate Change Performance Index (CCPI), published by Germanwatch and the Climate Action Network. But, despite David Cameron's affection for huskies and promise to have the greenest government ever, our relative performance has declined over recent years. Ed Miliband, the last Labour Secretary of State for Energy and Climate Change, was instrumental in securing the Copenhagen Agreement and was deeply involved in negotiations around the world. David Cameron, though, took only three years to abandon climate change as a major UK priority and tell his people to 'cut the green crap'. In 2016, the Department of Energy and Climate Change (DECC) was disbanded and rolled into a new Department for Business, Energy and Industrial Strategy (BEIS). And, as of 2017, Britain had slipped to fifth place in the Germanwatch and Climate Action Network tables. Their analysis of our performance is worth reading:

With a very high performance especially in the GHG

emissions category, e.g. with the third highest rated emissions reduction target, the United Kingdom holds the 5th rank in the CCPI. From national experts, the UK receives only low ratings for current policies, both domestically and regarding its performance in international climate diplomacy. National experts warn, like some other European countries, the UK's relatively high score stems from a lag effect: with the exception of a bold promise to phase out coal power, for which the UK deserves credit, policy from 5–10 years ago is responsible for low carbon investment and the UK's falling emissions. Experts agree that future carbon reductions are at real risk: the government has failed to deliver a policy framework for renewables from 2017 onwards, and as a consequence the UK's Treasury expects renewables investment to fall by 96 per cent by 2020. The continuation of several other important policies, including the carbon floor price and zero carbon homes, also seems to be at risk. Without significant change in policy in the next years, experts would expect the UK to drop in the [tables].

This intensely depressing assessment of our recent performance is directly down to Conservative priorities. Moving DECC into BEIS is one of those things politicians do when they want to send a message. As Ed Miliband noted at the time, departments set priorities and shape outcomes. In de-prioritising climate change and making it subservient to the needs of business, the government were almost certainly listening to the climate change-denying tendency in their own ranks. But they couldn't have been more wrong-headed. The direct effects of climate change will damage global businesses. Even the City of London isn't immune. Climate-related disasters like droughts and hurricanes, for example, are hitting insurers and reinsurers, for example Lloyds of London. The United Nations found that between 2005 and 2015, there were 335 weather-related disasters each year across the globe, almost twice the number from 1985 to 1994. Insurers are also worried about the cost. The real-terms cost of natural disasters was about $30 billion annually in the 1980s. It's now $182 billion a year – six times more even when accounting for inflation. Globally interconnected supply chains are also much more sensitive to disruptions in the vast array of locations they and their suppliers, distributors and customers operate in.

Beyond that, green energy is a huge emerging new growth sector globally. Britain should be trying to lead this industry to enhance our future prosperity. There is a global race on renewables. Al Gore, the former US Vice President and climate change campaigner, recently noted in an interview on *The Bernie Sanders Show* that the fastest growing job in the US, according to the US Bureau of Labor Statistics, is windmill technician. Germany announced in 2011 that it would phase out nuclear and prioritise renewables. Some critics said renewables couldn't possibly replace the megawatts produced by nuclear power plants. How wrong they were. On one day in May 2016, over 85 per cent of electricity produced in Germany was from wind and solar, so much that it caused a downward spike in the overall cost of energy. In the second quarter of 2017, 30 per cent of all energy produced in Britain was from renewables. In September 2017, a landmark occurred in Britain that critics of renewables had claimed wouldn't happen for years: the price of offshore wind went below that of nuclear, and by quite some margin. And yet, of the companies that operate in the renewables sector, Britain has only four of the top 200 according to Clean200, which produces annual analyses on the market. China has sixty-eight, the US has thirty-four, Japan has twenty and Germany has nine, including the top company, Siemens. Once more, the lack of a coherent industrial strategy has meant that the UK is missing out on the myriad opportunities available to lead in this new sector.

The politics of climate change and renewable energy are quite clear. In the government's published polling on climate change, available from the Department for Business, Energy and Industrial Strategy's website, in the latest tracker, 71 per cent of people say they are very or somewhat concerned about climate change. Seventy-nine per cent of people support the greater usage of renewables, with only 4 per cent opposed. Six in ten people said they would support a large-scale renewable development in their area. The opposition comes from vested interests like major oil and gas companies.

On the domestic front, our most pressing environmental challenge today is air pollution – in particular, levels of nitrous oxides, which the Environment, Food and Rural Affairs Committee declared a 'public health emergency' in 2016. The government's own scientists have found that 'air pollution has negative impacts on human health and the environment. Long-term exposure to particulate matter contributes to the risk of developing cardiovascular diseases and lung cancer.' A lot of the reporting on air pollution has been either hysterical or hysterically ill-informed. The truth is that air pollution has dropped markedly over the past few decades but there has been a particular recent and acute problem with nitrous oxides and particulates from diesel cars. In the UK today, about half of cars run on diesel. Sadiq Khan has taken the lead as Mayor of London on providing real facts on air pollution, acknowledging the improvements over recent years but putting plans into place to deal with nitrous oxides hotspots. It's a good example of serious, evidence-based and effective policy-making. His plan will reduce exposure to nitrous oxides by 96 per cent by 2020. The last Labour government made huge progress on our general environment: on water, our beaches, leading internationally on climate change. This was achieved with the assistance of EU directives and regulations, which Britain helped to formulate and pass. That progress appears to be in reverse now in several key areas, despite all those fine words from David Cameron and the presence of the purportedly green Liberal Democrats in the coalition government.

CRIME

The final component of squalor that concerned William Beveridge in the midst of the Second World War and the Commission on Social Justice in the 1990s was crime. In both periods, there was an acute sense of crisis, linked to a moral panic over young people. In the war, hundreds of thousands of young people had been evacuated away from their parents. Many of those young people would never see their conscripted fathers again. Hundreds of thousands more remained in towns without much supervision. There was a predictable rise in hooliganism, gang violence and petty crime. In 1997, crime had just reached all-time peak levels in the UK-wide crime survey. On both occasions, the incoming Labour government responded to soaring crime levels by being both tough on crime and tough on the causes of crime.

The Attlee government introduced the Children Act 1948, creating a comprehensive, locally administered childcare service, and the Criminal Justice Act 1948, which set up youth facilities that sought to retrain delinquent children through corrective training and, where necessary, a period of preventive detention. Attlee's government also outlawed whipping, hard labour and many of the excesses of the old penal regime.

The Blair government came into office with huge ambitions to revolutionise the approach to crime, which had soared in Britain, reaching its peak in 1995. A government statement of the time explained: 'In 1991, 5.3 million crimes (excluding criminal damage under £20) were recorded by the police. This compares with 4.4 million crimes in 1990 and 1.6 million in 1970. There has been an upward trend in recorded crime rates since the 1950s.' In the context of what can only be described as a crime wave, Tony Blair wrote in the *New Statesman*:

> Our approach is rooted in our belief that society needs to act to advance the interests of individuals. For crime, ultimately, is a problem that arises from our disintegration as a community, with standards of conduct necessary to sustain a community. It can only be resolved by acting as a community, based on a new bargain between individual and society. Rights and responsibilities must be set out for each in a way relevant for a modern world.

He was speaking in contrast to the rhetoric of the Thatcherites who claimed that there was no society – that it was individuals who were responsible for crime and nothing whatsoever to do with the broader social context.

On this, Tony Blair was right, and crime dropped at a precipitous and quite extraordinary rate in Britain over the following years. There were the usual Conservative commentators that claimed it was all statistical manipulation, but even the Tories have to acknowledge the extraordinary effect of Labour's policies. Nick Hurd, the Policing Minister, acknowledged in September 2017 that crime in Britain was down 69 per cent since its 1995 peak (but only because he was trying to spin the largest increase in recorded crime in a decade on his watch). His deception is easily revealed.

Criminology has allowed us to learn a lot about crime in recent decades, particularly the conditions under which people commit crimes and how to stop them from doing so in the first place. Mechanisms like surveillance help to dissuade potential offenders from crossing that line since, if they think they're going to get caught, they're much less likely to offend. Furthermore, our social mores have changed. Evidence suggests that in recent decades we in Britain, as well as many other countries in the West, have become less tolerant of violence. Bullying in schools has become less and less acceptable, especially since the scrapping of the odious Section 28; corporal punishment at home is not countenanced; and we have become less permissive of abusive, especially discriminatory, language.

We better understand criminogenicity – what makes people start committing crime – too. Studies have shown that delinquent behaviour tends to start at around twelve to fourteen years of age and tail off around twenty-one to twenty-four years. This period correlates with a natural liminal stage in a young person's development, when peers replace parents as key influencers until romantic partners take over. Around 56 per cent of offenders do so for the first time under the age of eighteen. A further 21 per cent first offend between eighteen and twenty-four – the transition to adulthood. After that, there is a natural decline in first-time offending.

Cutting youth crime and youth first-time offending is critical to an effective law and order strategy. The bulk of crime and first-time offenders can be dealt with by devoting attention and resources to dissuading young people and young adults from delinquency.

The focus by government and criminal justice lobbyists on how recidivism varies by how individuals are treated when they are already in the criminal justice system – whether they are sentenced to community punishments or the secure estate – is only part of the story. Recidivism is best explained by the fact that persistent reoffenders have personalities that are psycho-social in nature. Put simply, this means that the most prolific offenders start early and have long criminal careers.

From these statistics, a clear message emerges: we must deal with offending behaviour early and preferably before de-linquency sets in. There is an economic message here too. The monetary value of crime in the UK was calculated at £60 billion in England and Wales in 1999. A US study shows that the cost of a high-risk youth to society is $2 million over the period they spend offending. So, early intervention is not just a good idea to stop young people becoming future offenders, it is economically wise. It's a good investment.

Criminals who persistently reoffend have identifiable char-acteristics that would allow us to identify families and indi-viduals with high criminogenic risk. We have evidence that some programmes are effective in reducing offending and in many cases the financial benefits outweigh their financial cost. Demonstrably effective intervention programmes include gen-eral parent education, parent management training, pre-school intellectual enrichment programmes, child-skills training, teacher training, anti-bullying programmes and multisystemic therapy (MST).

It is worth noting that half of all offences are committed by unconvicted males. However, while it would be justifiable to target intervention programmes on high-risk persons who are likely to get convicted, it would also be desirable to implement those programmes that focus on the whole community, includ-ing those like SureStart, as well as measures designed to reduce childhood poverty.

The two major institutional innovations in the Crime and

Disorder Act 1998 – the Youth Justice Board and the Youth Offending Teams they co-ordinated – were at the heart of New Labour's youth offending policies.

Youth Offending Teams – multi-agency partnerships of childcare, healthcare and policing specialists embedded in local authorities – dealt with young offenders from arrest, through court, managing their punishment in the community or the secure estate, all the way to reintegration. Labour later added prevention work to their remit and resourced them with expertise on gang behaviour, restorative justice and more. We also gave them considerable latitude for innovation and sharing of ideas.

Labour's policies helped to arrest the unrestrained growth in crime that had occurred under the Conservatives and radically reduced youth crime. Labour judged, correctly, that the right way to cut youth offending and the number of young people in prison was to stop them turning to crime in the first place. Prevention professionals, armed with an understanding of the criminogenic factors outlined earlier, identified high-risk families and intervened to help young people before they crossed into offending.

We also improved schools, created schemes like SureStart and the Educational Maintenance Allowance (EMA), and raised 1 million children out of poverty, all of which worked to reduce offending.

This, as we know from the economics of offending, had considerable benefit to the state, particularly expense in the criminal justice system, policing and eventually in net economic benefit for young people that go on to lead productive lives that are not mired in criminality.

It is worth noting here that this wasn't much talked about outside of specialist circles. The Conservatives, utterly baffled at Labour's success, just pretended it wasn't happening. And many prominent 'prison reformers' expended huge amounts of chutzpah having a go at Labour for its 'tough-on-crime' rhetoric, forgetting the other half of the equation and the remarkable success it was having.

The effects of Labour's policies continued to be felt until the Tories started dismantling them. The Youth Offending Teams had their resources cut drastically, as did local government, leading to the closure of SureStart centres and children's facilities. EMA was also withdrawn. It was profoundly short-sighted and, alongside the cuts to police numbers, this led in 2017 to the biggest increase in crime for a decade – 10 per cent in recorded crime and 18 per cent in recorded violent crime. All of this will have an effect that will endure. It will harm communities, divide people and mean thousands of people who could have been saved from a life of crime will continue down a chaotic pathway. Worst of all, it will mean thousands of fellow citizens will suffer the harm and indignity of becoming a victim of crime. In short, we will all pay for the narrow-minded false economies of austerity policies.

The story across almost every measure of squalor – homelessness, poor housing standards, the environment and crime – has been one of considerable improvement thanks to serious intervention and clever policies by the Labour Party between 1997 and 2010, and retrenchment since then under the coalition and Conservative governments. We should be proud of that in the Labour Party. But there's also an underlying story that Labour didn't manage to put in place the fundamental structural reforms that would keep things getting better. In particular, the relationship between capital and labour remained out of kilter in the housing market and Labour didn't have the time to take advantage of the growing renewables sector to fundamentally rebalance our energy mix and industrial policy in the sector. Given time after 2010, and had we won in 2015, our policies and priorities would, we hope, demonstrate a greater political will to do so, particularly after the housing crisis exposed the problems in the market. There is no doubt they must be major political ambitions for the next Labour government.

CHAPTER SEVEN

DISEASE

Created shortly after the Second World War, the NHS is the most universally cherished achievement of Attlee's Labour government. It is seen around the world as a beacon of British civilisation and holds a special and central place in Britain's identity as a nation; one of the reasons Danny Boyle made it a centrepiece of his showcase of British culture at the London 2012 Olympics opening ceremony. But why is it so cherished? Because it recognises that some things are too important to be left to the 'free market'. Because it responds to need regardless of personal income. This is at the core of its success.

The majority of British people alive today were safely delivered in an NHS hospital. The NHS has helped to eradicate or seriously diminish the prevalence of many once-deadly communicable diseases, like tuberculosis, measles and polio. All British citizens, regardless of wealth, have been able to take advantage of rapid advances in pharmaceuticals, medical technology and techniques in recent decades; poorer citizens in many other countries would not have been given such equitable access. As a result, British people live far, far longer and enjoy better overall health than ever before. A child born in 1901 in Britain could expect to live around fifty years or so. A century later, a child born in 2001 could expect to live over seventy-five years. The ONS predicts that by the middle of the twenty-first century, life expectancy will reach 100 years.

The second extraordinary thing about the NHS is that it is paid for by all of us. It is a truly heart-warming notion to think that when we get poorly, every one of our fellow citizens has contributed to ensuring we get better. It is as pure and profound an expression of compassion and solidarity as you can get. Free at the point of access, from cradle to grave, paid for by each according to their means. It is the essence of democratic socialist values, and a perfect example of collective solidarity. No wonder it is so popular and inspiring.

The success of the NHS, however, has had huge knock-on effects on every area of social policy.

Take housing, for example. Because British citizens now live much longer, it means we are far less likely to pass on our houses to our children when they are in their young adulthood – instead they must wait until much later in life. That simple fact increases demand for housing considerably; indeed, extended lifespans is one of the biggest components in the housing crisis we face today.

It has also altered the demand for education, since longer lives mean we can afford to spend more time educating ourselves in preparation for our longer working lives. (If you thought you might only spend thirty years working, rather than fifty years, you'd be more reluctant to give up an extra few years to education.) It also increases the demand for mid-career education, as our economically active lives can span entire industrial cycles. Someone who started working in the 1970s would have seen the nature of the workplace change radically and our economy's composition change substantially. The ability to retrain is even more important than ever before.

The NHS's success has also had knock-on effects on the service itself.

Before it was created seventy years ago, children would die in the thousands of now easily preventable diseases like pneumonia, meningitis, tuberculosis, diphtheria and polio. The infant mortality rate – i.e. the number of children dying before they turned one – just before the Second World War, in 1938, was around 6 per cent. By 2015, that figure was 0.4 per cent. Indeed, it has gone down consistently every year in all but two years since the NHS was created. An international team of researchers led by the University of Bristol and funded by the British Medical Research Council, the Department for International Development and the European Union, has shown that even sufferers of HIV – which has caused millions of deaths – are now able to live for as long as people without HIV, if they are given effective, early treatment.

While this is all good news, the sheer success of the NHS in delivering high-quality healthcare to all citizens means we are now more likely to live long enough to encounter diseases and conditions like cancer, cardiovascular disease, dementia and deterioration of our musculoskeletal system by wear and tear. Indeed, the leading cause of death in Britain in 2016, according to Department of Health statistics, was dementia.

The number of people in their fifties is now far higher than the number of people in lower age brackets. This issue of changing demographics is being confronted by all those societies that have developed successful healthcare systems. Proportionately, citizens in their late middle age are over-represented within our age pyramid compared to citizens in younger age groups – and that means that in ten years or so we're going to have a real challenge as this age group reaches retirement age. Though a challenge, it's a great one to have, because it flows from the huge success of earlier social policy. It does, however, signal the need for a fundamental restructuring of our health and social security system to cope with future demographics. We're going

to need to ensure our young people are much more economically active and productive in order to pay for the retiring baby
boomer generation, who tended not to have as many children
(which is why we have been highly reliant on migration to bol-
ster the numbers of economically productive people that pay
taxes in Britain and support our older citizens).

The average 65-year-old costs the NHS 2.5 times more than
the average thirty-year-old. An 85-year-old costs more than five
times as much. That is because chronic conditions, like cardiovascular disease, diabetes and dementia, require long-term
clinical management. By the age of sixty-five, most people will
have at least one of these illnesses. By seventy-five they will
have two. Despite, or perhaps because of this, the global life
sciences industry has spent a fortune on discovering drugs and
developing protocols and techniques for intervening medically
to manage these problems.

The number of people dying as a result of cardiovascular disease went down by 70 per cent between 1970 and 2013, according to a study published in the *British Medical Journal*. Even
cancer is not the death sentence it once was – half of people
now survive for a decade or more. The NHS, the pharmaceutical industry and the array of scientists and medics in hospitals,
universities and research institutes around the world have done
an incredible job in changing our health and how we live. But
it all costs money.

In 2015/16, we spent £144 billion on the NHS: around 20 per
cent of total annual public expenditure. It is the second biggest
area of public spending after pensions (the rising cost of pensions itself being a reflection of how long we live). In real terms
(after adjusting for inflation) we spend ten times more than we
spent each year in the first decade of the NHS. Public spending
on health in the UK rose by an average of 3.7 per cent per year

between 1949/50 and 2013/14 in real terms. Public spending on health outpaced economic growth over this period and, as a result, public spending on health as a share of UK GDP has more than doubled from 1949/50 to today.

The period between 1999/2000 and 2009/10, when Tony Blair and Gordon Brown dealt with the underinvestment of the Thatcher years, saw a huge rise in health spending. It rose from 5.0 per cent to 7.8 per cent of GDP. Remember that next time someone asks why Labour didn't spend on one priority or another: just the increase in the NHS was quite staggering in absolute terms. That's why the NHS today is the fifth biggest employer in the world, with 1.7 million staff. It stands only behind the US Department of Defense, the Chinese People's Liberation Army, Walmart and McDonald's.

The proportion of total UK government spending devoted to health also rose from 9.3 per cent in 1949/50 to 18.1 per cent in 2013/14. That means that of every £5 spent by the government, nearly £1 goes to the NHS. If the NHS needs more resources because of understandably growing demand, that just squeezes everything else in the budget – social security, education, defence and the rest of the government's spending priorities. It's why driving efficiency in the NHS has always been so important. Making the money stretch further is a priority for governments that want to liberate more cash to spend on other things.

Let's put that £144 billion into context. We spend just over £102 billion a year on education, £34 billion on public order and safety and just over £2 billion on unemployment benefits. The NHS, while incredibly cheap by international standards, is a big portion of UK public spending. But other countries do spend far more on healthcare as a proportion of their economy. The OECD tries to compare total healthcare expenditure across countries. This is made slightly more difficult because in many countries there is both public and private purchase of health-care. Their data shows that, in 2014, we spent a total of 9.9 per cent of GDP on healthcare in the UK. In Germany, they spent 11 per cent; in France 11.1 per cent and in the USA, despite their well-known problems with coverage, they spent a staggering 16.6 per cent. That's the premium you pay for having private companies involved in every stage of your health system.

The central question for healthcare in Britain is becoming 'what are we willing to pay to get the services we expect?' The truth is that we will need to address both efficiency and absolute spending if our NHS is to be fit for purpose in the twenty-first century. That almost certainly means we will have to spend more. Indeed, money is at the very heart of the NHS's stresses and failures. Budgets may have risen beyond the rate of inflation consistently until very recently, but demand has also continued to rise. Every year the media report on a 'winter health crisis', with waiting times soaring, non-urgent operations cancelled, and patients being turned away from A&E for non-emergency conditions, as happened again in December 2017. We know as well that the time people spend waiting in A&E to be treated or have to wait to get a GP appointment is rising. Anyone who has had to have an operation in recent years for something non-urgent, like a knee reconstruction or cataract surgery, knows the wait can be months long and they can all too often be postponed if the system is under particular pressure.

The reason for this is that whereas our health system, for the main part, works effectively to deliver healthcare – hence the improvements in lifespan and general health – it is very heavily stretched, especially so in some parts. It's worth looking at what and where things are going wrong to better understand why it's happening and how we can fix it. The most acute pressures are noticed by patients in A&E, in getting a GP appointment, in waiting times for procedures and in the adult social care system.

In 2016/7, there were a record number of A&E attendances in the UK – 23 million, equivalent to around one attendance per three people. Once a patient attends A&E, they will be initially assessed rapidly and clinical staff will make a judgement on whether they need to be prioritised – this is called 'triaging' patients. Someone with trouble breathing, for example, will be examined carefully and, if showing signs of acute distress, admitted and given emergency treatment. That person would always be dealt with more quickly than someone coming in, for example, with a twisted ankle after slipping on some ice.

Labour introduced a target that 98 per cent of all patients should be seen within four hours of attendance. The coalition government reduced this target to 95 per cent of all patients to cover up growing waiting times. However, performance deteriorated further. Last year (2017), only 89 per cent of people were seen within four hours of arriving at an A&E. On average, patients spent around two and a half hours in total in A&E from arrival to departure, up from around two hours in 2011 and 2012.

So, beyond the raw number of attendances, what else explains the crisis in A&E departments? It's a complicated story. All too often reporting of crises focuses on immediate problems in one hospital or another rather than trying to understand the underlying problems and how they are or are not being addressed.

Of the 23 million people attending last year, 37 per cent were discharged without follow-up, and 19 per cent were discharged with GP follow-up. Only 20 per cent of patients required admission to hospital. Services like NHS Direct and its successor NHS 111 have helped to alleviate some pressure on A&E departments by providing advice to those who aren't sure what to do in the hours that their GP surgery isn't open. They can help divert people from A&E to other services, thus reducing the overall load on A&E as well as the number of people who will wait the longest in A&E, because they have been assessed in triage as being non-urgent. A report by the Health Select Committee illustrated the sorts of numbers going through the system, saying: 'On average each day in 2015/16, the NHS saw nearly 63,000 people through its A&E departments ... and offered over 38,000 NHS 111 calls.'

Meanwhile, the number of staff working in A&E has increased: consultants by 37 per cent in the past five years; non-consultant doctors by 19 per cent; and nurses by 17 per cent. Yet the United Kingdom has one of the lowest ratios of emergency doctors to attendance in the developed world. The Royal College of Emergency Medicine has said it is the lowest in the developed world.

At the same time, the Royal College reports that

since 2010–11 the total number of beds has decreased by 8.91 per cent (12,875) and the number of general and acute beds has declined by 6.44 per cent (7,127). The combination of increased demand and diminished physical capacity has led to a predictable increase in rates of bed occupancy. Since 2010–11 general and acute bed occupancy has increased from 86.3 per cent to 91.2 per cent. This is the figure recorded at midnight – daytime occupancy rates frequently exceed 100 per cent in many hospitals. Such occupancy levels mean there is no surge capacity, rendering hospitals hostage to fortune.

It is true that the number of beds overall in the NHS has reduced drastically in recent decades, in great part because of improvements in how we manage patients and clinical innovations. Procedures like keyhole surgery, improvements in anaesthesia and also simply a better understanding of when people need in-patient treatment and when they are better off at home have all contributed to a reduction in the need for beds. However, it is also quite clear that we have serious problems with the number of A&E beds available. They appear to have been cut too far to meet demand. There is some evidence that this is because the complexity of problems of patients presenting at A&E is increasing; the number of emergency admissions to A&E has increased in recent years much faster than the rate of attendances.

This will, in part, be down to the number of older patients attending, who have more complex health needs in general and therefore require more sophisticated clinical scrutiny. There is also a serious problem with beds being taken up in A&E by those needing transfer to other types of wards and facilities. One of the fastest growing causes of delayed transfer is a lack of capacity in the adult social care system, administered by local councils, which have suffered particularly deep cuts under the coalition and Conservative governments. If patients are not fit to go home on their own, hospitals have no choice but to keep them under supervision. Some hospitals have even gone so far as to hire domiciliary care workers so that patients can be taken to their homes and cared for there, freeing up beds for new acute cases.

Apart from A&E, the other way most of us access healthcare is through our GP. If you've tried to get an appointment recently, it will be no surprise to you that the statistics show we are waiting longer to see a GP and that the time available per appointment is being reduced. This is a clear sign that the general practice system is under increasing strain.

A survey by NHS England reported that a fifth of patients

wait a week or more to see their GP or are unable to get an appointment at all.

The survey of more than 800,000 patients showed that the proportion of patients waiting longer than a week to see a doctor rose 56 per cent in five years. The number unable to get an appointment rose to 11.3 per cent. A separate survey of 830 doctors by the GP magazine *Pulse* in 2017 suggested that average waits for an appointment are now thirteen days, up from ten days two years ago.

If and when you do get an appointment, they are on average shorter than the recommended fifteen minutes needed for a proper assessment. A study by Cambridge University, published in *BMJ Open* in November 2017, found British patients are seen for on average nine and a half minutes per appointment. That's less than in the US, Canada and most European countries.

There are around 51,000 GPs in the UK, 42,000 of whom are in England. GPs in England deal with 340,000,000 consultations a year. That number has been growing very fast; the Health and Social Care Information Centre found that the average member of the public sees a GP six times a year and that this is double the number a decade ago. Demand is being driven by a host of factors but an ageing population and people with more complicated conditions such as diabetes and heart disease, which are in turn connected to soaring obesity rates, increase the workload considerably. Despite a government pledge to increase the number of doctors working in general practice by 5,000 by 2020/21, the number of 'full-time equivalent' GPs fell by 0.3 per cent in 2016.

The problem is that it takes ten years to train a GP. You need a degree in medicine, which takes five years, then a two-year foundation course in general training, then a further three years of specialist training in general practice. So, even if we expanded the number of medical places today, it would still take a long time for that measure to bear fruit. In the interim, Britain has had to import general practitioners from overseas. Leaving aside the impact that has had on other countries' health systems and the lost investment made by their education systems (which can be really problematic), this is complicated and expensive to implement. The NHS is currently planning to recruit 2,000–3,000 GPs from overseas and will pay £100 million to international recruitment agencies. A long-term plan to ease the stresses on British GPs, to encourage them to open their own practices in areas of need and to encourage medics into general practice is needed, but it is not clear the NHS currently has the resources to implement such an ambitious plan. And nor will sky-rocketing tuition fees or Brexit help either.

The same pressures can be seen in our hospitals. The 2016 annual report on waiting times for non-essential surgery by the Patients Association, an independent health and social care charity, showed that the total number of patients waiting over eighteen weeks for operations in 2015 was 92,739, a huge increase over the 51,388 patients waiting the same time in 2014. Average waiting times for five procedures (hip replacement, knee replacement, hernia, adenoid and tonsillectomies) have risen above 100 days. This represents the highest average waiting time in the six years that data has been collected by the Patients Association. The report also found that hospitals cancelled an average of 753 patient surgeries 'on the day' in 2015. Shortages in equipment or beds were the most common reasons for cancellation. Again, the picture is one of a system under strain: of rising demand and an organisation that simply doesn't have the resources it needs to meet that demand.

The final part of the health system that is under critical stress is our adult social care system. Adult social care – and meeting the challenge of its future funding – was the principal cause of Theresa May's extraordinary turn of fortunes in the 2017 election; her plan to have people fund their own social care through a wealth tax was deeply offensive to many Conservative voters – who believe in keeping as much of their wealth as possible – and was quickly dubbed a 'dementia tax' by her opponents. Unreformed, the adult social care system is going to collapse under the weight of the growing number of older people with health conditions that require some form of supervision or help, and there is a huge funding shortfall. The Conservatives' reluctance to proceed with the Dilnot reforms to social care and their decision to sabotage Labour's attempt to reach a cross-party consensus on this issue in the 2010 election had come back to bite them. The catastrophic Conservative campaign in 2017 seems to have put paid to the idea that the wealthiest older people should have to pay for social care through their assets, but it has not put paid to the ongoing need for new sources of finance for social care to be found. The can cannot be kicked down the road forever.

In 1948, hospitals were brought under the control of the new NHS, but social care was left under the control of local authorities, which are legally required to meet the needs of their communities. The sort of care required varies by age. People over sixty-five are most likely to need physical help, but a substantial proportion require help with memory or cognition. For those younger than sixty-five, who make up a quarter of those getting local authority help, the most likely reason is either a learning disability or mental health problems. But enormous cuts in recent years to local authority funding – the most squeezed part of the public sector – have put the system under huge strain. The Local Government Association, health charities and the Association of Directors of Adult Social Services all estimate the shortfall in adult social care funding to be around £2.5 billion by 2020.

This has meant unpaid 'informal' carers – mainly women – have had to take on a huge amount of the workload. According to a major National Audit Office (NAO) report in 2015, £19 billion was spent by local authorities in 2012/13, while the value of informal care and support was estimated at £55 billion. Around 2.1 million people in the UK received some form of informal care in 2014, according to the Office for National Statistics. The proportion receiving 24-hour care has increased considerably in the past decade. The NAO concluded:

> Pressures on the care system are increasing. Providing adequate adult social care poses a significant public service challenge and there are no easy answers. People are living longer and some have long-term and complex health conditions that require managing through care. Need for care is rising while public spending is falling, and there is unmet need. Departments do not know if we are approaching the limits of the capacity of the system to continue to absorb these pressures.

All these problems – with A&E, GP services, elective hospital procedures and adult social care – are a reflection in great part of the chronic under-resourcing of the NHS. This is not a matter of debate between the political parties. Both Labour and the Conservatives accept that an ageing population, rising costs, rising public expectations – driven in part by technical advances that mean we are capable of dealing with more health problems – and rising obesity are driving up demand and the overall cost of healthcare.

The NHS's own *Five Year Forward View*, published in

November 2014, identified a shortfall of £30 billion in England alone. That's around 5 per cent of the total tax take in the UK; as much as the total amount of council taxes raised in the UK or one sixth of UK income tax returns.

In terms of the number of doctors, the OECD found in 2017 that the UK has fewer doctors per head of population than most other member countries. They calculated the UK has 2.8 doctors for every 1,000 people. Austria has 5.1 and Germany, Italy, Lithuania, Norway and Switzerland all have more than four doctors for every 1,000 people.

The OECD also found that in the UK we only had three hospital beds per 1,000 people in 2011. This was far behind the majority of other Europe countries. Germany has 8.3; Austria 7.7; Hungary 7.2; Czech Republic 6.8; Poland 6.6; Estonia 5.3; and Slovenia 4.6. Only Sweden had fewer, with 2.7 per 1,000 population.

Other countries have allocated more resources to meet the demand in their countries and that is, in great part, because they raise more revenues from taxes than we do to spend on health-care. That might sound surprising since we spend what sounds like an enormous sum of £140 billion a year on healthcare. But that is actually a smaller proportion of our total national income than is spent on health in many other developed countries. If we spent the same as, say, Germany, as a proportion of our Gross Domestic Product, we could bridge the gap between demand and supply.

It would mean a serious conversation between politicians and the public on how to deal with the problems of under-funding in the NHS. These are not new problems, but they are undoubtedly being exacerbated by insufficient annual increases in the NHS's budget and the inexorable and counter-productive cutting of council social care budgets.

Democratic socialists must also look at how we can work together – as a nation – to alleviate the pressures on the NHS. The UK actually has serious health inequalities. In short, the poor are much more likely to get ill. They have worse nutrition, and have higher rates of obesity, cardiovascular disease and diabetes – all of which are huge burdens on the NHS. In 2008, the Labour government led by Gordon Brown asked Professor Sir Michael Marmot to review the link between socioeconomic status and health. In his report, published in 2010, he introduced his analysis in stark terms:

> People with higher socioeconomic position in society have a greater array of life chances and more opportunities to lead a flourishing life. They also have better health. The two are linked: the more favoured people are, socially and economically, the better their health. This link between social conditions and health is not a footnote to the 'real' concerns with health – health care and unhealthy behaviours – it should become the main focus.

Professor Marmot updated his analysis in 2017, when he stated:

> The longest life expectancy in the country was in the richest borough, Kensington and Chelsea: eighty-three for men and eighty-six for women. By contrast, the lowest life expectancy was in the North: Blackpool, seventy-four for men; Manchester, seventy-nine for women.
>
> Even more dramatic than these regional inequalities are the inequalities within local areas. In Kensington and Chelsea, life expectancy was fourteen years shorter among the most disadvantaged compared to the best off. Alarming, but perhaps not surprising. Kensington and Chelsea may be the

richest local area in the country, it is also the most unequal economically.

In the Wirral, containing Angela's constituency of Wallasey, life expectancy can vary by over ten years, even though communities are geographically close together. East of the M53 motorway, which runs down the peninsula, is where poorer health outcomes can be seen in Birkenhead and Seacombe, with the richer west side of the Wirral such as West Kirby and Heswall having much longer life expectancy.

As in our analysis of inequality when it comes to the evil of want, inequality matters in healthcare. Both authors completely endorse Professor Marmot's conclusions, in which he 'identified six domains that cause health inequalities and where action is required to reduce them: early child development, education, employment and working conditions, minimum income for healthy living, healthy and sustainable places to live and work, and taking a social determinants approach to prevention'. Public health education – delivered by the NHS, local authorities, through education in school and beyond – is an essential component of bringing down demand for NHS services. If we can make ourselves healthier through voluntary modification of our consumption and behaviour, the cost of healthcare would of course come down.

However, there is another problem that makes that task more difficult. In Britain and across the developed world, our diets contain too many calories – chemical energy – and thus make us fat. We drink too much alcohol and we smoke. All of these are human behaviours that bring us pleasure and are actively encouraged by private companies comprising what can only be considered an Obesity and Ill-Health Industry, profiting through making us ill, and encouraging us to consume as many of their products as possible. A rich array of product designers and scientists study the mechanisms of human pleasure and addiction in order to physically entice us into consuming more. Marketers cover up any potential harmful effects and use exceptional levels of mendacity and misleading imagery and statements to psychologically persuade us to consume more. There is now a positive correlation between poverty and obesity which would have been unimaginable only a few years ago. We need much more governmental intervention to correct this inaccurate food labelling and advertising to children. Misleading promotional material needs to be clamped down on and we need far better education on nutrition in schools. The Conservatives would dub this an expression of a 'nanny state' (which is ironic, considering half of them had nannies themselves). The truth is that we need to do this if we are to protect children and parents from an industry that spends vast amounts of money and time trying to deceive and cajole.

The Obesity and Ill-Health Industry also attaches itself to sports, fashion, music and other forms of entertainment. What did smoking have to do with Formula 1, for example? What does alcohol have to do with football? Why do sugary cereals that tempt young taste buds all have cute comic characters on the front? There is a direct linkage between the increase in healthcare demand in the UK and the pernicious activities of the Obesity and Ill-Health Industry. Brits are today over three stones heavier than fifty years ago. As of 2015, according to the OECD, over a quarter of British adults are not just overweight but obese. Over 60 per cent of adults are overweight. A growing number of children are also obese. The rate has almost doubled in the past twenty years to one in eight children. A study by the American management consultancy, McKinsey, estimated costs to the British economy of over £15 billion in treating obesity-related medical conditions, including diabetes.

A guide as to how we might take on this industry can be found in how we dealt with the huge and powerful global tobacco industry. Smoking rates in the UK have been cut drastically since we got serious, using a mixture of taxation to increase prices, legislation to cut the spaces in which people can smoke, health warnings on packaging and education in schools to reverse the tobacco industry's decades of propaganda aimed at persuading our citizens that smoking was safe, cool and attractive.

The owners of companies that profit from obesity will cry foul, of course, but to improve the lives of British people, the amount of time they spend in good health and therefore our productive capacity as a nation, to cut costs in the NHS and to ease the burden on our amazing healthcare staff, we need to take on the Obesity and Ill-Health Industry. We must use the power of the state and every bit of determination as individuals not to allow ourselves to be duped by fat cats who profit from making us overweight and unwell.

CHAPTER EIGHT

LONELINESS

It was in an interview with *Woman's Own* magazine, in 1987, that Margaret Thatcher first stated: 'There is no such thing as society.'

It's a quote that is often used to contrast the atomised individualism of Margaret Thatcher's politics with the communalism of the Labour Party and of democratic socialism. The intent of her words was somewhat more complex than that stark, memorable phrase might imply. As she herself opined in her autobiography: 'They never quoted the rest.' She explained:

> I went on to say: There are individual men and women, and there are families. And no government can do anything except through people, and people must look to themselves first. It's our duty to look after ourselves and then to look after our neighbour. My meaning, clear at the time but subsequently distorted beyond recognition, was that society was not an abstraction, separate from the men and women who composed it, but a living structure of individuals, families, neighbours and voluntary associations.

From that broader explanation it becomes clearer that Mrs Thatcher was in fact drawing, yet again, on the teachings of Friedrich Hayek. Hayek believed diffused market-based mechanisms were far superior to centralised planning when it came to making decisions. He said that the taking of innumerable decisions on prices in a free market better marshals scarce economic resources by aggregating the distributed knowledge of lots of people. He compared that favourably to the idea that a central government should set those prices and thereby control economic life. In his writings, Hayek also applied these ideas to society itself. He believed 'spontaneous evolution' was preferable to 'intelligent design' in ordering social infrastructure and relations too, so that people could live good lives based on a more natural order. This ignores the truth that human beings are natural co-operators who live in communities of mutual interest and thrive best in that context. We are not made to be atomised individuals.

This idea has been used over the past four decades to tear down many of the aspects of our state that define a civilised society. Mrs Thatcher's fundamental approach to policy-making was to end universality and state provision in favour of the so-called 'free market' and to encourage both volunteering and individual self-reliance to fill in any gaps and provide support for those who simply cannot thrive in a society without a safety net. Similarly, we see Hayek's disdain for any form of central planning in David Cameron's Big Society. Cameron himself stated in a muddled revision of Thatcher's maxim: 'There is such a thing as society, but it's not the same as the state.' He and George Osborne showed what this means in practice by stripping back funding for services such as libraries, SureStarts, youth centres and – significantly – adult social care across the country through huge cuts to local authority budgets, while suggesting that individuals might band together to provide those services under the 'Big Society' banner.

The result of this activity has been the sustained degradation of the social infrastructure that underpins communal relations in Britain. Many of the buildings that were the sites of social interaction and the institutions and programmes that encouraged people to come together, mingle and share their lives, have disappeared. This all happened at the same time as capital took the whip hand over labour and squeezed more hours and energy out of workers, limiting the ability of individuals to enter into voluntary co-operation when they weren't at work. This pincer action – on institutions and individuals – has led to a continued loss of meaningful and satisfying social interaction in Britain and a substantial increase in loneliness, one of the most modern and most pernicious of the evils that Britain faces today.

Loneliness is not being alone. In modern Britain, especially in our cities, few of us are truly alone. The Mental Health Foundation, who have studied this phenomenon, state:

> Loneliness, then, is not being alone but a subjective experience of isolation. It is inevitable that all of us will experience this feeling at one time or another, whether it's a brief pang of being left out of a party or the painful sensation of lacking a close companion. Life-changing events, such as moving to a new town or a bereavement, can lead to acute loneliness. But it is the time factor that decides how harmful loneliness may be: research shows that 'loneliness becomes an issue of serious concern only when it settles in long enough to create a persistent, self-reinforcing loop of negative thoughts, sensations and behaviours'. In other words, it is long-term, chronic loneliness that wears us down rather than loneliness that is 'situational' or passing.

This is precisely the sort of loneliness that modern society imposes on more and more of our citizens.

A study by the Mental Health Foundation found that in the

UK, one in ten of us feels lonely often and 48 per cent of people think we are getting lonelier in general. There are two groups that appear to have a particular vulnerability to loneliness: the elderly – which may come as no surprise given the adult social care crisis facing Britain – and also young adults – a phenomenon that has only recently started drawing attention from policy-makers. It isn't just the elderly and young adults. Many adults, even those who co-habit or are in a relationship, feel alone. Loneliness is subjective and can be self-reinforcing. If we are lonely, we can start to change our behaviour in response to that sense of social alienation.

What makes loneliness really worrying is that it seriously harms our overall mental and physical health. There is a growing body of academic and scientific research quantifying how, why and to what extent loneliness affects us. What we now know is that loneliness is more than just a malady of the mind; it's fundamentally antithetical to human nature. We are simply not built to operate as atomised individuals.

Truth be told, humans are a relatively physically weak, slow and vulnerable species. Our bipedal posture limits our speed; we don't have offensive adaptations like claws; our teeth evolved for an omnivorous diet in which most of our calories come from non-meat sources; we lack fur or camouflage; and our skin is so fragile papercuts are a health hazard in our offices. What has made humans so extraordinarily successful and dominant as a species is our ability to co-operate. We evolved the capacity to create a far broader range of vocalisations than any other species to help us communicate with one another in languages of our own creation. We have evolved abstract reasoning, an innate desire for reciprocity, an aversion to cheating; a whole range of evolutionary modifications underpinned by complex neurological and other physical adaptations that further shape our cognition and behaviour. In short, we are adapted to be highly social animals that experience and enjoy a range of meaningful co-operative social interactions. Mrs Thatcher presented her folksy aphorisms about self-reliance and individualism as though they were based on common sense: in fact, she was just wrong. They were quite the opposite.

George Monbiot, the *Guardian* journalist who has done sterling work both highlighting and seeking to personally address loneliness through his *Breaking the Spell of Loneliness* album and tour with Ewan McLennan, has collated the latest findings on loneliness and our health:

> Social isolation is as potent a cause of early death as smoking fifteen cigarettes a day; loneliness, research suggests, is twice as deadly as obesity. Dementia, high blood pressure, alcoholism and accidents – all these, like depression, paranoia, anxiety and suicide, become more prevalent when connections are cut. We cannot cope alone.

Professor John Cacioppo at the University of Chicago, a social neuroscientist, has been at the forefront of producing scientific evidence of the physiological effects of loneliness: a rise in stress hormones as well as corollary decreases in immune function and cardiovascular function.

Loneliness in modern Britain is felt in every age group, social class and type of household. But we do know that there are certain risk factors: living alone, not working or a significant life event that disrupts our social circles, such as a death, moving to a new community, or leaving the parental home.

Loneliness in older people has had some attention thanks to charities such as Age UK, the Campaign to End Loneliness and more. They have reported:

Seventeen per cent of older people are in contact with family, friends and neighbours less than once a week and 11 per cent are in contact less than once a month;

Over half (51 per cent) of all people aged seventy-five and over live alone;

Two fifths of all older people (about 3.9 million) say the television is their main company;

Sixty-three per cent of adults aged fifty-two or over who have been widowed, and 51 per cent of the same group who are separated or divorced, report feeling lonely some of the time or often;

Fifty-nine per cent of adults aged over fifty-two who report poor health say they feel lonely some of the time or often, compared to 21 per cent who say they are in excellent health;

A higher percentage of women than men report feeling lonely some of the time or often.

For the main part, central government has washed its hands of the need to intervene to help stave off loneliness. The Care Act 2014 actually increased the requirements on councils, specifically to avoid for as long as possible the point at which older residents need to enter residential care by providing support in homes. However, as a result of cuts to councils, we will be spending £6 billion less on adult social care in England this year than in 2010. Defunded councils, barely able to provide those duties that are mandated by law, have lost so much capacity that no sensible person could lay the blame at their feet. With the squeeze on council resources, direct provision is disappearing. Day centres and sites for social initiatives such as lunch clubs are being sold off by local authorities to protect core services. Labour and Conservative councils alike are trying to expand their capacity by taking a co-ordinating role with the NHS, the police and a network of voluntary services that has emerged to try to reach into the crevices in which we have warehoused thousands of lonely older citizens and provide a loving, helping hand.

Cutting funding is especially damaging when you consider the demographic pressures in Britain. The ONS, in a report on loneliness, states:

> The average age of the UK population is expected to increase over the coming decades. We have projected ... that the number of people aged eighty and above is expected to more than double by 2037 and the number of people aged over ninety is expected to triple. The number of centenarians show an expected increase of sevenfold ... from 14,450 in mid-2014 to 111,000 in mid-2037.

There are always glimmers of hope. Social entrepreneurs such as Alex Smith, of North London Cares, South London Cares and Manchester Cares, try to bring together older and younger residents so they might form meaningful relationships and a sense of community. As they say on their website:

> We do this because London is a place of extremes. While our capital is one of the most dynamic places in the world, full of cultural and economic opportunities and a hotbed of innovation and change, it can also be anonymous, lonely and isolating.
>
> For our older neighbours in particular, many of whom have spent a lifetime in their home neighbourhoods in Camden and Islington, the rush and pace of the city can often now feel too much. Getting around can be frightening, and trends

including globalisation, gentrification, migration, digitisation and the housing bubble are transforming our communities faster than ever.

The multiplying effect of those pressures is that many older people have deep roots – from Kilburn to Kentish Town – but few connections. Meanwhile, young professionals – often graduates from across the country and around the world – can have hundreds of connections in the social media age, but no roots in their communities.

However, no matter how much the voluntary sector does, they will never have the capacity – at scale – to generate sufficient funding to match growing demand. And there is another problem: quite often, misconceived regulation can throttle the voluntary sector's capacity to initiate change. A Joseph Rowntree Foundation article by Tracey Robbins stated in 2013:

> Regulations around insurance, safeguarding and health and safety frustrated other ideas such as a pop-up café for a neighbourhood with no community centre, and reduced it to a coffee morning in a church – although 100 people each week still came. Restoring a village cinema for all ages became a film club mainly attended by adults. Intergenerational drama never happened as youth providers could not work outside their remit. The examples go on and on. Practical, simple interventions were seen as too risky, too hard and were therefore diluted or deferred.

Members of the Campaign to End Loneliness have discovered that even living in a care facility is not, in itself, a cure for loneliness, and again found stifling regulations to be part of the problem. They reported in 2015:

There is a growing understanding that communal living is not an effective antidote to loneliness, and that, in fact, older people in residential care demonstrate worrying levels of loneliness and isolation.

Experts acknowledged this issue and recognised that the vast majority of current initiatives were aimed at older people living in the community.

Some experts argued that the limitations on opportunities for social interaction among those in care settings were primarily a product of the barriers created by the high levels of physical disability and cognitive impairment that exist among most residents of residential care. However, others perceived additional barriers created by a culture of risk aversity among care home owners and a failure by practitioners and commissioners to recognise the need for individuals in care homes to maintain social connections beyond their interactions with other residents.

What galls most is that whereas this government has prioritised its obsession with eliminating 'red tape' for businesses (quite often so they can continue sharp practices), they have singularly failed over seven years to think more creatively about eliminating bottlenecks for looking after vulnerable members of our community.

At every level, whether in terms of matching funding to demand; sorting out the regulatory framework; providing meaningful co-ordination as only the state can do at a national level; or even showing that they grasp the scale of the problem, the Tory government has completely failed.

Moreover, while the ongoing crisis of how we care for our elderly has been botched by David Cameron and now Theresa May, a new crisis is starting to emerge: loneliness among young people.

A spate of studies in recent years has shown that young people are increasingly feeling more lonely and anxious than any other age group. Body dysmorphia is driven by 'perfect body' images which grace the covers of magazines and today proliferate on 'curated spaces' like Instagram, in which young children are encouraged to study poses, lighting and makeup to ensure they take the perfect photo to display to the world.

In 2010, the Mental Health Foundation found loneliness to be a greater concern among young people than among the elderly. Those aged 18–34 were more likely to feel lonely often, to worry about feeling alone and to feel depressed because of loneliness than those over fifty-five.

In 2014, the insurer Aviva released its latest Health Check UK Report. In it, they confirmed that 18–24-year-olds are now more likely than older people to state they feel lonely. They found:

- Over a quarter of 18–24-year-olds suffered anxiety last year.
- An astonishing 48 per cent of 18–24-year-olds say they often feel lonely.
- Constant social network connection is doing little to alleviate loneliness.
- Panic attacks are now common for one in seven 18–24-year-olds.

It is an utterly modern paradox: we have never been more connected and yet felt more alone.

As reported in *The Guardian*, Professor Maureen Baker, chair of the Royal College of General Practitioners, said in 2016:

[Loneliness] figures highlight worrying trends, particularly regarding the growing number of young women accessing mental health treatment. Society is changing – even in the last seven years, social media, for example, has increased in popularity and the number of platforms people might be present on has multiplied.

As a result, young people are facing unprecedented pressures, not just over the emergence of cyberbullying and revenge porn, but constant exposure to unattainable aspirations of what they should look like, and be like.

A series of studies has shown that the modern focus on individuals in economic and social life rather than communities has had an impact on social connection by driving a bigger wedge between those at the top and those left behind. A 2009 study by the World Health Organization found that unequal societies have higher levels of mental health problems and that injustice and inequality are 'deeply toxic'.

Those under forty have grown up under Thatcherism but those under twenty-five are our first truly digital generation. A study by researchers at the University of Pittsburgh has found that 'the more time young adults spend on platforms such as Facebook, Twitter, and Pinterest, the more likely they are to feel cut off from the rest of society' and that 'more than two hours of social media use a day doubled the chances of a person experiencing social isolation'.

The researchers posited three explanations. One is that social media displaces time for real-life experiences. Second, that social media may encourage feelings of exclusion, such as seeing others enjoying themselves while the viewer is isolated. And finally, that exposure to deliberately idealised and exaggerated representations of other people's lives may provoke envy and feelings of insufficiency. Every generation has this phenomenon, of course, whether it be the rich kid at school with the brand-new Nike trainers while a poorer child can feel the holes under their big toe in their no-brand shoes, or the one whose parents own the big house down the road, while a poorer child lives in a small flat with their parents on a deprived estate. Nowadays, though, technology has hyper-powered our awareness of how others live and the inequalities that birth confers upon us, while our economic system has both narrowed our children's opportunities to get on in life and extended the sheer scale of those inequalities. When we couple that with the degradation of our social infrastructure for young people – youth clubs, parks, after-school clubs and so much more – can it be surprising at all that young people are so angry and frustrated with politics here and in countries that have gone down a similar route?

Loneliness, then, we would argue, is a direct result of the injection of market fundamentalism into the public sphere in a number of areas. We have outsourced the state's role in helping to support meaningful and satisfying social interaction among elderly citizens to the voluntary sector, while the private sector – Facebook, Twitter and Instagram – plays the same role for our youngest citizens. Unfortunately, the voluntary sector simply does not have the scale to fund and deliver services to the growing number of people in need of a helping hand and a little bit of love in their lives. And while social media, the private sector's solution to a lack of social interaction, can be great at times – especially for those people that already feel engaged in society – it has played some part in increasing the loneliness and anxiety for those who are less engaged. Together, this has driven an increase in the prevalence of loneliness, which is making us sicker and less happy as a nation.

And that, surely, is the point. It makes no sense that we are spending less as a state on the maladies that drive people to mental and physical ill-health – and therefore reliance on our overburdened NHS – to say nothing of the personal misery of an unfulfilled life. It is empirically self-defeating to cut £6 billion from adult social care and hundreds of millions from our social infrastructure when the effect is a major increase in demand to the £140 billion health system. If you wanted to think of it in terms of a business, what do we think the effect is to the productivity of our workers if they are anxious, lonely, stressed and unhappy?

This is yet another frustrating example of the stultifying didacticism of Hayekian ideology triumphing over both common sense and the corroboratory scientific evidence. As we have shown, it is based on a fundamental misreading of human history and human nature. The results of the short-termism, solipsism and greed of Hayek's political project will require patience, compassion, pragmatism and intelligence to turn back the tide and build a cohesive, mutualist, happy and strong society.

CHAPTER NINE

MENTAL HEALTH
AND ILLNESS

It seems remarkable today but, seventy years ago, in 1948, when the National Health Service was founded, we hadn't yet found a vaccine for polio or diphtheria; thousands of children died or were left severely disabled. The first antibiotic, penicillin, had only been on sale for two years, and streptomycin, which cures tuberculosis, was still years from being discovered. Even so, our understanding of and ability to treat mental health effectively was simply medieval by comparison.

Psychiatric care in England dates back to 1247, when a priory on the site of what is now Liverpool Street station started to provide shelter for the sick and infirm. It came to be known as Bedlam. It was only in the Victorian Age, after the passage of Wynn's Act of 1808 and the Shaftesbury Acts of 1845, that the state started to build a network of 'asylums' on the outskirts of major cities 'for the regulation of the care and treatment of lunatics' in rural environments. Even then, people suffering from mental illness were crammed into these asylums by magistrates without any real psychiatric evaluation. The administrators had no drugs with which to manage mental illness; the 'treatment protocols' were less about treatment and more about observation, supervised activity and restraint when symptoms worsened.

The situation was worse still for women. Those with postnatal depression, stress or anxiety would find themselves detained and labelled hysteric. Many women in the 1920s were admitted as social punishment for being 'immoral', i.e. sexually active or difficult. It was seen as a means of controlling them, although many would then become institutionalised and go on to spend the rest of their lives incarcerated. When Angela first worked for the Confederation of Health Service Employees, COHSE (now part of UNISON), some of the victims of this awful policy were still alive and being cared for in the remaining mental institutions. The system was coercive, conservative and in some cases actively abusive, with drugs sometimes used simply as a chemical cosh rather than having any therapeutic use.

By the 1930s, two major treatments were developed in Europe. The first was electroconvulsive therapy, which entailed passing a current through the brain to induce a seizure. The second was the lobotomy, a horrifying procedure in which steel spikes were inserted into the brain to crudely sever connections to the frontal lobes. It earned its creator, Egas Moniz, the Nobel Prize, but had thankfully fallen into disrepute by the 1950s because of its terrible effects.

It wasn't until the discovery of lithium for mania and chlorpromazine, an anti-psychotic, in 1949 and 1950 respectively that pharmaceutical therapies became available to doctors. It made an immediate impact. Since then, we have expanded the range of drugs available for use across a wide array of mental illness: antidepressants; antipsychotics; anxiolytics for anxiety; mood stabilisers; depressants and stimulants. The development of new forms of therapy, in particular Rational Emotive Behaviour Therapy and Cognitive Therapy in the 1950s and 1960s, also expanded the range of options available to psychiatrists.

Over time, stigmas around mental illness have been

challenged, new drugs have been discovered and the range of psychotherapies available has expanded. Our ability to help people with mental illness has improved substantially in a short period of time. However, the British state has not always done a great job in treating mental health as a serious problem, despite the great trauma it can cause to people and our growing understanding of just how prevalent mental illness can be in the population.

1948 was not the turning point it might have been for the treatment of mental illness in the United Kingdom. The medical profession was starting to realise the interaction between physical and psychological health, local authorities were beginning to provide some care in the community, and charities dedicated to helping those with mental illness were springing up. The new National Health Service, however, did not treat the mentally ill as it did the physically ill; mentally ill patients continued to be housed within the asylums and mental hospitals. By the mid-1950s, there were 150,000 people in these institutions.

It wasn't until 1959 that things started to change. The passage of the Mental Health Act saw medical professionals take over from judges and magistrates in deciding who needed to enter a mental hospital. But the institutions remained in place. Two years later, however, attitudes towards mental health were transformed as Ministry of Health civil servants realised the enormous possibility of psychiatric drugs and care in the community. In 1961, the government started to consider shutting down the asylums in favour of greater community care provision for mental health patients and moving treatment of acute mental illness to general hospitals, thus reducing the number of psychiatric beds by 75,000.

It was as radical a plan as the building of the original asylums. From the 1970s onwards, the number of psychiatric beds fell, with the decline accelerating in the 1980s as more care was delivered in community settings. This wasn't uncontroversial; many saw the changes as an excuse for cuts. Press reports of people with serious mental health problems committing crimes raised the hackles of the public. The murder of Jonathan Zito by a paranoid schizophrenic, Christopher Clunis, who had been discharged from a psychiatric care setting, led to frenzied headlines in the tabloid press and deep doubts about care in the community.

The truth is that the transition to community care was complicated. It required new techniques, skills and resources. It called for outreach in place of treatment in institutionalised detention settings. The potential rewards to individuals were substantial though: socialisation and independence have been shown to improve quality of life and reduce the likelihood of admission to psychiatric care units. But this required money. As Angela recalls from her time in COHSE, few people wished to keep the old institutions open, but the fact is that it was much more expensive to look after people properly in their own settings in the community than it was to warehouse them out of sight and out of mind, and the funding simply wasn't there. Once again, the Conservatives were focused on saving money, rather than making sure the transition was adequately financed, and as a result, a great many vulnerable people – especially those who could not look after themselves or make decisions – were let down. This caused a complete lack of public understanding and lots of prejudice against people with mental illness, fuelled by the reactionary tabloid press.

By the time of New Labour, the considerable challenge of transforming the treatment of mental illness away from hospitals towards a community model continued, helped by a substantial increase in spending. Although the IPPR's

Commission on Social Justice had not mentioned 'mental health' at all in their report, New Labour's evidence-driven ethos encouraged the commissioning of a raft of studies to improve the community care system. Right-wing tabloids continued to decry the system, highlighting cases in which people with psychiatric illnesses committed serious crimes, and the government was often on the back foot.

It was only as we moved from the twentieth to the twenty-first century that policy-makers started thinking about general mental health rather than mental illness as a central policy concern. In the early 2000s, Lord Richard Layard, an economist at the London School of Economics with a particular interest in happiness and mental health as well as reducing inequality, produced a series of works that looked at how greater access to psychotherapy could be economically beneficial, chiefly by reducing expense to the welfare state and improving overall economic productivity. A young Ed Miliband and Gordon Brown took a special interest in his work.

In 2008, Labour introduced Improving Access to Psychological Therapy (IAPT), a primary care service that extended the availability of psychotherapy far beyond the segment of the population that had been the focus of psychiatric care for most of the period since 1948. Assisted by the growing public and political openness to talking about mental health, the new approach gained cross-party support. The Health and Social Care Act 2012, passed by the coalition government, made it a requirement for the NHS to place mental health on a par with physical health. The coalition government, to its credit, stated its desire to expand IAPT, and extend it to children and young people, but it has been plagued by insufficient funding and staffing.

Today, we are on the cusp of a third revolution after the asylums and care in the community. The drugs, the technologies, the therapies and the clinical protocols have evolved and improved rapidly. We have cross-party agreement that mental healthcare has to include helping people to live healthier lives overall, not just dealing with serious mental illness. We have a much more progressive public discourse on mental health, aided by high-profile people such as Alastair Campbell, Kevan Jones MP and Charles Walker MP, who have been incredibly brave in talking openly about their own mental health problems. Mindfulness and meditation classes are now commonplace not only in the posh enclaves of Notting Hill but far more widely.

We understand that the stresses of modern life can contribute to the degradation of our mental health and so – as we are trying to do with physical health – we aim to nip it in the bud. We have a long way to go to deliver on our aspiration of preventing mental illness before it manifests by protecting the mental health of our citizens. One approach we might consider is that of the Mental Health Foundation, which recommends a 'life-course', with 'interventions and approaches across the lifespan, including before birth, early family-formation years, adolescence, adulthood and working age, and older adulthood. In each area, different challenges present themselves, as well as opportunities to intervene and support mental health.' That's going to require a lot more innovation to join together the myriad institutions that have the capacity to intervene and improve mental health; it's not just the NHS, but an array of state services that will be required. It's also going to require funding.

So, what does the mental health of the nation actually look like? Firstly, it is important to realise that measuring the actual frequency of mental health disease in society is beset with problems. Diagnostic practises vary across the country, and NHS treatment statistics by definition exclude people who haven't been diagnosed and so underestimate the true number. Measuring change over time is even harder. As we've become a more open society and started discussing and helping people to understand their own mental health, more people have been aware that what they may have thought of as a sense of overwhelming sadness or apathy, for example, is in fact a curable form of depression.

The Adult Psychiatric Morbidity Study is carried out every seven years by the NatCen Social Research with Leicester University for the NHS. It tries to build a truly representative picture of mental health across the country by asking questions about mood and behaviour to identify any problems. It's not perfect, but it gives us a picture.

Their most recent report contains some key statistics:

TRENDS IN MENTAL ILLNESS

One adult in six had a common mental disorder (CMD): about one woman in five and one man in eight. Since 2000, overall rates of CMD in England steadily increased in women and remained largely stable in men.

Young women have emerged as a high-risk group, with high rates of CMD, self-harm, and positive screens for post-traumatic stress disorder (PTSD) and bipolar disorder. The gap between young women and young men increased.

Most mental disorders were more common in people living alone, in poor physical health, and not employed.

TRENDS IN TREATMENT AND SERVICE USE

One person in three with CMD reported current use of mental health treatment in 2014, an increase from the one in four who reported this in 2000 and 2007.

Since 2007, people with CMD had become more likely to use community services and more likely to discuss their mental health with a GP.

There is a particular concern about young people in much of the recent analysis of mental health in Britain. A 2017 study, undertaken by academics from University College London and the University of Liverpool and funded by the Economic and Social Research Council, found that 24 per cent of fourteen-year-old girls and 9 per cent of boys have depression: over 200,000 in total. This is double the rate compared to a decade earlier. The survey found that girls from lower income groups were more likely to be depressed than higher income groups. *The Guardian* analysed NHS data in September 2017 and found that 'the number of times a girl aged seventeen or under has been admitted to hospital in England because of self-harm has jumped from 10,500 to more than 17,500 a year over the past decade – a rise of 68 per cent. The jump among boys was much lower: 26 per cent.' The report's author identified highly visual social media, such as Snapchat and Instagram, as driving this anxiety and depression.

A New York University professor, Adam Alter, specialising in how the psychology of marketing and addiction works, explained to *Business Insider*:

> The minute you take a drug, drink alcohol, smoke a cigarette if those are your poison, when you get a like on social media, all of those experiences produce dopamine, which is a chemical that's associated with pleasure.
>
> When someone likes an Instagram post, or any content that you share, it's a little bit like taking a drug. As far as your brain is concerned, it's a very similar experience. Now the reason why is because it's not guaranteed that you're going to get likes on your posts. And it's the unpredictability of that process that makes it so addictive. If you knew that every time you posted something you'd get a hundred likes, it would become boring really fast.

One of the problems with Instagram is that everyone presents the very best versions of their lives. So, you can curate Instagram, you can take 100,000 shots if you want to before you actually share anything. What that means is, every time you look at someone's feed, you're getting only the very best aspects of their lives, which makes you feel like your life, in comparison, with all its messiness, probably isn't as good. Seeing the best version of everyone else's life makes you feel deprived.

This is especially true in richer countries. A 2009 WHO study found – remarkably – that mental health problems are far worse in richer countries, like the UK, that are socially and economically unequal, because 'greater inequality heightens status competition and status insecurity across all income groups and among both adults and children'. The report's author explained that she had looked at international studies on 'mental health, inequality and resilience' and concluded that 'injustice and inequality are deeply toxic to us'.

It seems almost cruel, then, to consider that the very creation of inequality as an incentive to economic growth – an idea at the very heart of market fundamentalism, with its worship of money as a proxy for success and virtue – is crippling the minds of those people who grew up in its shadow and are now living in a society in which its effects have been fully manifested. Turbocharged by new technology – which is itself owned by some of the richest people in the history of humanity – our youngest citizens are facing those inequalities in visceral, visual formats on a daily basis. A recent report by the Royal Society for Public Health, *#Status of Mind*, based on surveys of young people, found that they themselves said that social media platforms made their anxiety worse. We need to start listening, understanding and taking action. Leaving aside the serious delays and under-funding of Child and Adolescent Mental Health Services (which do of course need fixing), it is the root causes we must address – and inequality is at the heart of it.

Beyond the clear moral imperative that we as a society should care about our fellow citizens' mental health, it's worth thinking about what happens when we fail to do so. The false economies of the current government's approach to spending are never starker than when looking at the sheer misery and cost of dealing with mental illness. When mental illness goes untreated, it can lead to catastrophic breakdown in people's lives. Stigma, embarrassment, as well as a lack of local provision, can all contribute to a failure to receive treatment. Sometimes it's just that the drugs don't work as they should. Some anti-psychotic drugs, for example, cause a condition called tardive dyskinesia with prolonged use, which causes involuntary movements of the mouth and of the body. Sufferers may stop taking their drugs due to physical impairment or social embarrassment, putting them at risk. Whatever the reason, untreated, mental illness can spiral rapidly, and as mental health worsens, a huge range of physical symptoms can appear. Increased levels of stress hormones can lead to problems like headaches, muscle pains due to tensing, gastrointestinal symptoms and a worsening of cardiovascular symptoms: it can literally cause a heart attack. If an untreated sufferer finds themselves unable to get up, or feels averse to social situations, they are at risk of losing their job or damaging their relationships, which can make things even worse. In extreme cases, they may end up on the wrong side of the law or find themselves homeless or forced to sleep rough.

Our prisons have for a long time been filled with people with unresolved mental illnesses. The Centre for Mental Health's deputy chief executive, Andy Bell, told *The Guardian* that the last reliable survey on the prevalence of offender mental health problems was carried out in 1998. One reason may be that the government simply doesn't want to admit the degree to which our soaring prison population is a symptom of systemic failures in mental healthcare provision.

Lord Bradley, a former Labour Home Office minister, was asked by the government in December 2007 to assess mental health problems in the prison system. His report revealed that 'the prevalence of psychiatric disorder is even higher among young offenders and juveniles, with 95 per cent suffering from mental disorder, substance misuse problems, or both'. The Prison Reform Trust, which campaigns to ensure our prisons are just, humane and effective, says that its own analysis shows

Ten per cent of men and 30 per cent of women have had a previous psychiatric admission before they entered prison. A more recent study found that 25 per cent of women and 15 per cent of men in prison reported symptoms indicative of psychosis. The rate among the general public is about 4 per cent.

Forty-nine per cent of women and 23 per cent of male prisoners in a Ministry of Justice study were assessed as suffering from anxiety and depression. Sixteen per cent of the general UK population (12 per cent of men and 19 per cent of women) are estimated to be suffering from different types of anxiety and depression.

Forty-six per cent of women prisoners reported having attempted suicide at some point in their lives. This is more than twice the rate of male prisoners (21 per cent) and higher than in the general UK population amongst whom around 6 per cent report having ever attempted suicide.

A National Audit Office report in 2017 noted that the government simply did not have the data they would expect on mental illness among the prison population. However, they did worry that

> rates of self-inflicted deaths and self-harm in prison have risen significantly in the last five years, suggesting that mental health and well-being in prison has declined. Self-harm rose by 73 per cent between 2012 and 2016. In 2016 there were 40,161 incidents of self-harm in prisons, the equivalent of one incident for every two prisoners. While in 2016 there were 126 self-inflicted deaths in prison, almost twice the number in 2012, and the highest year on record.

Our prison system is there to both punish and try to rehabilitate those that have committed criminal offences. It should not and must not become a warehouse of those we have failed to help adequately. It is not only morally unacceptable, but self-destructive economically. The vast cost of our prison estate could be reduced considerably if we provided targeted intervention for those prisoners who are clearly suffering from mental illness and ensured that, within prison, offenders have their particular problems – whether that be mental illness or substance abuse – dealt with appropriately.

The same toxic mix of moral injustice and economic self-destructiveness is seen in another social evil that is often a direct result of mental illness: rough sleeping, which has been getting worse and worse over the past seven years. The government's own figures show that the estimated number of rough sleepers in Britain has risen from 1,768 in 2010 to 4,134 in 2016. You'd think the Conservatives in government would have noticed, since the highest rate of rough sleeping is in the Conservative local authority area of Westminster itself, home to Parliament and Whitehall, with 260 counted in 2016.

The government's own analysis says: 'Of those rough sleepers who had a support needs assessment recorded, 43 per cent had alcohol support needs, 31 per cent drug support needs and 46 per cent mental health support needs, with 13 per cent having all three needs and 26 per cent having none of these three needs.' That means 74 per cent of all rough sleepers had a diagnosable mental illness or substance abuse problem.

Because rough sleeping is highly visible (unlike homelessness more generally, where someone doesn't have a permanent home but may be living in council-funded temporary accommodation or in a hotel), it of course garners a lot of political attention. Local authorities understand that you need integrated teams comprising health, social care, welfare and housing to deal with these problems, but the cuts to their budgets simply have not helped at all.

The raw economics, calculated by homeless charity Crisis, are that it costs the state substantially less to deal with someone's problems early (on average less than £1,500) than dealing with it once the problem is entrenched (£20,000 per year in health, policing and social services per rough sleeper). The failure to fully fund rough sleeping prevention and assistance services is a classic example of a false economy and one that causes huge misery.

The only country in Europe that has managed to resist the rising tide of homelessness and rough sleeping is Finland. Finland decided to take an approach to housing that saw it as an absolute right and basic need. So, they decided that anyone that was sleeping rough should immediately be given a secure, permanent dwelling. So, for the young person kicked out of their family home, the drug addict desperate to get back on their feet but with nothing stable in their life, the person who lost his job and sank into severe depression, they will provide them with stability and compassion. This has allowed people to turn around their lives, become part of society, access help, get back to work and start paying rent. You can imagine the howls of the Hayekians, but in fact, Sajid Javid, the Secretary of State for Communities and Local Government and a self-professed Thatcherite, is implementing three trials in Manchester, Merseyside and the East Midlands. It is an approach that has the potential to show just how effective taking the market out of basic needs can be – and how compassion and social solidarity can be the catalysts for people to realise their full potential.

The final social evil that we must look at when we think about untreated mental illness is that of suicide. Suicide and self-harm are not mental health problems in themselves, but the Mental Health Foundation states that 90 per cent of all suicides have been 'found to be associated with a psychiatric disorder'. Suicide rates in Britain have been falling since a peak in the recorded rate sometime during the Great Depression. The lowest rate ever recorded was in 2007, just before the banking crisis and recession; a third of the rate in 1934. Since then, the rate rose by about 10 per cent but is now declining once again. Part of this is due to specific policies addressed at making it more difficult to commit suicide – such as detoxifying the domestic gas supply, fitting cars with catalytic converters and banning certain pharmaceuticals that are particularly dangerous in overdose. Part of it is that we have created quite an effective working relationship between government, local authorities and charities.

But, as we are frequently reminded, suicide remains the biggest killer of men between the ages of forty and fifty-nine. Male suicide rates are much higher than female rates: around three times as high. One reason for this is because older men are the least likely to seek help for psychiatric illness, as opposed to a physical ailment for which they would go to a doctor, and instead tend to 'self-medicate' with alcohol or drugs, both of which have serious neurological effects that can exacerbate symptoms and cause a downward spiral in mental health.

The answer is a mix of everything we've discussed above: to ensure that when people do seek help they can get access quickly; that we try to eliminate the stigma around mental illness; and, given a raft of evidence that people with a low perceived socioeconomic position are much more at risk of mental illness, that we address some of the social inequalities that can make people's mental health deteriorate in the first place.

There can be no doubt that Britain has achieved a considerable amount since Beveridge's time and indeed in the past few decades when it comes to mental health. We've made great strides in eliminating the stigma of mental illness and in improving the quality of care. However, we have so much further to go. It is imperative we ensure that we treat mental illness in the same way we would physical illness: everyone has an absolute right to quality care, free at the point of access, when things go wrong. However, it's also imperative that we treat mental *health* (as opposed to illness) – to ensure our population is happy and reduce predictable stressors – much as we seek through our physical public health programme to prevent diseases such as obesity, diabetes and cardiovascular problems before they manifest. It is also undoubtedly true that we cannot afford to allow budgets to continue to be squeezed and cut when they need instead to be increased. And it is also going to be increasingly important over the next decade to address a looming crisis in an age in which inequality is ever more visible, and the mental health of many people – especially our young – is being damaged by the inevitable economic consequences of Hayek's market fundamentalism.

CHAPTER TEN

BIGOTRY AND INTOLERANCE

Pastor Martin Niemöller was a German Protestant and human rights activist who was detained in Sachsenhausen and Dachau concentration camps in the Second World War. Before his imprisonment, Niemöller had been sympathetic to the Nazis and to their anti-Semitism. It was only when they took control of the Protestant church that he became a resistor. After the war, he wrote a short poem that spoke to his and Germany's wilful ignorance of the murderous hatred that had grown in their society. The poem also reminds readers of how those who peddle blame and hate always expand their targets; that hatred becomes an end unto itself.

> First they came for the Communists
> and I did not speak out
> because I was not a Communist.
> Then they came for the trade unionists
> and I did not speak out
> because I was not a trade unionist.
> Then they came for the Jews
> and I did not speak out
> because I was not a Jew.
> Then they came for me

and there was no one left
to speak out for me.

Britain has made huge progress in confronting, discussing and addressing bigotry in our society. In 1992, the Commission for Social Justice was curiously cautious about not spending a lot of time thinking about discrimination on race, gender, religion, disability or mental health, although it did devote a lot of time to class. In 1942, Beveridge would not have understood much of our contemporary debate on discrimination. He may not even have recognised our modern diverse society.

Because democratic socialists believe profoundly in equality, we have been in the forefront of the battles to fight all forms of discrimination. This commitment is about the kind of society we wish to live in. It is about building social solidarity and ensuring that all our citizens, whatever their gender, ethnic origin, disability, belief, socioeconomic class or sexual orientation, are treated first and foremost as human beings with rights to respect and equal access to economic and political opportunity. Discrimination prevents individuals from reaching their full potential and that damages our society as a whole. Just as we must fight to end undeserved privilege so we must act to open up life chances and opportunities to all. In this time of anger, resentment and rising populism fuelled by hate, we all have a duty to acknowledge the human rights and dignity of every human being.

There are a number of ways in which people are discriminated against, including on the basis of gender, sexuality, race, religion, disability and class. Discrimination can be direct or indirect, and the perpetrators can be individuals, groups, institutions and even the state itself.

In the UK we have made great progress in legislating against hatred and discrimination and we can be proud of this but we are clearly not there yet. There are still powerful forces of intolerance and of outright hatred within our society who wish to preserve the privileged access to opportunity which they believe is theirs by right. The snarling faces of Britain First are at one extreme. But discrimination is usually more subtle than that. The persistent gender pay gap; the CV with an 'ethnic' name less likely to progress to interview even if the work experience it contains is identical to a CV with a 'British' name; the worsening structural impediments to social mobility which hold working-class people back; the effective exclusion from work of the majority of people with disabilities; the horrifying fact that eight out of ten young trans people have self-harmed and that the number of lesbian, gay and bisexual people who have experienced a hate crime rose to 16 per cent in 2017, according to Stonewall. So, where are we today, and how far have we got to go?

WOMEN

Women comprise just over 50 per cent of the population and yet do not hold 50 per cent of jobs. The more senior the roles, the fewer women will be found. Angela was especially struck by the dwindling number of female ministers she encountered at meetings of the EU Council of Ministers as the councils she attended on behalf of the UK government became more senior. When she attended the Environment Council or the Social Affairs Council, there were many women, but when she became a Treasury minister and attended the Economic and Finance Council (Ecofin), it was overwhelmingly male. A glance at the G7 or G20 leaders photo calls demonstrates just how far the world has to go to include women fully in political life. As a result of exclusion and discrimination, women have less income, wealth and opportunity, and are disproportionately more likely to be victims of sexual violence, domestic violence and discrimination in the workplace. Recently we have been reminded of the extent of the misogyny that is endemic in our society: from Gamergate to the Harvey Weinstein scandal, which has spawned the inspirational Time's Up movement in response. Nor has the treatment of women in politics improved as they have become more involved in higher-profile roles. Angela was no supporter of Mrs Thatcher but was nauseated by the sexist attacks she endured, such as exhortations to 'ditch the bitch'. Hillary Clinton suffered relentlessly appalling treatment in the 2016 US presidential election, including – uniquely – directly from her opponent on the stump and in the televised debates. Social media has normalised vicious misogyny in the UK and it is coarsening our politics in the UK.

The End Violence Against Women Coalition, a campaigning group founded in 2005, published a list of key statistics that makes for gruelling reading:[2]

- In 2016 there were 2 million female victims of domestic violence.
- Two women every week are killed by a current or ex-partner and other close relative.
- Only 15 per cent of serious sexual offences and 21 per cent of partner abuse incidents are reported to the police.
- More than 100,000 women and girls in the UK are at risk of and living with the consequences of female genital mutilation, forced marriage and so called 'honour-based' violence.
- Girls in schools in the UK are experiencing high levels of sexual violence and harassment, as alarmingly evidenced by Parliament's Women and Equalities Select Committee.

Prosecution rates for sexual violence are worryingly low. Newspapers love to cover miscarriages of justice for accused men but the thousands and thousands of trials that never go forward because of prosecutorial reticence are never heard about, despite the fact that at the heart of each is a traumatised woman whose life has been utterly changed by the violence she has endured.

Despite the Equal Pay Act 1970 and the Sex Discrimination Act 1975, which were put on the statute book by the formidable Barbara Castle, equality has still not been achieved. On remuneration, the gender pay gap between full-time workers has been driven down by successive administrations aggressively pursuing this as an issue, but it remains at 9.1 per cent as of 2017. As Frances O'Grady, the TUC's first ever female general secretary, archly noted, it would still take decades for women to get paid the same as men at the current rate of improvement. Worse still is the gap for mothers. According to analysis by the Institute for Fiscal Studies, after childbirth the pay gap increases to 33 per cent after around twelve years. The wage gap is particularly serious for women with lower socioeconomic status, i.e. low levels of education and few qualifications. Part of the problem is the very high cost of childcare in the UK. This has worsened following government spending cuts, which have also led to the cuts to SureStart centres and the failure to ensure that all parts of the country have access to high-quality childcare. OECD projections show that by 2030, 'if the share of women working reached the same level as for men, annual growth rates in GDP per capita would rise by 0.5 percentage points in the UK. The boost to economic growth would be even higher if women's working hours increased too.' It is a catastrophic waste of women's ability, potential and our nation's economic prosperity. Facilitating women to work by investing in childcare and elder care provision would quickly pay for itself and yet the progress made by the last Labour government has since stalled.

Women also remain stubbornly locked out of Britain's boardrooms and the top levels of our professions. The Directory of Social Change's analysis of 339 corporate boards showed the overall percentage of women was 22 per cent. Cranfield School of Management found the proportion of women holding the most influential non-executive positions, such as chairman and senior independent director, in the biggest 100 companies in the UK is just 8 per cent. Meanwhile, John Allan, the chairman of Tesco, opined:

> If you are female and from an ethnic background – and preferably both – then you are in an extremely propitious period … For a thousand years, men have got most of these jobs, the pendulum has swung very significantly the other way now and will do for the foreseeable future, I think. If you are a white male, tough. You are an endangered species and you are going to have to work twice as hard.

Nine out of the twelve members of Tesco's board and Executive Committee are white men; there are no ethnic minorities. We are in the extraordinary position of being in the midst of a full-fledged backlash against the progress of women, when, in reality, not that much has changed.

Women's equality is a core goal of the Labour Party. Progress has been made but there are stubborn reactionary forces that have yet to be overcome. Since the financial crisis, the EU's Gender Equality Index found we have made no progress on tackling inequality, lagging behind our neighbours, including France, Holland, Finland, Sweden and Denmark. The results are shaming. Critical, sustained and significant action is required to fix this ongoing moral injustice and profoundly economically damaging state of affairs.

LGBT

It was thirty years ago, in 1988, that the Conservative government put the infamous Section 28 onto the statute book. It banned local councils from 'intentionally promot[ing] homosexuality or publish[ing] material with the intention of promoting homosexuality' in its schools or other areas of their work. The legislation was wildly popular with the right-wing tabloid press, as well – depressingly – as the Catholic Church, Church of England, Muslim Council of Britain and the Salvation Army. It was cruel and bullying because it signalled an official disdain for the struggles of lesbians, gay men and bisexuals to come to terms with their sexual orientation and be themselves in a society which often regarded them with fear and contempt. Its characterisation of LGBT relationships as 'pretended' further signalled that it was OK to single them out and have no respect for them as human beings. The fact that it applied to schools prevented teachers from dealing with homophobic bullying and protecting genuinely vulnerable pupils who were left to cope alone.

Fifteen years ago, this disgusting, cynical, pandering piece of legislation was taken off the statute books in the Blair government's Local Government Act 2003. This was after a titanic battle with the House of Lords, which had defeated an earlier attempt. New Labour made huge strides on countering discrimination against LGBT people. They equalised the age of consent; ended the ban on LGBT people serving in the armed forces; gave LGBT people the right to adopt; banned discrimination in the sexual offence laws; banned discrimination in the workplace;

created the Equality and Human Rights Commission to help enforce the equality laws; included homophobia in the definition of hate crimes; created civil partnerships, finally giving official recognition and legal rights to LGBT relationships; and introduced the Equality Act. The hardest battles were fought over equalising the age of consent, which was only put onto the statute book by invoking the Parliament Act, because the House of Lords simply would not pass it. Likewise, the battle to end discrimination in the provision of goods and services on the grounds of sexual orientation was fiercely resisted by some but put on the statute book nevertheless. All of this progress has changed political debate so radically that by the time the Conservatives finally came close to winning an election in 2010, they had had to install a leader who promised to consult on gay marriage if elected.

And yet, despite all this progress, there is still far to go in society to achieve real LGBT equality. A 2017 survey of more than 5,000 LGBT people in the UK by YouGov for Stonewall, a remarkable and brave charity that has done so much to combat anti-LGBT hate in the UK, makes for stark and depressing reading. They found that:

- One in five LGBT people have experienced a hate crime or incident because of their sexual orientation and/or gender identity in the past twelve months.
- Two in five trans people (41 per cent) have experienced a hate crime or incident because of their gender identity in the past twelve months and one in six LGB people, who aren't trans (16 per cent), have experienced a hate crime or incident due to their sexual orientation in the same period.
- Four in five anti-LGBT hate crimes and incidents go unreported, with younger LGBT people particularly reluctant to go to the police.

- More than a third of LGBT people (36 per cent) say they don't feel comfortable walking down the street while holding their partner's hand. This increases to three in five gay men (58 per cent).
- One in ten LGBT people (10 per cent) have experienced homophobic, biphobic or transphobic abuse online directed towards them personally in the past month. This number increases to one in four for trans people (26 per cent) directly experiencing transphobic abuse online in the past month.

Beyond outright hate crimes, LGBT people still have to deal with negative depictions in the media and the press. It is noticeable that as communities become more visible, confident and accepted, reactionary elements of society – the forces of conservatism – increase their opprobrium: in recent months and years, the number of anti-trans headlines seem to have flourished. In November 2017, *The Sun* newspaper, outraged at children being taught about transgender rights and tolerance, splashed their front page with an enormous headline: 'The skirt on the drag queen goes swish, swish, swish.' In playgrounds, pubs and elsewhere, words like 'poof', 'faggot' and 'dyke' are still in common parlance. Even the word 'gay' has come to mean 'bad' in street slang.

The battle against homophobia has been long and hard; there has been great progress, and society has been changed in many ways, yet we have a long way to go if we are to change the equal rights that been legislated for into a reality for every LGBT person in our country.

RACE

Just fifty-four years ago, in 1964, Conservative MP Peter

Griffiths campaigned to win his seat in Smethwick with the slogan: 'If you want a nigger for a neighbour, vote Liberal or Labour.' Forty years ago, white people in Britain could walk into a pub past signs reading: 'No Irish, No Blacks, No Dogs.' Just fifteen years ago, Imran was assaulted in London for no reason other than being a 'Paki' by a skinhead with a key held between his fingers, hitting with such ferocity that it shattered the bony orbit that surrounds his left eye and sliced into his face. We may not have had legalised racism, segregation or discrimination, as in the United States under its Jim Crow laws, but it existed nonetheless throughout society. Hailing a cab, trying to get a job, renting a house or even going to an unfamiliar barber would be fraught with the potential for racial discrimination.

We should be glad, therefore, that Britain has done more than almost any country in the world to deal with racism over the past few decades. The Race Relations Act 1965 was a Labour Act, opposed ferociously by the Conservatives, that made it illegal to refuse access on racial grounds to public places such as hotels, restaurants, pubs, cinemas and public transport. Refusing to rent accommodation to people because of their race was banned, and inciting racial hatred became a criminal offence. Eleven years later, the Race Relations Act 1976 introduced offences of direct and indirect discrimination and the Commission for Racial Equality was created to take a hard look at the state of race relations. More controversially, the Macpherson Report into the Metropolitan Police response to Stephen Lawrence's murder was brutally direct in accusing the entire organisation of being 'institutionally racist'. Those who have worked with the police since know how hard they took those words and how much they have worked to reform.

Racism appears, at times and in some places, to be in remission in the UK. *Spectator* journalist Clarissa Tan wrote about this retrenchment in an article entitled 'Britain has many major problems – racism isn't one of them':

> In the 1990s, the British Social Attitudes survey found that 44 per cent of people said they would be uncomfortable if their children married across ethnic lines. But that is changing dramatically: according to a recent British Future report, only 5 per cent of those aged between eighteen and twenty-four would mind their children marrying someone of a different ethnic background.

That's a heartening statistic, and yet a study by the University of Manchester (*Equality, Diversity and Racism in the Workplace*) found that a third of the 25,000 employees they surveyed had witnessed or experienced racism. One Indian respondent said he was called a 'Paki' by his office manager, and another witnessed colleagues making 'monkey noises' and placing bananas on a Ghanaian colleague's desk. Another respondent said that his team ordered sharing starters at a restaurant, but opted for pork-based dishes so their Jewish boss could not eat them.

The Race Disparity Audit commissioned by Theresa May, at the urging of black groups such as Operation Black Vote, reported in 2017 and found that while 'the gaps between groups have narrowed significantly, there is still a way to go before we have a country that works for everyone regardless of their ethnicity.'

Operation Black Vote's Simon Woolley, writing in *The Times* on the launch of the audit, said:

> The beauty, however, with having a lot of data in one place is that you can cross-reference. You see that young black men are three times more likely to be unemployed, and yet much more likely to have a university degree. So these

young men and women are doing everything society tells them to do – 'if you want a good job, then study hard' – and too many of them still can't find employment. But it's not just the data that should inform this discussion but also those personal stories about black men and women changing their African and Asian-sounding names just to get a job interview.

Discrimination imposes a huge toll on its victims, making them question their identity and appearance. There is a significant market for skin-lightening creams and treatments in the UK among the BME population. Some of the treatments contain harsh chemicals that can have horrible, scarring side-effects. Even Nivea and L'Oreal have faced controversy after marketing products that purport to lighten skin, an extraordinary example of capitalism's amorality in pursuit of profit. The unfairness of racial discrimination is so damaging to the psyche that it can lead to the very segregation that racists then use to justify their suspicion and 'othering' of minorities.

Across various headings – including Communities, Poverty and Living Standards, Education, Employment, Housing, Policing, Criminal Justice, Health and the Public Service Workforce – the Race Disparity Audit found signs of progress, signs of retrenchment and clear opportunities for improvement. In a book that seeks most of all to find solutions to the inequality that blights our society, it's worth citing its findings on poverty.

Asian and Black households and those in the Other ethnic group were more likely to be poor and were the most likely to be in persistent poverty. Around 1 in 4 children in households headed by people from an Asian background or those in the Other ethnic group were in persistent poverty, as were 1 in 5 children in Black households and 1 in 10 White British households. Households of Bangladeshi, Pakistani, Black, Mixed and Other backgrounds were more likely to receive income-related benefits and tax credits than those in other ethnic groups. The ethnic minority population is more likely to live in areas of deprivation, especially Black, Pakistani and Bangladeshi people.

The TUC's 2015 report, 'Living on the Margins', found that BME people are disproportionately affected by the growth we identified earlier in precarious work with fewer employment rights.

TUC research also indicates that workers from ethnic minority groups have been disproportionately engaged in agency work in the UK following the recession. While just 11 per cent of UK employees are from black and ethnic minorities, they hold 17 per cent of temporary jobs and 21 per cent of agency jobs.

Over forty years since the Race Discrimination Act was passed, it is clear that we still face an enormous task to make Britain a less hostile, more welcoming, better integrated, fairer place to live. This is compounded by an apparent surge in anti-immigrant sentiment in the US and Europe. For those of us committed to a Britain free of racial prejudice, we will need to consider whether more robust intervention will be necessary to rectify the imbalances in our society driven by prejudice. Ideas like name-blind job applications and the setting of binding targets for the elimination of race-disparities have their place to play in righting historic wrongs.

RELIGION AND BELIEF

Both of your authors are atheists and humanists, and yet we've watched with genuine concern over recent years as a surge of – in particular – anti-Semitism and Islamophobia has washed over British politics and society. Britain is not an especially religious country overall. Over a quarter of British people hold at least one anti-Semitic view, according to a study conducted by the Institute for Jewish Policy Research. More than half of Muslims questioned held at least one anti-Semitic attitude. Meanwhile, when British people were asked by YouGov in 2015 if they held a positive or negative view of Islam, 61 per cent said their view was negative.

We both believe that it is wrong for institutions or individuals to discriminate based on religion or belief. We both believe that people have the right to practise their religion in any way they see fit, within the confines of our laws and as long as they are not directly harming others. The UK is unusual in that it has an established Church and a head of state who leads that Church. But we also have many religious traditions and have largely developed a climate of respect and co-operation between them. We may not have a formal separation of Church and State, as America purports to have, but as the US proves through its frequent, deliberately visible, grandiose and often quite hypocritical displays of religiosity by the ruling classes, legal status is irrelevant unless secular, tolerant values are at the heart of all our communal institutions and interactions.

The dangerous Islamophobia of groups such as Britain First – whose page has nearly 2 million 'likes' on Facebook – some of UKIP's upper echelons and provocateurs such as Katie Hopkins need to be actively resisted and countered through both inter-faith and community displays of co-operation and mutual understanding. Similarly, the appalling rise in anti-Semitism within society has to be constantly and vehemently challenged.

Where Muslims, Jews, Christians and people of all faiths and none should be in agreement is that there is more that unites the moderate many than divides us; we have more in common with each other than we do with the intolerant purveyors of hate who seek to divide, destroy and reverse decades of progress.

DISABILITY

According to the charity Scope, there are around 13.3 million disabled people in the UK, almost one in five of the population. Only one in six disabled people were born with their disabilities. The majority acquire their disability later in life. Seven per cent of children, 18 per cent of working-age adults and 44 per cent of adults over state pension age are disabled. In January 2016, the UK employment rate among working-age disabled people was just under 50 per cent, compared to 84 per cent of non-disabled people. Scope calculate that a 10-percentage point rise in the employment rate among disabled adults would contribute an extra £12 billion to the Exchequer by 2030.

Discrimination against the disabled is a pernicious social and economic problem for Britain. Despite Parliament having passed legislation to deal with disability discrimination, we are still chronically under-serving our disabled citizens. The trade union movement has done much to make workplaces and public spaces more accessible and yet MPs hear every day from their constituents about the iniquities suffered by those who live with a disability. Since the era of austerity this has become much worse.

The most commonly reported impairments by disabled people are mobility (52 per cent); stamina, breathing, fatigue (38 per cent); and dexterity (27 per cent). It is surely not beyond the ken of humankind to design spaces that can accommodate these disabilities, yet such reasonable accommodations are often touted as part of 'Elf 'n' safety gone mad', sneered at by right-wing pundits and so-called taxpayers' lobby groups (actually funded by vastly rich plutocrats who don't want to spend their money on such changes). There is also a serious pay gap between the disabled and non-disabled. An Equality and Human Rights Commission report found that 'the disability pay gap in the period 1997–2014 was 13 per cent for men and 7 per cent for women.'

The public-sector union UNISON has outlined how we might evolve to deal with disability in Britain through its 'social model of disability'. They explain that

it is the way society organises itself and people's attitudes that stop disabled people from taking an equal part in life, rather than their physical or mental conditions or ailments. As a union we campaign on important issues such as:

- Inaccessible workplaces;
- Information systems that are not designed for disabled people;
- Negative attitudes and prejudice from employers.

This can be extended beyond 'employers' and 'workplaces' to all other spheres of society. It makes sense for shop-owners to make their shops open to more people who might purchase their goods, just as it makes sense for museums and galleries to allow more visitors to get inside. It is actually not so much 'health and safety' as it is good old-fashioned British common sense.

CLASS

Possibly one of the clearest forms of discrimination in the UK today is class. At a middle-class dinner party, outright racism, sexism or bigotry against LGBT people would be less likely to be tolerated now, but class discrimination is embedded in our society. From education, to the job market, to access to services, to their ability to get on the housing ladder, people from a lower socioeconomic status are less advantaged than those from higher classes. Both of your authors were born into working-class families, and we have both witnessed the levels of disadvantage and discrimination against working-class people, as well as the ebb and flow of improvements with change as governments change.

The Conservatives' Social Mobility Commission, formerly headed by Alan Milburn, a New Labour Cabinet minister, did a considerable amount of work to analyse the nature of class disadvantage and make recommendations for its improvement. Alan eventually quit the Commission when he realised its recommendations were being ignored for the main part and often undermined by policies set by the government. In his work, however, he found disturbing facts.

On housing, for example, Alan concluded:

Home ownership helps unlock high levels of social mobility but it is in free-fall among young families. Owning a home is becoming a distant dream for millions of young people on low incomes who do not have the luxury of relying on the bank of mum and dad to give them a foot up on the housing ladder. The way the housing market is operating is exacerbating inequality and impeding social mobility.

On jobs for young people that have worked hard and succeeded economically, Alan found:

Unpaid internships are a modern scandal which must end. Internships are the new rung on the career ladder. They have become a route to a good professional job. But access to them tends to depend on who, not what you know and young people from low-income backgrounds are excluded because they are unpaid. They miss out on a great career opportunity and employers miss out from a wider pool of talent.

Even if those young people get a job, the Social Mobility Commission found that people from working-class backgrounds who get a professional job are paid an average of £6,800 (17 per cent) less each year than colleagues from more affluent backgrounds. Access to Britain's traditional professions such as medicine, law, journalism and academia are dominated by those from advantaged backgrounds. The Commission found, for example, that 'nearly three quarters (73 per cent) of doctors are from professional and managerial backgrounds with less than 6 per cent from working-class backgrounds'.

Class discrimination even exists in our most privileged institutions, like the City of London. There is a pub by London Bridge in the City of London called the Barrow Boy and Banker. 'Barrow boy' was a term used for street-hawkers, selling fruit and veg from a cart. Their quick mouths and faster-still mental arithmetic were iconic. When those young men managed to get a professional job in the City, they found themselves on the trading floors. The bankers, by contrast, were the posh folk running the merchant banks. Whenever anything goes wrong in the City, we rarely see the bankers being blamed; quite the contrary, they remain feted and have caps doffed to them wherever they go. It's the Cockney-accented 'spivs' on the trading floor that are the focus of intense hatred, despite the fact that the rules and operating models are set by the bankers upstairs and their public-school and Oxbridge contemporaries in government. Class runs through every aspect of our society from the top to the bottom.

Class, race and gender are also deeply interlinked. The assault by Margaret Thatcher's government on single mothers was both gendered and class-based discrimination. The persistent targeting of Muslims by right-wing newspapers and political groups is both race-based and class-based: the Women and Equalities Select Committee published a report in 2016 explaining that Muslims suffer serious economic disadvantages, with an unemployment rate more than twice that of the general population.

The persistent failure to address class is unsurprising when you consider the extent to which Parliament has been dominated by those from higher socioeconomic backgrounds. It is still rare for someone born into a working-class family to find themselves in Parliament. This is partly due to structural exclusion, partly because working-class people are not given the encouragement in either our educational system or life in general to aspire for high office. Both our politics and, more importantly, our country are much the worse for it.

Intolerance, bigotry and hatred are deeply entwined, and while we have made progress in this sphere in our society, there are signs of fracture. Reactionary forces, such as those that have empowered UKIP, Le Pen and Trump, are growing in confidence. Identity politics is starting to clash with social democratic politics as well as conservative politics. It will be necessary in the twenty-first century to take stock in a substantive way and plot our course to more tolerant societies. Technology may indeed be part of the solution. Without modern technology, we'd have a much poorer understanding of the world around us and the commonalities we share. But there is a darker side too.

As our shop floors disappear, we have fewer opportunities to mix with people with different opinions, from different hometowns and cultures. We are less likely to know our neighbours than ever before. A YouGov poll in 2015 found that '65 per cent of British people say they would not call any of their neighbours "good friends"', 'an even greater majority (67 per cent) have not invited any neighbours into their house for a meal or drink in the past year' and 'only 32 per cent of people living in urban areas know all five of their nearest neighbours' names. In rural areas most (51 per cent) do, and in town and fringe parts 47 per cent do.'

Benedict Anderson, a political scientist, wrote a book in 1983 called *Imagined Communities*. In it, he hypothesised that the printing press and the creation of media written in a common vernacular allowed the creation of nationalism by making it 'possible for rapidly growing numbers of people … to relate themselves to others in profoundly new ways'. The emergence of online disaggregated publishing platforms, like blogs, Twitter and Facebook, has allowed for the creation of even more granular communities with their own normative values, common knowledge and even language. Furthermore, the richness of communication has reduced. Think about text messages and the number of times a recipient has misinterpreted levity for anger, opprobrium or nastiness. A tweet is a geographically dislocated burst of communication to someone without a hint of context, mood or tone, and, most importantly, the instant feedback you would get if you said something to someone else in person: a look of shock or hurt, tears of pain.

These pose a serious threat to the Enlightenment project of greater commonality, exposure to and debate of ideas, and to social democracy's most fundamental characteristic: solidarity. As technology extends our reach as well as our ability to listen and talk to other people, we will have to be even more vigilant that we ensure our communications are tolerant, respectful and inspire solidarity. At the very least, all social democrats should set themselves that target; because one thing we know is that once a movement allows itself to be defined by hatred rather than a desire to improve things, there is no end to the horrors it can cause.

PART 3

DEMOCRATIC SOCIALISM IN THE TWENTY-FIRST CENTURY

CHAPTER ELEVEN

THE HISTORY AND FUTURE OF DEMOCRATIC SOCIALISM

ORIGINS OF SOCIALISM

Socialism was forged in tumultuous times, in which rapid social and economic change was causing great hardship. The emerging philosophy took a variety of forms from its very inception, ranging from the utopian ethical views of English socialists such as Robert Owen, Edward Carpenter and William Morris, to the Marxist vanguardism of Lenin and Trotsky, the gradualist Fabians such as Sidney and Beatrice Webb, the Christian socialists, the nascent trade union movement, the industrially based guild socialists, syndicalists and everything in between.

It was during the French Revolution of 1789–99, following an explosion of egalitarian ideas, when early socialist ideas began to be put forward as assumptions about the moral legitimacy of absolutist rule by monarchs slowly gave way to the emerging democratic age. In his 1754 *Discourse on the Origin of Inequality*, the idealist French philosopher Jean-Jacques Rousseau asserted that law must be made for the good of society as a whole, not merely to protect the interests of a privileged few. His melding of humanism, romanticism and social contract theory formed the building blocks of what would become democratic socialism. While Rousseau predated socialism, it could not have been developed without the egalitarian and democratic shift inspired by his writings.

While many different interpretations of socialism developed in parallel and, ironically, in competition, initially there was much common ground due to widespread agreement on the huge injustices that had to be fought. The evils of untrammelled capitalism were in the sights of socialists of all types. It was hard to witness with equanimity the effects of the developing capitalist society on the lives of those who lived through these times. All socialists fought against poverty, exploitation and squalor, especially that which emerged from the Industrial Revolution of the nineteenth century. This created vast urban conurbations and the cruelties of the factory system, which were well documented in the UK by writers such as Dickens and Engels. Socialists of all kinds believed that there should be rights for workers who at that time had none. They believed everyone deserved to live in a good society where all could flourish, free from the waste of capitalist crisis and class privilege, free from the fear of poverty, illness, malnutrition and early death. They rejected the rule of competition and the free market in favour of fraternity and co-operation. They aspired to something higher than work slavery and stunted lives for those who were without property or independent wealth. Ethical socialists emphasised a more egalitarian society with opportunities for personal expression, leisure and fulfilment for all.

From the beginning, then, despite its variants, socialism became almost a generic term for a political creed that sought economic and social development in a different way than liberal, *laissez-faire* capitalism was delivering. Under this broad umbrella shelter all of socialism's many adherents. These range from Marxist revolutionaries who believe in the dictatorship of the proletariat and the dominance of one Communist party in an authoritarian regime, to the democratic socialists in Scandinavia, the German SPD and the UK Labour Party, who believe in the parliamentary road to socialism within the rule of law and an accepted democratic system. After the Second World War and subsequent decolonisation, countries in Asia, Africa and Latin America developed their own versions of socialism, in keeping with their own local traditions. As a result, the blanket meaning of the term continued to be stretched as it evolved to meet many culturally specific requirements. The development of feminism and environmentalism were later to challenge and enhance the meaning of the concept. The drive for social justice and equality continues to be a common theme binding disparate movements together, as does a desire to harness and use market forces rather than submit blindly to the wildly unequal income, wealth and opportunity distribution and intermittent crises that the errone-ous 'rules' governing the 'unfettered market' deliver.

THE BIRTH OF THE LABOUR PARTY

As the Industrial Revolution grew apace in Britain, socialist ideas became stronger in reaction to the appalling conditions that emerged in the urban slums and factories. In response to a positive desire to create a more equal society, devoid of the huge inequalities in wealth and privilege, many campaigning organi-sations sprang up with the aim of turning this hope into reality. They created trade unions to fight for fair pay and rights in the workplace, for the enfranchisement of women and the working class, for sanitation and access to medical care, for education and decent housing.

The rapid social and economic changes that occurred during the Industrial Revolution in the UK created the conditions for the Labour Party to be forged as a new expression of the collective political aspiration of the emerging working class. Progressives were still agitating for the completion of the universal franchise in the UK, as the already established Tory and Liberal parties sought to win the newly enfranchised working man to their cause. Women would not get the vote until 1918, and it was not until 1928 that suffrage was broadened to give them electoral equality with men.

Labour evolved out of many social reform movements, most notably the British trade union movement, the Independent Labour Party (ILP), the Marxist Social Democratic Federation (which quickly left) and the Fabian Society. One of the first major tasks was to wean a large part of the trade union movement off their political connection to the Liberals. Labour was, from the beginning, dedicated to winning power through parliamentary endeavour so that it could make the lives of working people better. This explicit commitment and its lack of individual membership in its formative years (see below) set it apart from many other socialist parties which were springing up across Europe, especially in the industrialising countries. It also attracted the exasperated ire and ridicule of revolutionary socialists, most notably Lenin and Trotsky, who were scathing about what they regarded as its reactionary leaders, who they believed were overly influenced by democracy and religion.

A key characteristic of the British Labour Party has been its ideological pragmatism. It was not until 1918 that Labour became explicitly socialist by adopting Clause IV of its new constitution, which outlined its aims and values. Yet even then, the 's' word was not mentioned, merely alluded to.

To secure for the workers by hand or by brain the full fruits of their industry and the most equitable distribution thereof that may be possible upon the basis of the common owner-ship of the means of production, distribution and exchange, and the best obtainable system of popular administration and control of each industry or service.[3]

One hundred and eighteen years after the formation of the Labour Party, its origins are set out succinctly on the party website:

The Labour Party was created in 1900: a new party for a new century. Its formation was the result of many years of strug-gle by working class people, trade unionists and socialists, united by the goal of working class voices represented in British Parliament. It was this aim that united Keir Hardie and the colleagues who gathered for the famous inaugural meeting of the Labour Representation Committee at Lon-don's Memorial Hall in February 1900. Ignored by the Tories and disillusioned with the Liberals, they gathered together to push for change.[4]

In 1900, the Labour Representation Committee came formally into existence. It was a body that accepted affiliated organi-sations rather than individual membership. It was not until Fabian and early British socialist Sidney Webb's constitution was adopted in 1918 that the Labour Party finally accepted individual membership and began to organise that member-ship in Constituency Labour Parties based on parliamentary boundaries. Prior to this, only the Independent Labour Party accepted individual rather than collective memberships. This unusual origin continues to explain the party's affiliated structure, which is regarded erroneously as incomprehensible and illegitimate by some observers. This collectivist origin also affects the distribution of power and voting rights expressed at Labour's supreme decision-making body: Annual Conference. The modern Labour Party still accepts the legitimacy of collective affiliation, with accompanying voting rights for those organisations that join as well as individual membership voting rights for the purposes of decision-making at the conference. The balance that should be maintained between the two types of voting, however, has been a matter of much dispute over the years on both the left and the right of the party.

From the beginning, the Labour Party existed explicitly to gain working-class representation in Parliament. With the adoption of the 1918 constitution, it also aimed to create a political mass-membership organisation in the country at large. This founding aim is stated in Clause I of the party's constitution: 'This organisation shall be known as "The Labour Party" (hereinafter referred to as "the party"). Its purpose is to organise and maintain in Parliament and in the country a political Labour Party.'

The huge disjunction created by the carnage and dislocation of the First World War exacerbated the desire for radical change. Despite the promises made, there was to be no 'land fit for heroes' awaiting those who returned home from the horrors of the trenches in 1918 – only more of the same grinding poverty, falling wages, hunger and humiliation. When the UK returned to the gold standard with the resulting crushing austerity in 1925, it was clear that pursuing the existing political and economic policies could only lead to a return to pre-war insecurity and unimaginable hardship. In fact, the narrowness of the political possibilities on offer combined with the radical nature of what the Labour Party stood for ensured it made rapid electoral progress at the expense of the Liberals in the early part of the twentieth century. Throughout this period, there was a genuine three-way split, with each of the main parties taking around 30 per cent of the vote share at elections – though this was not proportionally reflected in the number of seats won in the House of Commons.

A SHORT HISTORY OF LABOUR'S POLITICAL INFLUENCES AND EXPERIENCES

Labour is a democratic socialist party that has consistently been more concerned with pluralism, pragmatism and praxis than being in thrall to any particular theorist. Many diverse views have flourished within the party, some becoming mainstream, because the party has always been a broad church. The experiences of governing have also influenced the development of Labour's thought and political programme, and we will consider key examples of these below, along with some of the main theories and influences that have helped shape the historical evolution of the party.

THE EARLY UTOPIAN SOCIALISTS

There was a genuine mix and ferment of ideas in the period before the coalescing of the forces which were to bring the Labour Party into existence. In the UK, there had been many earlier strands of socialist thought which did not put at their centre the demand for a revolutionary overthrow of the state. Rather, they emphasised a more evolutionary transformation of the economy and society. Robert Owen was an early pioneer. His New Lanark model community was initially about employer philanthropy, but it turned into a more holistic co-operative ideal. In 1832, after returning from the United States following the failure of a co-operative venture there, he established the giant Grand National Consolidated Trade Union (GNCTU). This rapidly gained half a million members and so alarmed the authorities that they responded by arresting and transporting the Tolpuddle Martyrs for daring to join it. The GNCTU collapsed after two years, unable to reconcile the difference between those who wished to fight for better wages and conditions and those, like Owen, who believed that the co-operative ideal was the way to reorganise the economy. Ten years after the demise of the GNCTU, the Rochdale Pioneers followed Owen's example and founded what was to grow into the modern co-operative movement. There is great merit in seeking to end the 'monoculture' of the PLC as the dominant form of company.

'LABOURISM' – THE UNIQUE DEVELOPMENT OF THE BRITISH LABOUR PARTY

Trade unions had a critical role in creating and sustaining the Labour Party. Indeed, we grew up thinking of Labour as the political wing of the trade union and labour movement. And, in many ways, it still is. It was born because the trade unions wished to take their destiny into their own hands. They wanted direct representation in Parliament for the working class. Rather than lobbying other political parties for the change they needed, they opted for self-reliance and self-organisation. Labour continues to be supported and sustained by those trade unions which remain affiliated to it, and although the membership of trade unions has halved in the past four decades and the density of trade union presence has been ruthlessly driven down in the private sector, this link is still essential. At 6 million members strong, trade unions still represent the largest organisation of civil society in the UK, and they are a vital conduit to what is happening in the UK workforce for Labour. In the 150th anniversary year of the founding of the Trades Union Congress (TUC), it is clear that trade unions have to reform and rebuild to maintain their relevance, especially in the private sector. A strengthening of trade union organisation is a prerequisite for the rebalancing of the share of national income that goes to labour, and a Labour government must help to make that possible.

The inescapable history of its trade union origins is lodged in the party's DNA and the political ideology of the party has since evolved within these bounds. Economically, Labour's thought owes at least as much to the analysis of Thomas Hodgskin (1787–1869) as it does to Karl Marx. This 'Labourism' distinguished UK Labour from its European sister parties which had developed along more classical Marxist lines, separately to the trade unions. It accounts for the fact that one of Labour's primary obligations remains to this day to protect the living standards of workers by political action. Labour still responds to the expectation of the trade union movement for the development of a society that meets the needs and wider aspirations of their members. This is both legitimate and desirable. However, the weaker the trade unions become, the more problematic Labour's dependence upon them is. For now, however, they remain a formidable strength.

The practical effect of 'Labourism' is to connect the Labour Party directly to the experiences and aspirations of many millions of those who work. That connection is a powerful tool in a participatory democracy. When women moved into the workplace in great numbers in the 1980s, their needs were rapidly reflected in changes to the bargaining agendas of their unions. Demands for childcare arrangements, maternity leave and flexible working hours suddenly predominated. And these changes were soon reflected in the development of Labour policy at

Annual Conference. Likewise, as memorably portrayed in the film *Pride*, the solidarity shown by LGSM (Lesbians and Gays Support the Miners) with striking Welsh miners was reciprocated in 1985 when the National Union of Mineworkers (NUM) supported the first motion at a Labour Party Conference demanding equal rights for LGBT people. This motion formed the bedrock of all the advances in LGBT rights which were legislated for by the Blair government when it came to office in 1997.

One of the results of 'Labourism' is that Labour has overwhelmingly been concerned with responding to the aspirations of millions of workers within a capitalist society rather than with the total replacement of the capitalist system itself. The overthrow of the state always seemed to be put off until after the latest pay negotiations.

MARX AND THE LABOUR PARTY

From its inception, many in the Labour Party were sympathetic to Marx's critique of the capitalist economic system in the volumes of masterly analysis that is *Das Kapital*. As we have seen, many who were inspired by Marx's thought at the end of the nineteenth century (including many members of the Social Democratic Federation) looked to the Labour Party as the focus for the self-assertion of the working class. After this initial involvement, however, Marxist internationals took differing strategic decisions regarding what their relationship with the British Labour Party should be.

For his part, Labour leader Keir Hardie was highly critical of what he regarded as the unemotional and dry nature of *The Communist Manifesto*, and accused Marx of reducing socialism, which at its heart was a crusade against selfishness, to a mere class faction fight. 'Socialism makes war upon a system, not a class,' he wrote in September 1903. For obvious reasons of political expediency, Hardie was less interested in Marxism and more interested in opposing the Liberal Party, which stood in the way of Labour's progress in Parliament. He was created in a 'Labourist' rather than a revolutionary mould. And, with the exception of the militant syndicalists and their successors in the grassroots Shop Stewards' Movement of the 1970s and '80s, so were the trade unions.

REVISIONISM – REFORM OR REVOLUTION?

At the turn of the nineteenth century, as the industrialised nations developed further, the gradually extending democratic franchise meant that the interests of the working classes could no longer simply be ignored by any political party. As socialist parties sprang up across Europe and began to establish themselves and demand social and economic change, there was a realisation that revolution may not be the only way to achieve the desired transformation of society. At the same time, contradictions in the scientific predictions of Marxist doctrine about how change would come led some to question its accuracy as well as its desirability.

The most prominent of these early 'revisionists' was the German leader Eduard Bernstein, who in his 1899 book *Evolutionary Socialism* noted that capitalism was proving supple and strong and that class conflict was diminishing, not increasing as Marx had predicted it would. He called for the achievement of socialism by what he called piecemeal and parliamentary means rather than revolution.

It was at this point that the greatest bifurcation in the approach to the methods needed to achieve socialism appeared. Was it to be reform or revolution? The battle of ideas between the revolutionaries and the revisionists was one of the key features of the development of socialist thought in the twentieth century. As the inevitability of the demise of capitalism seemed to recede into the far distance, revisionist thought and the idea of 'democratic socialism', which emphasised reform rather than revolution, acquired increasing importance. After the Russian Revolution in 1917, though, it was the revolutionaries that dominated the theoretical and the political scene.

The Fabian Society, which began in 1884 and was one of the founding organisations that created the Labour Party, was famously interested in the 'inevitability of gradualism', believing that the tide of democratic collectivism, not a revolutionary rupture, would mean steady advances towards the desired goal.

The Labour Party's lack of revolutionary zeal has been a source of constant frustration to the many socialist splinter groups in the UK, who have spent their time denouncing it as hopelessly unrevolutionary. However, despite their ideological disapproval, the Labour Party has transformed Britain for the better even though it was in government for only twenty-two years and nine months throughout the entire twentieth century.[5]

R. H. TAWNEY

If anyone can be said to have provided a uniquely English philosophy for the Labour Party in Britain, it was R. H. Tawney, a Christian socialist who abhorred poverty and deprivation. He was also a believer in British democracy, fighting against what he regarded as Prussian militarism on the Somme during the First World War. He was critical of utilitarian individualism as it had developed after the Reformation, which he blamed for creating a dangerous division between commerce and social morality. He was especially coruscating about what he saw as the idolatrous 'worship of wealth', which he believed characterised the immorality of capitalist societies. He felt that there was a disorder in social values caused by the capitalist emphasis on individual rights without any discussion of the function individuals should play in a healthy society. Because this abstracted the rights people expected from the social purpose for which they should be used, it was all too easy for individuals to pursue their own interests and material wants regardless of the effect on others. Because of this mistake, he believed that individual gain and self-interest had come to dominate society. The society which resulted then existed purely to promote the acquisition of wealth rather than the common good. He called for the creation of a functional society that would emphasise the performance of duties rather than the maintenance of rights and give social purpose precedence over material gain. In a healthy society, he believed, there should be duties and obligations to society rather than rights against society. His book *Equality* (1931) is a damning critique of the class system operating in Britain, and in it he wished for the creation of an equality based on esteem, dignity and what he referred to as common humanity, not class snobbery and undeserved privilege.

He regarded the definition of liberty as far wider than the right of freedom from restraint. Rather, freedom was the right to act positively for the community and to accept some social rules to prevent the abuse of power. His observations still resonate very powerfully today. This is especially true in our modern era of hyper-consumerism dominated by sophisticated advertising, exhorting everyone to pursue wealth and material gain to the exclusion of all other considerations.

THE EXPERIENCE OF GOVERNMENT

From its birth, there has been a pragmatic edge to the ideological positions taken by the Labour Party. It has always fought shy of being too ideological in its approach to the theory of politics and has changed and developed in response to the challenges of being in government. Over time, there have been differing views on the role that nationalisation and state ownership should play in Labour's political programme. There have been especially fierce arguments about the relative merits of unilateral or multilateral nuclear disarmament, and the Independent Labour Party (ILP) disaffiliated from the Labour Party in 1932 over the latter's insistence that ILP MPs take the Labour whip and defer to Labour policy rather than their own, usually more left-wing, policy stances. While not particularly focusing on them, Labour has rigorously policed its ideological boundaries when it thought it necessary to do so. After the ILP disaffiliated in the 1930s, the Socialist League was formed by *Tribune* founder Sir Stafford Cripps to agitate within the party for more left-wing policy positions. It was finally proscribed, and he was temporarily expelled for making a nuisance of himself. The Communist Party of Great Britain tried to affiliate on several occasions but was always rebuffed. In 1933, Labour finally decided that individual membership of the Communist Party would be a bar to joining the party. Attempts at entryism by other far-left parties have periodically caused Labour to act, not least in the 1980s, when the Militant Tendency was expelled.

Throughout its existence, the Labour Party has encompassed contending approaches to the theory and practice of achieving a socialist society in Britain. Utopian socialists focused on the form an ideal society would take and worked to bring it about initially in experimental miniature. Many Marxists had a 'scientific' theory of the economic conditions that had to be achieved before the overthrow of the existing order could bring about the new society. The trade unions tended to be more interested initially in improving the pay and working conditions of their members and focused on building their own organisational strength to increase their chances of success. They forged truly working-class institutions that have helped shape our country's history for the better. They wanted direct representation of the working class in politics as an extension of their belief in self-reliance. The Fabians believed more in an elite rule of the enlightened middle class, using the levers of the state gradually to deliver the transformation required. As Marxism developed and theories about the inevitable overthrow of capitalism were refined, 'revisionists' opted for reform rather than revolution. Since Labour had been created explicitly to obtain direct representation in the legislature, it was hardly surprising that the parliamentary road was the one taken by Labour in the UK.

Following the obvious successes of economic planning in the context of wartime, the Labour Party developed a form of 'corporate socialism', which it put into effect alongside creating the NHS and the welfare state after the Second World War. Labour was a victim of its own success in the years that followed. After it had alleviated many of the most egregious hardships of poverty and mass unemployment which were so obvious in the inter-war years of slump and the resulting political volatility, it soon became clear that a different economic approach to the organisation of society was needed to guarantee Labour's continuing relevance in this rapidly changing world. Labour MP Anthony Crosland focused on equality, opportunity and ending the unfair class system which so distorted opportunity and life chances. He caused outrage in the party by doubting the importance of nationalisation to this project. Harold Wilson returned Labour to power with an appeal for a profound modernisation in the face of a new industrial age forged in the 'white heat' of the technological revolution, which he believed Britain must be prepared for. However, catching the zeitgeist in a notable speech and developing a vague commitment to economic planning did not produce a new and successful economic model that would project socialist values into the future. And he struggled to do so in office.

While the achievements of the Wilson Labour governments were truly impressive in the social sphere, they were not able to cure Britain's economic ailments. There was a failure to modernise and move on from ossified, backward-looking policy and old shibboleths even though times were rapidly changing. Often Labour resembled a religion bound by an unchanging creed rather than a democratic socialist party with a need to evolve to retain its appeal to voters. As a result, the Labour governments of the 1970s succeeded Ted Heath's failed Tory experiment with industrial coercion by attempting a social partnership which proved politically unsustainable for long enough. It ran into the sand of temporary prices and incomes policies, public expenditure cuts and rising trade union anger. This paved the way for the election of a reactionary right-wing Tory government led by Mrs Thatcher, which most definitely did have an economic and political plan. The ideas of Friedrich Hayek were now to form the basis of a new settlement, and we are still suffering the baleful consequences.

As Labour fell into recrimination and internal power struggles, the huge scale and ambition of the radical right-wing project only gradually became clearer. It was nothing less than the end of the post-war consensus and the inauguration of the age of market fundamentalism across the globe. Eighteen years of uninterrupted Conservative rule followed, which dismantled a great many of the gains Crosland had assumed would never be reversed. When Labour finally returned to government in a landslide larger than that achieved in 1945, it was espousing the 'Third Way', which sought to accommodate the perceived constraints imposed on democratic socialism by globalisation. Thus, the Third Way accepted the economic conditions as presented – with no thought of trying to influence them. Much of great use was achieved in thirteen years of Labour government, but 'New Labour' as a concept was killed by the global financial crisis of 2008. The question to be answered now is: what comes next?

THE LESSONS OF TONY CROSLAND AND
THE FUTURE OF SOCIALISM

One of the most important contributions to 'revisionism' in the UK was Tony Crosland's *The Future of Socialism*, published in 1956. It was written when Labour had been out of power for four years, after the 1945 Labour government had achieved the vast majority of its transformational programme and, exhausted by the demands of the war, had run out of steam. The Conservatives had grudgingly accepted Labour's post-war settlement, especially the creation of the NHS and welfare state. They had even thrown themselves into the resulting house-building effort and focused successfully on wooing the industrial working class, as democratic electoral politics in the post-war era demanded they must.

Crosland was frustrated that Labour had not used the four years in opposition to think more clearly about how socialism needed to evolve to remain relevant in the rapidly changing circumstances of the new era. He argued that Labour in government had transformed pre-Second World War capitalism out of all recognition and, as a result, socialism too had to be refined to reflect this success. He felt that, despite the huge advances made in dealing with the worst aspects of poverty, social distress and physical squalor still existed, that inequality and class privilege had not been banished, and that public services also needed strengthening to ensure that a fairer society could emerge.

Crosland felt that the economic insights of J. M. Keynes meant that future slumps could and would be avoided and that growth could be harnessed further to enhance the life opportunities and prospects of all people. He felt that old-style nationalised state monopolies, organised in a top-down 'Morrisonian' way, were bad for freedom. He favoured instead what he referred to as diverse, diffuse and pluralist patterns of ownership for industry. He advocated a social revolution in the distribution of property and egalitarian reforms which would alleviate class inequalities, especially in relation to access to private schools and the creation of comprehensive schools. He advocated a fairer distribution of private wealth, and echoed Robert Owen and the early utopian socialists, rather than Sidney Webb, when he suggested updating the very restrictive laws on censorship, divorce, women's rights and homosexuality, which still made Britain a drab and repressive place in which to live. In a famous dig at Sidney Webb, he drily observed (as a well-known and prodigious drinker himself) that total abstinence and a good filing system are not the right signposts to a socialist utopia.

The Future of Socialism was widely acclaimed upon publication and still stands as one of the more important attempts by a major political figure in the UK to evolve the notion of what socialism should come to mean after the transformative success of the 1945 Labour government had completely changed the terms of political trade.

Predictably, the book was viciously attacked by the right-wing Tory press, but it was also attacked by the Labour left. Principally, the left felt it had abandoned nationalisation as the means of reaching socialist ends and was therefore deeply flawed. The Conservatives attacked it because it suggested an evolution of socialist aims which they recognised would be popular and compelling in future electoral contests. It was brimming with ideas on how Labour should move forward in a way that no other contemporary publication achieved. Between 1964 and 1970, Harold Wilson's Labour government was to implement parts of it, especially its suggestions on social reform. However, educational and class privilege were to prove harder to dismantle.

Rereading *The Future of Socialism* today, with hindsight, it is hard to avoid the criticism that it was far too complacent about the prospects of ongoing economic success. It was virtually silent about the rising power of feminism and what was then becoming known as environmentalism. Also, it had no clear theory of the role of the state – an omission which to this day remains uncorrected.

What also becomes painfully clear upon rereading is that the confident assumption that the progress that had been made towards a fairer society would inevitably be sustained, and, indeed, would continue and deepen, was proved by events to be very wrong. Nevertheless, we can forgive Crosland's mistake as a product of his intellectual confidence after Labour's successful 1945 government, when the tide of history was flowing in the direction of collectivism and state intervention as the way to secure a fairer society. After all, the planned and centralised state implemented in Britain by the National Government during the war had outperformed the Nazi state and, with American support, won the war. Rationing had actually led to a decline in malnutrition among the British population, despite the hardships of war and blockade. Planning for fairer shares for all as well as economic efficiency had become popular since it was so obviously superior to the system of inter-war slump and misery it superseded. At this time, confidence that this success would persist was high, even if ultimately it was not to be proved correct.

This new post-war consensus, which rejected *laissez-faire* economics, was dominant and seemingly unassailable. This in turn was because the appalling results of the untrammelled 'free market', especially mass unemployment and the rise of fascism and world war, were still all too fresh in the popular memory and few wished for a repeat of the misery it had caused. Moreover, war experience had ensured that civil servants, too, had the confidence to deliver planning effectively, as well as the intellectual underpinning to justify the state doing so.

Unsurprisingly, Crosland completely failed to spot the intellectual revival in the discredited ideas of *laissez-faire* economics led by Friedrich Hayek, who published his seminal polemic, *The Road to Serfdom*, in 1944. And Crosland certainly did not predict the advent of Thatcherism, which was to dismantle bit by bit his overconfidence that the *laissez-faire* beast had indeed been vanquished for ever.

THE LESSONS OF THE ALTERNATIVE ECONOMIC STRATEGY

The 1970s was a time of great upheaval in British politics, with the crumbling of the post-war consensus and the first emergence in the mainstream of the hard-right libertarian ideology which has been at the centre of the Conservative Party's political and economic approach ever since. As high unemployment was accompanied by high inflation, it became clear that, in the absence of suppressed demand (a feature of persistent mass unemployment and slump), Keynesian ideas were failing to manage the economy effectively. The commodity price shocks in the middle of the decade, especially the huge increases in oil prices after the Yom Kippur War in 1973 and the emergence of OPEC[6] as a more assertive cartel during these years, sent inflation soaring, which in turn provoked ever-increasing wage demands and industrial unrest. Unemployment had soared above the million mark by 1972 – a level which was then regarded as socially unsustainable by the generation of politicians who had lived through the mass unemployment of the inter-war years and seen the rise of fascism as a result of it. The system of fixed international exchange rates against the dollar, which had endured since the end of the Second World War, had also broken down and the pound was floated in 1972, allowing Heath to avoid the stigma of devaluation which had so dogged the Wilson government of the 1960s. The UK joined what was then known as the Common Market in January 1973 after Parliament approved the terms that had been negotiated on a free vote. Everything was changing. This realisation that the post-war consensus was crumbling led to a reassessment in sections of the Labour Party too. As the Wilson and Callaghan governments struggled with public expenditure cuts and incomes policies, others developed what became known as the Alternative Economic Strategy.

The decade had begun with the shock defeat of Wilson's Labour government in the 1970 general election, which the Conservatives won with a majority of thirty seats. They fought the election on a proto-Thatcherite agenda which had been formulated by Ted Heath and his shadow Cabinet during an away day at the Selsdon Park Hotel in Croydon. It was a radical free-market agenda designed explicitly to take the government out of the marketplace. It advocated corporate and individual tax cuts, legislation to restrict the power of trade unions, tough law-and-order policies and immigration control. In the event it was quickly abandoned by Ted Heath, who found he could not keep the government out of the marketplace even if he had ever really wanted to. Under pressure, he rescued Rolls-Royce from bankruptcy in January 1971 and found himself doing the same

for the Upper Clyde Shipbuilders five months later. His attempts to curb trade union rights ran into fierce resistance from
the unions who simply ignored the requirements of the new Industrial Relations Act. Their defiance was successful, at least in
the short term. The government effectively abandoned its own
legislation and struggled to cope with waves of strikes for higher
pay as rising inflation squeezed living standards. Heath invoked
emergency powers when the dockers and the power workers
went on strike and, during the two miners' strikes he had to
contend with, introduced the three-day week and a system of
rolling power cuts, causing a run on candles which Angela still
remembers. Mrs Thatcher never forgot Heath's 'betrayal' of
the 'Selsdon Park programme' and she subsequently became
the lady not for turning, regarding compromise as surrender.
She ruthlessly pursued the right-wing market fundamentalist
agenda that Heath had abandoned.

While the libertarian right were on the intellectual ascend-
ency in the Conservative Party, the Labour Party was searching
for a radical programme that would replace the failing post-
war consensus on progressive principles. What emerged was to
become known as the Alternative Economic Strategy (AES).
It was partly forged during Tony Benn's period as Secretary of
State for Industry and by the academic work of the Cambridge
Economic Policy Group of Wynne Godley and Francis Cripps.
It was supported by the syndicalist revival of the Militant Shop
Stewards' Movement, which was playing a prominent role in
the outbreak of industrial unrest in the trade unions. The Institute for Workers' Control, which focused on developing new
forms of industrial democracy, was also influential as these new
approaches were being developed.

The AES was designed as a conscious break with the consensus 'corporate socialism' of Attlee's Labour government.

It involved proposals to reflate the economy to increase both output and employment. To ensure that the money spent on stimulating demand would not leak out and simply benefit foreign producers, the AES advocated import controls to protect UK industries as well as controls on foreign outflows of capital from the country. It suggested the creation of a national enterprise board, which would co-ordinate price controls and compulsory planning agreements with all the top companies operating inside the UK, mandating levels of employment and investment. There were proposals to nationalise key industries and bring major banks and financial institutions under state control. There were also to be selective subsidies to industry to help modernisation and investment. There would be new powers for trade unions to bargain and for workers to have democratic control in their workplaces, as well as policies to encourage work-sharing and employment subsidies. The UK would be withdrawn from the Common Market and there would be major cuts in defence spending, including the end of the UK's independent nuclear deterrent, which then consisted of Trident's predecessor: the Polaris system. Income and wealth would be redistributed and there would be an expansion of social services. It was not until after Labour's two narrow general election victories in 1974 that the AES was to be fully developed and campaigned for throughout the structures of the party. But, perhaps sensing its otherworldly nature, the Wilson and Callaghan governments rejected this approach. Crosland was scathing and described the AES as having been written by people who didn't live in the real world.

It was certainly very utopian and reads more like a hopeful shopping list of idealistic policies than a serious programme for government. While it consisted of an academic economic theory that may have looked plausible in a classroom, it was unconnected to political reality and simply impracticable. When challenged about the likelihood that its retreat from open trade into protectionism would provoke retaliation from those countries whose imports were to be restricted, the Cambridge Economic Policy Group's dubious response was that this would not happen if the import controls were applied correctly. However, the UK has always been an open and trading economy, and was likely to suffer badly in a trade war. Moreover, returning to capital controls just as others were abandoning theirs gave too much of a sense of backward-looking yearning for an era long gone. There were certainly some good elements included in the AES, but it is hard to take seriously as a practical programme of measures which could have been implemented or which would have worked. It had too much of a 'stop the world we want to get off' feel about it. It advocated strict protectionism for one of the most open trading nations in the world. It seemed to have no coherent plan about how to deal with retaliation from our trading partners if they did not approve of us preventing their goods coming into the UK but expecting our exports to be unaffected.

When it was finally incorporated wholesale into Labour's 1983 election manifesto, Labour collapsed as a viable alternative to Mrs Thatcher's Conservatives, winning only 27.6 per cent of the vote and failing to capture a majority of the votes of trade unionists for the first time in its history. Undoubtedly the SDP breakaway accounted for some of this catastrophe, but so did the unrealistic manifesto plan for the institution of an economic autarky and rationing of foreign exchange in a rapidly globalising world. Angela can remember forlornly canvassing for Labour with the manifesto in hand in Oxford East, which was then the most marginal constituency in the country. She still remembers the looks of pity on the faces of some of the voters she spoke to when she dared to brandish this document. And she remembers Conservative candidate Steven Norris, who imported cars into a constituency which contained the Cowley car manufacturing plant, beating Labour's Andrew Smith in what should have been a Labour constituency. So catastrophically did the manifesto go down with voters that Gerald Kaufman famously described it as 'the longest suicide note in history'. The Conservatives obviously agreed, because they bought 1,000 copies of it solely to hand out to and frighten voters.

With the defeat of the Callaghan government and the election of Margaret Thatcher in 1979, the long intellectual and political domination of market fundamentalism had begun. In 1983, the British electorate chose a hard-right free-market programme rather than an otherworldly option for a siege economy that turned its back on the world. It took many more years for the disadvantages of the institution of a hard-right market fundamentalist economic plan to be appreciated more fully by the British electorate. The lack of a practical, forward-looking, progressive response to the challenges facing Britain in the 1970s meant that ideologically the field was vacated to the forces of market fundamentalism. Labour were to be out of power for eighteen long years. And the battle to end the economic and political domination of hard-right ideas is still to be completed.

THE LESSONS OF NEW LABOUR AND THE THIRD WAY

The Third Way was an attempt to reconcile traditional social democratic concerns for social justice with what sociologist Anthony Giddens regarded as the unchallengeable constraints imposed on national governments by the phenomenon of globalisation. Giddens was a critic of postmodernism who believed in a more holistic view of how societies worked and interacted. He also believed that the phenomenon of rapid globalisation had changed the meaning of national sovereignty and limited the scope that governments had to act effectively in the domestic sphere. The rising tide of individualism had also weakened the bonds of 'solidarity' and switched the focus much more onto the pursuit of personal, rather than communal, fulfilment. This was the very thing that R. H. Tawney had criticised when he observed it in the 1920s. Giddens, however, felt these increases in individual self-determination and empowerment were to be encouraged, and there was a welcome commitment to broaden out inclusion and increase diversity in his writings. There were responsibilities as well as rights for individuals implicit in this new settlement. A decline in deference and tribalism was weakening traditional political affiliations, which would continue to loosen the hold the major parties could command over the loyalty of voters.

Giddens asserted that while governments still had a role (defending the country and making the law), globalisation and the rise of transnational corporations had made politicians less influential and civil society was correspondingly more powerful. As a result, the traditional 'right' and 'left' conceptions of politics were increasingly anachronistic and needed to be superseded by the creation of a 'radical centre'. Economic prosperity had to be achieved in an open, globalised marketplace. This meant that social justice could only be advanced with the proceeds of growth rather than funded by tax increases: redistribution, not 'pre distribution'. There could be no useful attempt to intervene in market distribution prior to the initial outcome, he held. If there was no growth, then there could be no progress towards a more just society. Government needed to reform social security to increase individual reliance and public services could benefit from an increase in private sector know-how to make them more responsive to those who relied on them.

In reality, the Third Way was an essentially pessimistic interpretation of the prospects that democratic socialist governments faced when they were elected to office in the latter part of the twentieth century. It contained no challenge to the economic status quo, instead requiring that a new centre-left government should accommodate the market fundamentalist assumptions which had established themselves globally in the Thatcher/Reagan era. Indeed, the Third Way contained no economic analysis about what was wrong with this system. Instead, it was accepted as an unchangeable *fait accompli*. Imagine how little the Attlee government would have achieved if it had thus constrained itself upon coming to office in 1945?

All too often, the Third Way appeared to consist of a 'triangulation' between left and right, which had the effect of alienating party activists and traditional Labour voters who felt it 'wasn't Labour enough'. It did triumphantly win the support of the country, however, who were sick of the Conservatives and reassured by the absence of the very things Labour activists wanted to see. And that was no mean feat. Labour was elected for an unprecedented three successive terms in office, but on reducing turnouts as apathy appeared to be making the largest gains among voters who were now coming to believe that voting never changed very much.

Those New Labour governments had a long and impressive list of achievements to their credit. There was huge investment in social housing, in modernising schools and transforming the NHS, in abolishing pensioner poverty and reviving our cities after decades of neglect. Discrimination against LGBT people was wiped off the statute book and the Climate Change Act created the foundations needed to tackle the existential threat of global warming. Much was achieved to hold inequality at bay and invest in Britain's people and its social infrastructure.

Unfortunately, New Labour's undoubted achievements were snuffed out in George Osborne's first ludicrously named 'emergency' austerity Budget in 2010, which simply cut public expenditure and, with it, Labour's legacy of advancing social justice. We have all now experienced how fleeting social advance can be if it relies solely on redistributing the proceeds of growth and fails to create institutions that can reflect and project Labour's democratic socialist values far into the future. With the exception of the National Minimum Wage, no institution, such as the NHS or the Open University, introduced by the Attlee and Wilson governments respectively, was created that projected Labour values into the future. That is what is needed to be a truly transformative government – and transformation is what is needed when we next have a Labour government.

THE FUTURE

Following the fall of the Berlin Wall in 1989, American political economist Francis Fukuyama wrote a hubristic essay entitled 'The End of History?', which he later turned into a bestselling book. In it, he claimed that the fall of Soviet Communism had ushered in the end of history, because Western liberal democracy had won the Cold War and was therefore the pinnacle of human sociocultural evolution. In its triumphalism, the book failed to acknowledge the problems that market fundamentalism itself had created or exacerbated in the remaining, now-dominant global economic system. Persistent poverty, inequality, unsustainable use of finite resources, the existential challenge of climate change, the tendency to concentrate wealth and power in the hands of fewer people: all of these flaws were overlooked. Following the global financial crisis of 2008 and the rise of political instability and unrest which has followed, we suspect that few people would be so sanguine about the perfection of the rampaging market fundamentalist version of 'Western liberal democracy' that has predominated since the fall of the Berlin Wall.

Democracy and liberalism do not have to be accompanied by market fundamentalist beliefs. The economic liberalism of market fundamentalism is not the same as social liberalism. In fact, the two are in contradiction, because the social solidarity necessary to support an open, tolerant society needs greater economic equality if it is to be sustained. We suspect that such a society, which seeks to alleviate poverty, injustice and war – in other words, Western liberal democracy without market fundamentalism – might just catch on. For some political thinkers, the search for a new, non-socialist alternative to capitalism has resumed.

Before we explain over the coming chapters how we would approach applying the democratic socialist values we hold to the problems of tomorrow, we wish to address a few of the new theoretical approaches that are *en vogue* on the left and in the wider labour movement today: accelerationism in its left-wing iteration, post-capitalism and 'fully automated luxury communism'. We also examine the 'Blue Labour' approach which emphasises the importance of family, faith and flag, and consider the case for introducing a universal basic income which springs from the view that the march of the robots will mean we are entering a post-work society.

ACCELERATIONISM

Capitalist transformation and the global marketplace has prompted wildly different responses from different groups. For example, it has given rise to the slow movement which strives for a more holistic and local integration of production, be it of food or clothes. The slow movement has recently manifested itself culturally, too, bringing us the unexpected pleasures of slow TV and the 168-hour epic reindeer migration from Lapland, filmed and broadcast in real time by Norwegian national broadcaster NRK. Others, however, have responded very differently to what they call the transformations of late capitalism. Instead of appreciating slow things, they glory in speed.

Accelerationists make a virtue of not trying to reform or resist the evolution of capitalism; they welcome it with open arms, especially the more aggressive, neoliberal, globalised variety that has been enabled by rapid developments in computer technology and processing speed. Accelerationists believe that this evolution should be actively speeded up, either because there is no alternative or because they wish to see the collapse of the entire system under the strain. Collapse will lead to chaos and then to the transformation they seek. They do not believe that capitalism and its development can be controlled or mitigated in any way, which eerily aligns them with basic tenets of market fundamentalism itself. Tellingly, the 'there is no alternative' mantra was first coined by Margaret Thatcher. You can't buck the market, they say, and if you can't beat it, you might as well join it. And yet the labour and trade union movement came into existence precisely to transform the system, by pursuing the patient and determined demands for change aimed at improving the lives of all. The unambiguous celebration of capitalism's instability and the complacent belief that its collapse will automatically lead to something better ignores the agency of those who work for collective social improvement as well as the lessons of history.

Accelerationists appear to be fixated on merging and fudging boundaries: between reality and the virtual world; between the digital and the human; and between fact and fiction. They are especially focused on going beyond the limits of the earth and colonising other planets. They frequently assume an end to resource scarcity, which will be achieved when humans are able to mine asteroids. All too predictably, taking their cue from Nietzsche and the will to power, what interests them is 'collective self-mastery' and 'command of the plan' married to the 'improvised order of the network'.[7] This approach is more about achieving power and control than anything that is recognisably progressive. It is at best 'post democratic'; at worst downright authoritarian. It is not democratic or socialist to celebrate the power and enrichment of a few or replace one powerful undemocratic privileged elite with another.

Nick Land, the nearest the accelerationist movement has come to a founding guru in the UK, celebrated what he called the dark will of capital to rip up political cultures and delete tradition in disturbing writings which were darkly nihilistic and anti-human. Creating what he called a 'group mind', the rogue CCRU (Cybernetic Culture Research Unit) at Warwick University, he declared that humans were something for 'it [a group intelligence] to overcome, a problem, [a] drag'. Accelerationists seem to be mesmerised by power and contemptuous of people. Little surprise, given this attitude, that there is a right-wing as well as a left-wing iteration. Accelerationism has directly spawned the odious alt right, NRx and the presidency of Donald Trump. NRx, the self-styled neo-reactionary movement, has had direct contact with Breitbart and Trump campaign mastermind Steve Bannon and openly admires white supremacists and Nazis. It wishes to abolish democracy, hates egalitarianism and argues for a return to authoritarian rule by powerful Wall Street businessmen and Silicon Valley entrepreneurs. It is the modern version of Ayn Rand's *Atlas Shrugged* and spouts just as unpalatable a set of semi-fascistic political beliefs.

There are those who see themselves as left-wing accelerationists (though many of them would argue that the political terms 'left' or 'right' are now meaningless), yet even these are worryingly sceptical of democracy and appear to be elitist. In *#Accelerate: Manifesto for an Accelerationist Politics*, Alex Williams and Nick Srnicek argue for the creation of an accelerationist's equivalent to Hayek's Mont Pelerin Society, the secretive network he set up in the 1940s. It is credited with creating and then propagating to devastating effect what has been dubbed 'the neoliberal thought collective' (NTC for short),[8] which ensured the continued influence worldwide of the dubious ideas of market fundamentalism. The accelerationists wish to use hi-tech social platforms to build a 'complex new hegemony' and, in the *Accelerationist Manifesto*, they talk of 'refurbishing mastery in a new and complex guise'. This is as revealing as it is disturbing, because the Mont Pelerin Society was and remains an unashamedly elitist network of the already powerful and privileged who meet semi-secretly to propagate their own self-interests in the guise of certain economic and political dogmas. As such, they are a top-down power structure that is unaccountable and undemocratic. No progressive movement that is interested in empowering the mass of people and achieving real 'bottom-up' democratic change would suggest the use of such a power structure to bring it about.

Accelerationists believe that Marx is outdated by cybernetic theory, but they retain a cod Marxist belief in the inevitability of the transformation of capitalism or its collapse. One of their cultural heroes is the relentless killer cyborg in the *Terminator* film series, first played by Arnold Schwarzenegger in the movies.

Revealingly, the accelerationists do not seem to be inspired by the human freedom fighter the terminator is seeking to destroy. (Personally, we were rooting for Sarah Connor.) This is millenarian, extremist, apocalyptic stuff out of which it is impossible to imagine anything progressive or socially desirable emerging. Wishing for the collapse of the system as an end in itself has never been the way of democratic socialists, who believe that by working together we can build a better society for the common good. The belief that the worse things are the better they are has been the approach of nihilists the world over and experience shows that what follows the collapse always seems to be brutal and inhumane.

A preference for collapse over reform would not have assisted the world's prospects during the global financial crisis in 2008, when an accelerationist approach might have indicated that it was better to let the entire financial system collapse, destroying people's savings and bringing down the political system with it. This is not politics. It is a dereliction of duty which could only have been seriously contemplated by irresponsible people who thought they would be personally insulated from the consequences. It is always the poor and vulnerable who lose out most as a result of collapse. Look at what has happened in Russia. There, the collapse of Communism led directly to mass larceny and the rise of the oligarchs, the creation of an amoral kleptocracy and steep declines in life expectancy for ordinary Russians. Authoritarian dictatorship rather than democracy is all too often the outcome of collapse. Accelerationism as a theory seems to care little about the continuation of democracy itself, and as the futurist movement in Italy degenerated into fascism, it appears that the tendency of accelerationist analysis to crave collapse indicates that its modern-day heirs may end up going the same way.

An engagement with accelerationism has spawned two off-spring on the left in British politics: post-capitalism and fully automated luxury communism.

POST-CAPITALISM

The post-capitalist approach speculates that the seeds of the destruction of the system have long been sown, and that it will indeed be superseded by something else. In the 1990s, Peter Drucker published a book called *Post-Capitalist Society*. In it he coined the term 'knowledge society', arguing that the internet age would usher in a transformation from an industrial to a knowledge-based system which would render obsolete the adversarial distinctions of labour and capital. This was an idea enthusiastically taken up by New Labour, but we do not believe it has come to pass. If anything, the intervening years have re-emphasised that the very adversarial contest of labour and capital is alive and kicking. And currently labour is losing. The labour share of national income has shrunk across the already industrialised nations as the owners of capital have taken a much larger share and levels of inequality have soared. And so, albeit in a modern guise, the political challenges facing democratic socialists are eerily familiar and we believe will endure for the foreseeable future.

American economic and social theorist Jeremy Rifkin celebrates the dawn of a new era and the coming of what he calls the 'collaborative commons'. He believes that this is enabled by the rise of a super internet which will produce a world of distributed and collaborative power. In his book, *The Zero Marginal Cost Society*, he argues that the costs of production are being lowered to such an extent that the traditional, vertically integrated corporation will be destroyed. This is the phenomenon that has already disrupted the music industry and made it virtually impossible for all but the most famous composers and musicians to be paid for their work. Rifkin regards this development as a new paradigm and the first new economic system to appear since the rise of capitalism and socialism in the nineteenth century. Currently he believes we are living in a hybrid society, where the new and the old systems are existing side by side. Rifkin believes that the collaborative commons will supersede capitalism, though how this will come about he does not really say. Rifkin's theory does not deal with the established vested interests of ownership of network infrastructures and the super-profits they are delivering to certain technology companies. Nor does he deal with the effects of the bombardment into personal timelines of mass advertising. This advertising is what pays for the system. As well as turbo-charging consumerism, it leads to the harvesting of mass data on every individual which can be used to build individual profiles of the behaviour of every user and to target political propaganda cheaply to everyone involved in the system. While this data could be used for good, it is predominantly being used currently to propagandise and to make monopoly profits for a few gigantic companies.

Paul Mason, in his book *PostCapitalism: A Guide to Our Future*, makes much the same case for the sharing and collaborative economy. He argues that this new world will evolve spontaneously out of the current system. Indeed, he believes that this is already happening. He cites myriad examples of resistance to oppression which he covered as a BBC reporter, ranging from the revolts of the Arab Spring to the heroic resistance to the extreme austerity that was imposed on Greece. He pronounces the proletariat dead and believes it will be superseded by a network of millions of individual, educated and connected human beings who will challenge and change the system. In reality, as the rest of the world industrialises, the proletariat and – we would argue – the new piecework-driven, apparently self-employed 'precariat' has never been larger. Indeed, it is possible in the UK to purchase these thought-provoking books online from Amazon and have them delivered the very next day, after an 'Amazombie' – working a twelve-hour shift in one of their 'fulfilment centres' for £8.20 an hour, who is expected to find 300 items in that time – has packed it for you. It will then have been given to a 'self-employed' courier who is expected to deliver up to 100 parcels a day, six days a week, being paid 48 pence a delivery. And if that wasn't enough, they also have to supply their own transport and fuel. To fight against exploitative employment conditions such as this, to create a more humane society, was why the Labour Party and the trade unions first came into being. Now we need to renew our efforts to do just that, not slink into history, discouraged and defeated.

There is certainly a place for idealism and vision in the fight to end the scourge of market fundamentalism and the exploitation it has brought in its wake, but the power of the state cannot be as easily dismissed as Paul Mason does. However networked and educated the individuals who occupied Tahir Square in Egypt were, the fact is that the military are now back in power and many of the protesters who occupied the square are in jail. These idealistic visionary accounts also tend to assume that technology is neutral as a medium, when it clearly is not. The internet did not come into being as a public good and nor did the World Wide Web, even though it was originally envisaged that way by its creator Sir Tim Berners-Lee. The reality is that it has evolved in an entirely different way. The technology has been ruthlessly commercialised, and the 'network' which now connects millions of people the world over has been created by corporations who have come to dominate the globe in rapid time. The libertarian approach of many in Silicon Valley is hard-wired into the design of the operating systems which now power the internet and it is not at all clear that building a 'collaborative commons' will be easy in such a hostile environment.

The new dominant corporations of our era have been very adept at designing the infrastructure to make colossal profits for themselves and the companies they have built. As we shall see below, they have used every trick in the book of every monopolist since time immemorial to exploit and keep their market power. They do not like paying tax to any government; they have installed free but proprietary operating systems and software; and they have quickly swallowed up any rivals they could not destroy. Much of the output available on the internet is addictive in the extreme, deliberately designed to keep people on the page in order to make money through advertising. This produces a very different internet experience than that which would have been produced if the internet had been developed as a public good, free of commercial advertising. It might be that, contained within the potential of all this technology designed for profit and exploitation, there is something kinder and better that can be grown and come to predominate. But many other nastier futures are just as plausible if there is not some sensible regulation of the internet, an enforceable internet bill of rights and a commitment to establish and maintain a trusted hub for the fact-based provision of information.

FULLY AUTOMATED LUXURY COMMUNISM

Fully automated luxury communism envisages a tech-enabled utopia just around the corner. It suggests that the advent of widespread automation should be speeded up so that human beings can enter a 'post-work' society in which robots and automatic production will remove the requirement to work for more than a few hours a week. Full automation of everything would go hand in hand with common ownership of all of it. In exchange for all this leisure time, people would be provided with a universal basic income, free housing, education and healthcare.

This unashamedly utopian vision contains no detail as to how we may get from where we are now as a society to this startling future. For one, how would we achieve common ownership of the automation of everything? At the moment, all this infrastructure is owned and controlled by corporations and individuals. It is also diffuse and global. So, are we contemplating fully automated luxury communism in one country or across the entire world?

All of this relies on a very optimistic view of the potential of technology to solve all practical problems and generate enough value to finance a world of mass leisure and luxury. But – and it's a big but – even if enough value were to be generated by mass automation, how would the redistribution to all citizens work?

There are other serious problems. Fully automated luxury communism has little to say about the environmental or energy constraints that will be barriers to luxury mass production, whether commonly owned or not, to say nothing of the recycling bills. Indeed, fully automated luxury communists suggest that the solution to the issue of the finite resources available on earth is to look to the stars. They claim that scarcity could be overcome by mining asteroids. But, again, this fails to deal with the issue of ownership and control. Elon Musk and his SpaceX company would be unlikely to hand over the profits of his space-mining ventures if they were to be successful, and as yet there is no extra-terrestrial law on the ownership of mineral rights on passing asteroids.

If all this utopian speculation sounds a bit too good to be true, that's because it is. And the luxury communists' view of the future does not accord with current facts or our experience of previous periods of rapid industrial change. The demise of work has been anticipated for over two centuries now and, despite the fact that we are about to enter the Fourth Industrial Revolution, work is still stubbornly failing to disappear. As the TUC points out in a recent discussion paper, 'Shaping Our Digital Future', breakthrough technologies have been disrupting the established order for over 250 years and in each case new technologies have resulted in more, not fewer, jobs. Far from disappearing, they say, jobs are more plentiful than ever. Statistics show that the UK employment rate is close to a record high. The real issue is the quality of the jobs available and the type of pay and conditions that come with them. Those issues are the core concerns of the labour and trade union movement and always have been. There is no discussion in this vision of a 'post-work' society of the desirability of separating people from the identity and satisfaction which have long been associated with work. Many of those who work with the unemployed will testify how destructive the lack of purpose and ability to contribute that often accompany joblessness are to individual wellbeing. Further to this, good work positively enhances wellbeing. It creates a sense of pride, belonging and purpose which helps make life meaningful. Luxury communists are silent on caring jobs. In their brave new world, who would care for the elderly or children? Housework and domestic labour would be unlikely to disappear, even if production and some services were automated and everyone was wearing self-cleaning clothes. Or doesn't domestic labour count as work in their view?

A UNIVERSAL BASIC INCOME

The idea of introducing a universal basic income has recently reappeared in left-leaning political circles and is on the global agenda, in part in response to the anticipated labour market disruption and loss of jobs caused by the march of the robots. The nature of the transition from the old to the new era is what worries policy-makers, but the advocates of universal basic income make strange bedfellows: from the super-rich tech elites of Silicon Valley, via Sir Richard Branson to the fully automated luxury communists. In the UK, both the liberal Royal Society for the Arts and the right-wing Adam Smith Institute are advocates. One of market fundamentalism's high priests, conservative economist Milton Friedman, proposed a version of universal basic income in his 1962 book, *Capitalism and Freedom*. Essentially, his idea was to introduce a negative income tax as a temporary transition on the way to what he called a 'transfer-free' society. By this he meant that the goal would be that no tax revenues whatsoever would be 'redistributed' from one individual to another by the state. The needs of the poor would be looked after by the voluntary action of civil society and charities, not government. This was a bit like an earlier version of David Cameron's 'Big Society', which is currently providing cover for the Conservative government's effort to dismantle the British welfare state. Unlike David Cameron, however, Friedman was quite explicit about his motives. He intended that the introduction of the universal basic income would enable big savings to be made in existing state expenditures, with even more to come in the future. He wished to eliminate state-funded social security payments and programmes such as old-age pensions, public housing, public health programmes such as Medicare and Medicaid, hospitals and mental institutions.

To Friedman and his intellectual aficionados on the market fundamentalist right, the universal basic income was a way of dissolving the state and the social security safety net completely over time. In this way, the state itself can come as close to being extinguished as possible. Some on the right even argued that non-taxpayers should be denied the vote as a logical extension of this system, where only those who pay taxes get a say and those who receive assistance should be grateful, but voiceless. Where market fundamentalists are concerned, it is important to appreciate the dynamics of any system they propose over time to discern their real end point. In Friedman's case, it was the smallest government expenditures possible and a return to Victorian systems of charity for the poor. President Nixon was similarly persuaded that introducing a universal basic income was a good idea, and he presented the Family Assistance Plan, which would have introduced it, to Congress in 1969. It was passed by the House of Representatives but rejected in the Senate and subsequently overtaken by the unfolding drama of the Watergate scandal.

The win for the hard right in the successful introduction of a universal basic income is that replacing all public payments and, over time, the provision of public services with a regular single payment would make it much harder to justify giving more specific support to particular individuals who may be in need, despite receiving their basic payment. The right would blame them for squandering their basic income and make the case against further, more specific support. Universal basic income is no substitution for a state tax and benefit system that is democratically accountable and decides how the social wage will be made up and at what level taxes will be levied and public services provided after consulting society as a whole in an election.

As French philosopher André Gorz observed in his book, *Paths to Paradise*, about the concept of an income for life detached from the requirement to work: 'The guarantee of an income independent of a job will be emancipatory or repressive from the left or the right according to whether it opens up new spaces for individual or social activity or whether on the contrary it is only the social wage for compulsory passivity.'

Thus, Gorz points out that context and political motivation are all-important in assessing whether a universal basic income would even be a desirable aim. In order to finance something better than a social wage for compulsory passivity, the universal basic income would have to be set at a very generous level, which would make it very expensive to introduce and much harder to gain political consent for. Politically, arguing for more focused support for individuals in need on top of an existing basic income payment would be hard. And any increase in the universal benefit will be prohibitively expensive and by its nature hard to deliver. The UK has always relied upon a mix of universal payments, such as child benefit (universal until very recently), and more focused benefits for those who must qualify for them. This may be messy, but it is more politically sustainable and more likely to alleviate real hardship than a universal payment to everyone, which will either be too small to be meaningful or too expensive to introduce in practical terms. A particular problem with the concept of a universal basic income is that it severs the relationship between need and access to social security benefits completely. This separation dispenses with the contract implicit in the UK's social security system since the Beveridge reforms that, collectively, society is committed to alleviating poverty and meeting the needs of all its citizens. This would be a major loss to the progressive character of the social settlement, which would be hard to replace once it had been dispensed with.

BLUE LABOUR

While the accelerationists rush head-long towards the future, however dystopian, Blue Labour looks backwards for its inspiration. Their response to the disruption caused by the rapid changes associated with 'modernity' is an urge to nostalgia and the invocation of a world long gone. We seriously doubt that this longed-for old world ever really existed, much like John Major's nostalgic memories of the village cricket green, warm beer and the cycling spinster in his disastrous 'Back to Basics' relaunch. The Blue Labour cry of 'family, faith and flag' neatly encompasses their rose-tinted view of the halcyon days of the working class, where everyone was fixed in their place, where jobs, communities and religious beliefs were unchanging and socially conservative – and the issues of feminism, anti-racism and LGBT rights had yet to rear their disruptive and challenging heads. In short, Blue Labourites seek political accommodation within a mythical, socially conservative, working-class world view. As the children of working-class parents and immigrants, we just don't recognise this lazy and insulting cartoon depiction. For one, the working classes have always contained as wide a range of views on social and religious issues as any other section of society. And not only are working-class people open to social change, their communities and their organisations were often at the forefront of it, as with the mining communities and unions support for LGBT rights in the 1980s. Aspirational working-class parents (like our families) were determined their children would use educational achievement to escape the narrow choices that had been their lot in life. Like everyone else, working-class communities want – even if they no longer expect – economic opportunities. They want fulfilling, well-paid work; they want opportunities to be available for them and their children. They are not a bastion of some kind of social reaction to be appeased or feared by Labour's more urban voters. Solidarity and collective endeavour were at the heart of how they survived, often under severe economic pressure, and these values nurtured the labour and trade union movement. Indeed, they still form a basis for a more inclusive and diverse politics, rather than the backward-looking, socially conservative nostalgia being peddled by some.

It is instructive that the nostalgic vision Blue Labour invokes tends to be set in the 1950s, before the hippies and the Beatles and the feminists blew Macmillan's tired repressive world of cosy conservative hypocrisy apart for good. That world is never coming back. We don't *want* it back. We welcome our new more diverse society.

CHAPTER TWELVE

AUSTERITY IN THE UK

History will record that the global financial crash in 2008 marked the beginning of the end for Hayek's market fundamentalist doctrines. The cause of the crash was readily apparent: failure of *laissez-faire* economics and the complexity of capital markets; the amorality of the globalised and greedy financial system and a lack of adequate regulation both domestic and internationally. As millions of Britons struggled with falling real wages ten years after the crash, the ILO global wage report for 2016/17 showed that the long-term decline of the share of national income taken by labour now lags behind growth and has resumed its thirty-year decline. Meanwhile, the Bloomberg Billionaires Index reveals that the richest 500 people in the world got $1 trillion richer in 2017 and now control wealth of $5.3 trillion – a quarter of the size of the US economy.

The truth is the industrialised world had been here before. After the market catastrophe of the Wall Street Crash in 1929, the foolish pursuit of orthodox economic policies by President Hoover had caused slump and depression, nearly destroying the entire world economic system. As the Great Depression set in and unemployment and destitution soared in the USA and then spread to the industrialised world, it took the election of F. D. Roosevelt to avert total disaster. His New Deal saved American capitalism by transforming it. He instituted huge investment in public work schemes partly financed by a significant increase in progressive taxation imposed on the highest incomes. The 1933 Banking Act (the Glass–Steagall Act) legislated for the separation of commercial from investment banking, stopping in its tracks the reckless speculation which had brought down the banking system and 'liquidated' many jobs and businesses. Strict banking regulation, progressive taxation and Keynesian stimulus steadied the ship. The rise of fascism and war in Europe demonstrated the real dangers of tolerating economic collapse because of wrong-headed economic orthodoxy.

There was déjà vu in 2008, therefore, when the banking system once more teetered on the brink of disaster and Lehman Brothers was allowed to fail by a US administration ideologically reluctant to shore it up. The resulting shock hit already fragile levels of trust in the highly leveraged and over-extended but closely interconnected global banking system. All interbank lending froze, causing an immediate 'liquidity' problem for banks, threatening their solvency and as a result their very existence. This sudden unavailability of money and credit would have destroyed the real economy if it had been allowed to continue unaddressed by government action. As it was, governments across the world were forced to put unimaginably vast sums of money into their banking systems to prevent them from collapsing. Some banks were nationalised, others recapitalised, and governments guaranteed interbank lending as well as giving protections to depositors so that the system could continue to operate. Without this action, the banks, which constitute the entire financial plumbing system of any modern economy, would have been destroyed, leading to an economic cataclysm with incalculable political consequences. The G20 meetings in 2008 and 2009 announced ambitious stimulus programmes to try to get the world economy moving again. A global depression was avoided, but the worst recession in eighty years resulted in a decade of lost growth and suppressed living standards in the UK. We were especially badly hit because of our oversized banking sector. Thus was the globalised banking system rescued from the consequences of its own greed and folly by the determined action of states around the world. It seemed as if market fundamentalism would never recover its dominance since it had been revealed to the world that its dogmas and doctrines were not only actively dangerous, but plain wrong. It was a bit like realising that the extreme anti-state author of *Atlas Shrugged*, Ayn Rand, ended her life relying on the very US state welfare programmes she denounced and abhorred in her vainglorious fascistic writings. This realisation, coupled with her own breathtaking hypocrisy, should have been enough to make her a laughing stock. Many now expected that the global financial crash would make a laughing stock out of market fundamentalism too. Unfortunately, logic has not prevailed over faith, Ayn Rand is still worshipped by extreme libertarians and market fundamentalism is still alive and kicking.

Within two short years, right-wing politicians across the globe were blaming governments for causing the crisis by 'overspending'. These fake assertions were being cheered on by the very same market fundamentalist shock troops whose greed and folly had caused the global financial meltdown in the first place. Governments took on the burden of rescuing the banks to save the economy, but now the debts that this essential rescue had generated were used as an excuse to demand huge cuts in the size of public spending and the state itself. This audacious pivot which blamed those who rescued the situation for causing the crisis was ultimately successful as a political ploy. And those of us on the other side of the argument need to understand why.

The rich and powerful vested interests enjoy superior narrative firepower because they pay for it. It was in their direct financial interests that market fundamentalist doctrines continue their dominance. The lesson for us on the left is that we rely far too much on the belief that the logic and truth of an argument can prevail over bare-faced but well-resourced lying. In other words, emotion and a good narrative beat logic and truth every time. The costs of the rescue now led the right to demand the implementation of a policy forged in the fires of market fundamentalist ideology. And we all got what they demanded: austerity.

In his ludicrously named 'Emergency Budget', staged in June 2010, George Osborne, the Chancellor in the Conservative–Lib Dem coalition government, deliberately stoked the politics of fear and alarm for his own partisan political ends. Even though Angela, who was then on the opposition Treasury front bench, thought June was a bit early for the pantomime season, the Chancellor announced for no obvious economic reason that eliminating the UK's post-2008-crisis borrowing deficit would be the new government's primary aim. He also stated that a current budget surplus would be achieved in five years, after which the sunlit uplands would beckon. He issued blood-curdling warnings about the awful fate that would await Britain if his 'fiscal consolidation' was not achieved in the five-year timescale he had set out. Labour's plan to complete the task in ten years and go for growth in order to shrink the deficit by investing and aiming for a larger economy was so dangerous it was like driving a crashed car straight into a brick wall! The country needed cuts and more cuts! Without his plan, he said, the UK would lose its triple 'A' credit rating, we would come to resemble the stricken Greek economy (trapped in the euro, unlike Britain), unable to finance its debts. In any case, what did we expect when Labour had maxed out the country's credit card with all that wasteful public spending?

Amidst all this political theatre, the Chancellor made another controversial ideological choice in that first Budget. He announced that 80 per cent of the fall in borrowing which would eliminate the deficit would come from public expenditure cuts, and that only 20 per cent would come from tax increases. Outrageously copying the inclusive social democratic rhetoric which had accompanied a Swedish example of fiscal consolidation following a banking failure there, he then announced that though the times ahead would be tough, we'd be 'all in this together'. He was implying to the country that the 'tough but necessary' choices he had settled on would at least be implemented fairly. He made 'austerity' sound like an unpleasant but necessary diet which would have to be endured and completed if the country were not to end up in A&E. After five years though, he promised, everything would return to normal. Recovery from the largest global financial crisis the world had experienced since the Wall Street Crash in 1929 would be straightforward, and the sooner it was done the better.

The reality was that he had taken advantage of the aftermath of the global financial crisis to pursue a specifically Conservative ideological plan to shrink the size of the state in Britain, successfully disguising it as an absolute economic requirement. This plan was sustained and put into effect by the support of the Liberal Democrats in government and in Parliament. The Chancellor's 'analysis' of the causes of the crash was not serious or remotely accurate. But it was a highly effective political narrative designed to divert the blame from the bankers and financiers, whose greed and recklessness had caused the crash, onto the Labour government which had been in office when it struck. Apparently, Labour spending money on building schools and hospitals had caused a recession in sixty-five countries! Of course, the 2008 financial crisis was not caused by Labour spending too much public money on schools and hospitals, but by greed and lack of effective regulation in the American subprime mortgage market and by incredibly risky behaviour in the global banking and finance sectors. This should have been but was not picked up by policy-makers, regulators and governments the world over, who had come to trust in their own complacent belief that globalised capital markets spread risk when the crisis demonstrated that they actually spread the contagion.

The 2010 Budget and the shift in economic policy that it signalled provided an opportunity to test the market fundamentalist dogma that spending cuts (and tax cuts) create recovery. And the experiment has been a resounding failure in its own terms. This is not a surprise. A recent study by the politically impartial US Congressional Research Service has looked at sixty-five years of US data and noted that cutting taxes does not lead to economic growth. It does, however, help the already-well-off increase their share of the economic pie at everyone else's expense.

Seven years after George Osborne's first Budget, the UK is experiencing the slowest recovery from recession since the Napoleonic War and the longest squeeze in living standards since Victorian times. And it gets worse. Our trend growth rate has halved to an anaemic 1.5 per cent a year, productivity continues to flatline and the million fewer public-sector workers who remain to run essential services are working harder for less. They have not had a real pay rise since the crisis. Those who rely on social security payments – be they disabled, ill or unemployed – have been hit very hard indeed. There has been a huge explosion in food-bank use as many are left short by benefit sanctions or delays in payment in a system that has been deliberately re-engineered to be more punitive and humiliating. The speed of the plans to cut spending announced in the 'Emergency Budget' and the fervent warnings about Britain's parlous Greek-style economic peril combined to create a double-dip recession with a triple dip being only narrowly avoided.[9] The completion of the Conservative–Lib Dem five-year plan for eliminating the deficit and achieving a budget surplus has turned into public expenditure 'austerity' with no end in sight. The result is a devastated public realm of huge local government cuts aimed most at the poorest areas; growing unmet need in social services as the population ages; soaring levels of homelessness; the NHS and education sector experiencing real-terms cuts and increasingly struggling to meet genuine need; the smallest army since the Boer War; a new aircraft carrier without any aircraft to go on it; police and fire service cuts in personnel pay and equipment; a dangerous prisons system; and a dysfunctional courts system where many are now left to represent themselves and justice can scarcely even be seen to be done. There are soaring rail fares and virtually no roads without a pothole. Thirteen more years of public spending cuts on the scale expected are simply unsustainable if we are to maintain the NHS and free education, let alone aspire to recreate decent pension provision and a social security system we can all rely on as our population ages.

And yet, if the primary aim of the Conservative government was to achieve a budget surplus, they could have done so by 2018, achieving a surplus of £5 billion, if they had not decided to cut taxes. Instead, they made a political choice to maintain the current account deficit because they prefer to keep the minimal state 'austerity' drive, which leads to deep cuts in government spending, going until the end of this parliament and beyond. A closer look at the out-turn for public spending and taxes in the 2010–15 parliament reveals an astonishing truth. In the event, public spending cuts bore not 80 per cent of the cost of deficit reduction as George Osborne announced they would in his first Budget. As the Resolution Foundation work shows, tax receipts actually added to borrowing by 0.1 per cent of GDP, which means that public spending cuts bore 100 per cent of the cost of getting the deficit down. Even maintaining taxes at their previous level would have contributed to attaining a budget surplus in the current parliament, but the temptation to cut taxes, especially the 50p rate, handing a bonanza to Conservative Party donors, was just too great. Analysis from the Resolution Foundation shows that the cost of tax cuts in the last parliament was £40 billion: £21 billion on increases to the personal income tax allowance, which helps the better off; £12 billion on cuts to corporation tax; and £6 billion on the suspension of the fuel duty escalator. If the Conservative manifesto pledge to continue increasing the personal tax allowance and the higher rate threshold in income tax is fulfilled, that will cost a further £2 billion – nearly half of which would go to the top 10 per cent. This leaves those who are poorer and on low incomes to bear the brunt of the cuts to public services and benefits while receiving little of the extra money distributed in tax cuts.

It is already clear that despite the inclusive 'all in it together' rhetoric, the cumulative effect of austerity policies has been to hit the poorest and the already disadvantaged hardest. The Equality and Human Rights Commission has recently published its analysis of the impact of these policies and it is an indictment of the effects of the choices this government has made about where the axe will fall. Overall, the EHRC found that the changes were regressive, with the bottom half of the income distribution losing more than the top 10 per cent. This only gets worse in the current parliament, where the effect of policy decisions already made but still to be implemented is yet to be felt. The austerity-induced changes will boost the share of the top fifth of the income distribution but at the expense of substantial reductions in the bottom half. The EHRC found that losses for black households are double those for white households, at 5 per cent of net income. The disabled have been particularly hard hit. For those households which include someone with a disability, there is a significantly worse outcome compared to those containing no one with a disability. Benefit changes will mean that cumulatively they lose £2,500 a year, and this rises to £5,000 if the family includes a disabled child. And lone parents, who are almost all women, will lose around 15 per cent of their income – around double the greatest losses of other family types. The EHRC analysis shows that women will lose more than men from the changes at every income level; £940 per year on average compared to £460 for men. No wonder the government has declined to publish an equality impact assessment of its tax and benefit measures, despite the Equality Act 2010 putting it under a legal obligation to do so. Here also lies the explanation for the huge rise in the use of food banks reported by the Trussell Trust, which is the largest provider in the country. They gave out 129,000 emergency food parcels in 2011 – a number which rose eightfold to 1,183,000 in 2016/17. The government has consistently refused to collect official statistics on the volume of emergency food parcels handed out in Britain, which, though it is slipping down the league, remains one of the richest economies in the world.

This telling analysis does not take into account the cuts to public service provision or to local authority budgets, which have done deep damage to our social infrastructure and our communities since the government's austerity drive first began in 2010. Excluding education, spending by local authorities in England for the financial year 2016/17 has been cut by 22 per cent since 2009/10. But this overall figure hides deep disparities between different local authorities. While local government finances can be complex, what is clear is that poorer, mainly urban local authorities that have smaller tax bases and were therefore more reliant on grants from central government have suffered far greater cuts than others. IFS figures show that on average they have had to deal with 33 per cent cuts while the richest areas have only lost 9 per cent.[10] The government's intention of abolishing the rate support grant completely by the end of the current parliament will end the redistributive capacity of local government finance. This is the exact opposite of a progressive tax system in that it condemns already poorer areas to rely solely on their own resources to meet the greater needs of their poorer local population. Hayek would have been proud of his conservative disciples.

CHAPTER THIRTEEN

THE SECOND
MACHINE AGE

The invention and application of mechanised production powered by steam was a great technological leap forward. It transformed the landscape of this country more rapidly than any other change had previously done. Vast brick factories, belching smoke stacks and the unending clamour of machines filled our towns and cities, blackening the air and the faces of the workers who were drawn to these new temples of industry and manufacturing. Thousands upon thousands of people moved from the country to the burgeoning cities. As the revolution gathered pace, it turned Britain into the workshop of the world. Huge fortunes were made as innovation developed rapidly and productivity soared. But the Industrial Revolution had a very dark side, creating intolerable conditions for millions of people. While the owners of the new factories and manufacturing sectors accrued greater and greater wealth, a draconian factory system emerged, with the new urban proletariat living in appalling slum conditions. Child labour was commonplace. Poverty and disease accelerated in the new urban environment as workers lived cheek by jowl, crammed into cheap and nasty slum conditions which took a terrible toll on health and life expectancy.

It was therefore no surprise that these unprecedented social conditions spawned a new political movement. Its raison d'être was to redress the huge inequality that had grown up between the owners of capital and those who laboured to create the profits. Socialism, in all its many forms, was a reaction to the unacceptable exploitation faced by the new industrial workforce enduring powerlessness and poverty in the rapidly growing urban areas. In the UK, the socialist movement agitated for reform. It wanted decent sanitation, safer conditions in the factories, limits on child labour, paid holidays and reductions in the hours that made up the working week. Reformers fought to establish rudimentary health clinics and educational opportunities for everyone. Trade unions and social reformers lobbied Parliament for change and finally organised to enter Parliament themselves to represent the working classes directly. Democratic socialist ideas were to be instrumental in creating a social welfare system in the UK after the Second World War, which included comprehensive unemployment insurance, access to free healthcare and an extended universal right to free education as well as access to affordable housing. There was an explicit promise to fight what William Beveridge had so strikingly called the five 'Great Evils' of want, disease, ignorance, squalor and idleness, which stood in the way of social progress. His report, dealing with the fragmentation of the social insurance system and suggesting the introduction of an entirely new social security settlement, had become an unexpected publishing sensation in the war years. It sold an astonishing half a million copies and became the foundation of a social security settlement which was a defining cornerstone of social progress when it was implemented by Attlee's Labour government after the Second World War. Democratic socialists, through campaigning and governing, forged a more humane and socially just society. Now, as we have seen from the earlier analysis of soaring levels of inequality and social injustice in our current system, the time is ripe to do this again – this time in our modern setting.

We are now, in the twenty-first century, faced with changes that are likely to be even more disruptive than those which first called Labour into existence over a hundred years ago. And the pace of this transformation is likely to be exponential not linear, as it was during the First Industrial Revolution. This presents great opportunities for the development of humankind, but it also requires a robust and clear strategy from a government determined to make this transformation work for all.

Humanity has been here before. We know from experience that some countervailing political force is needed to ensure that the change that is upon us is shaped in the interests of the whole community and that the transition from the old economy to the new is properly planned and managed. We need to evolve a new form of socialism for this second machine age, to make sure that the outcome is both socially and environmentally sustainable.

We wish to explore ways in which a reinvigorated democratic socialism can ensure that we create an economically vibrant, socially just, environmentally sustainable future for all in the face of what is expected to be the most disruptive exponential change the human race has ever experienced.

WHAT IS THE FOURTH INDUSTRIAL REVOLUTION?

The First Industrial Revolution harnessed the power of steam. The Second and Third Industrial Revolutions used electricity to mechanise production and then information to automate it. Now humanity is on the cusp of the Fourth Industrial Revolution. It is already radically reshaping our world and the pace of change and innovation is accelerating.

The Fourth Industrial Revolution is about the fusing

together of technologies. It blurs the lines between the physical, digital and the biological world. The scale of change is set to be huge and it will be felt at whole system level as well as by individuals. It is being driven by innovations which include the collection of huge quantities of data and the computing capacity to analyse and deploy it in ways we cannot even yet anticipate.[11] Automation is now advancing rapidly. Robot design is progressing in leaps and bounds. Many of our workplaces already have their tasks routinely ordered and distributed to the human workforce by algorithms. Angela saw this when she visited a closed supermarket warehouse where food orders placed over the internet by customers were being put together for delivery to their door. A computer was directing the people gathering the orders which aisles to go to and in what order to ensure the most efficient use of their time fulfilling the orders. This happens in telecoms too, where the computer will suggest to the engineer how faults should be identified and addressed in each case. These algorithms are capable of learning from human patterns and improving over time. They will in the end be likely to replace humans altogether in performing some of these routine tasks. The second machine age is defined by Brynjolfsson and McAfee[12] as the automation of many cognitive tasks which make humans and software-driven machines substitutes not complementary. Millions of jobs currently in existence across the globe are likely therefore to be destroyed by this type of automation. The authors cite the algorithms that are even now marking the work of university students without the intervention of any human being. The advent of driverless cars will render millions of taxi and lorry drivers redundant. Despite the huge changes which are expected, we are optimistic about the outcome of this turbo-driven change. It has always been the case that change has created many new jobs as well as destroying existing ones. The transition, however, can be brutal, and sensible societies should plan to preserve their civilised values as technological innovation changes the world around us and especially as it changes the world of work.

Medicine, too, will be transformed by the Fourth Industrial Revolution. Imagine a British doctor wearing a virtual-reality headset that allows him to navigate through a 3D model of a beating human heart, his view soaring through chambers and vessels until he finds a weakness in an atrial wall, at which point he marks up what cuts and seals need to be made. The movements and data are sent through to a surgical robot 100 miles away, where the exact same movements are executed on the patient with flawless precision. Artificial intelligence helps the robot react to the beating of the heart, even dealing with a momentary flutter. Almost all of this is already possible, and its routine deployment will radically change the nature of how we organise the diagnostics and treatment of our own citizens, and even citizens in far-flung places who require the expertise of our brilliant doctors and surgeons.

Today, similar techniques model entire production lines for manufacturing trains or cars in virtual reality. This enables any flaws in design to be pinpointed and ironed out before the line is even built, which is delivering huge increases in manufacturing efficiency. As the industrial 'internet of things' develops, it is likely that much more manufacture will be performed by robots in increasingly automated 'brainy factories' overseen by a relatively few human technicians. Production can be performed remotely to design, and very small-scale personal manufacture of bespoke items will become common. Factories are likely to become much more automated, eventually dispensing with the need for a human presence altogether, except perhaps for the occasional technician.

Developments such as this will not just be confined to the manufacturing sector. Utilities will become more automated, too. Water pipes which alert systems engineers when they need to be repaired are currently being installed in the UK. Robotics and sensing technologies are likely to revolutionise agriculture also, and lead to significant increases in efficiencies as well as major job losses in the sector. In Japan, the company Spread has already developed a 'Technofarm', producing indoor, factory-farmed lettuce with a minimal human presence, using resources much more efficiently and completely avoiding the need for pesticides.

Thanks to the plasticity of the human brain, electronic implants can allow people who are paralysed to control robotic arms by the power of their thoughts. This development has the potential to transform the economic prospects for disabled people, who may be able to enjoy or regain their independence and ability to function in a way which would once have seemed impossible to contemplate. Autonomous self-driving vehicles are being tested in Milton Keynes and robots are becoming more ubiquitous and more sophisticated. Machine learning is advancing so fast that there are now real ethical debates about how to ensure that artificial intelligence does not become completely autonomous of humans and grow into a threat to us all. And as the Pentagon's bid for $12 billion to pursue AI-controlled weapons systems demonstrates, warfare is going to be transformed by these processes too.

Bioscience offers the possibility of gene editing to avoid genetically inherited illnesses. The potential is now emerging to augment human capacities too. These developments require an ethical debate about whether they should be pursued and to what end. Humanity and machines can be combined already to achieve more productive work. Super-strong 'exoskeletons', which are worn and controlled by human beings but can lift and move huge weights, are no longer science fiction – they are being developed to be deployed now. (As a long-time admirer of Ripley from the *Alien* film franchise, Angela already has one on pre-order.)

If nanotechnologies and quantum computing can be successfully developed and deployed, this offers a potentially huge leap forwards in computing capacity, which in turn enhances the potential speed of development in every area of scientific research. Connecting all of it will enable the collection, exchange and analysis of unimaginable quantities of data. It is estimated that, by 2021, there will be 46 billion sensors animating the 'internet of things' (the network of physical devices connected to the internet) in the world. That is close to six for every person on the planet. In 2013, technology company Cisco noted that 13 billion devices were connected worldwide. They are estimating that this will rise to an astonishing 500 billion by 2030. There are already more electronic components that run modern computers than there are leaves on the earth's trees.[13]

The implications of these developments, both ethical and political, are worthy of intense public debate. Data collection and accrual on identifiable individuals is now commonplace. Sensors, which collect data and send it back to operators or manufacturers for their use, are included in almost everything you purchase and much else besides – in your iPhone, your Fitbit, your smart meter and your increasingly automated car. It will not be long until they are included in your washing machine, your toaster and just about everything else you bring into your house or use at work. Every time you casually click on a licence agreement, someone is getting vast amounts of data about you.

All this is generating a 'data boom', the implications of which are only just beginning to be considered by the manufacturers, let alone by the customers and users of these 'smart' goods.

THE SPEED OF CHANGE IS INCREASING

Hermann Hauser has identified the emergence of what he calls 'general purpose technologies' (GPTs) twenty-four times in world history.[14] These technologies are examples of drastic innovation which are so profound that they disrupt entire systems. The steam engine, electricity and the invention of the computer are all examples of GPTs. After their invention, literally everything changed. Hauser posits that there were only nine in the first nineteen centuries of the Common Era[15] – the printing press being one of the most important of these and the effects of which most closely resemble that of the World Wide Web. There were eight new GPTs in the twentieth century, with the remaining seven arriving at an accelerating rate in the twenty-first. Hauser believes that there are six different waves of computing, the final one, based upon machine learning and the development of artificial intelligence, being the most powerful and unpredictable of all the GPTs ever invented, involving, as it might, the emergence of superintelligences. GPTs are defined by their capacity to be totally disruptive of the existing order, and because of this they always cause massive job losses and change on a huge scale. For example, the advent of the railway cost coachmen, stable boys and farriers their livelihoods, to say nothing of those who worked on the previously dominant transport system, the canals. In the past, however, it has taken time for these new technologies to become fully established and disseminated across the economy, since money had to be invested in appropriate infrastructure and the appropriate machinery had to be built. In contrast, the speed of the arrival of the new technologies of today, their low-cost and rapid scalability are unprecedented. This leaves little time for individual displaced workers or society to adjust to the change.

THE NETWORKED WORLD

We are living through an era of exponential change and it is driven by the increasing power of computing and data analytics. In 1965, Gordon Moore, who co-founded Intel, predicted that the power of computers would double every eighteen months while the cost would fall. This became known as Moore's Law, and it has been an accurate extrapolation of the exponential rate of progress to date because the computer industry took it up as a challenge and made it a self-fulfilling prophecy. While future progress will inevitably be harder to achieve without significant new innovation, Moore's Law has moved computing from the basement into everyone's pocket. Thus, the computing power of your iPhone is far greater than that which was available to astronaut Neil Armstrong as he piloted the *Eagle* to the first moon landing in July 1969. The cost of computing has fallen by 33 per cent a year since 1992; data storage costs by 38 per cent. This has enabled an explosion of new ways of communicating, purchasing and problem-solving that has completely transformed the way we live and relate to each other. In this increasingly networked world, people sat next to each other on the bus no longer communicate because they are too busy talking to someone else on their personal networks in cyberspace.

HUGE NEW MONOPOLIES NOW DOMINATE NEW TECHNOLOGIES

The World Wide Web was invented in 1989, yet iPhones did not exist until 2007. Their emergence had to await the creation of powerful Wi-Fi-enabled mobile telecoms, which became available from 2001. The astonishingly rapid rise of the company behemoths of this second machine age gives a clue to the accelerating pace of development. Facebook was created in 2004 and, as of February 2018, has a value of $511 billion. Google, created in 1998 and floated in 2004, is worth $766 billion. Twitter, which went online in 2006, has seen its initial market capitalisation fall from $31 billion to $24 billion because it wasn't growing its user base fast enough. YouTube was created in 2005 and sold to Google a year later for $1.65 billion. The market capitalisation of Apple, Google, Microsoft, Amazon and Facebook combined is now $3.57 trillion[16] of the $280 trillion of global value. Wealth is concentrating rapidly in fewer hands. Recent figures from the Credit Suisse Global Wealth Report show that the richest 1 per cent of the world's population now own 50.1 per cent of its wealth. The poorest 3.5 billion people own just 2.7 per cent of it. These companies have established globally monopolistic positions in a remarkably short space of time. They have more money and more information about citizens' lives that most states.

The sheer volume of users and interactions these companies handle is astonishing. Close to 9 billion videos are now watched daily on YouTube. In the first quarter of 2017, Facebook passed the two-billion monthly user mark, Google's Gmail has 1 billion monthly users and Twitter has 328 million. It is estimated that over half the world's population, nearly 4 billion people, now have access to the World Wide Web and that number will only go on growing. The information that is generated by their individual interactions with this technology is valuable in itself. Those who have access to it are only just beginning to understand how it might be analysed and monetised. Aside from the data which quite properly belongs to any business, more generalised collecting of 'raw' data is now proceeding apace. Companies are therefore intent on collecting this data and storing it in what are known as 'data lakes'. They are certain it will be useful in the near future, even if they don't quite know what to do with it now.

It is becoming clear, using our current business models, that those who have the data are collecting what they believe could be a very valuable resource in the near future. Whether they are correct depends on the accuracy and success of the analytics which underpin developments in so-called big data. So far this has been especially useful in analysing existing medical research papers and discovering hitherto unknown connections. The Brexit vote in the UK and the election of Trump to the US presidency demonstrated that it is a powerful force in politics too.

Because the dominant business model in use today gives away content for free, it relies on advertising for its revenues. The increasing sophistication of the collection of highly individualised information appears to be turbo-charging the effectiveness of advertising and, by extension, political propaganda. It achieves this by tailoring highly effective individual messages to millions of unsuspecting voters. Such personalised advertising fails to distinguish between truth and fiction, or, indeed, facts and so-called alternative facts. If unchallenged, this technique undermines the basis on which all democracies are designed to work – the ability to distinguish between truth and fiction by unbiased access to the facts.

EFFECT OF THE FOURTH INDUSTRIAL REVOLUTION ON OUR ECONOMY, SOCIETY AND POLITICS

Rapid industrial change threatens to hit the poorest hardest, exacerbating already high levels of inequality in our society. In terms of job losses to automation, it threatens to hit developing nations harder than those which have already developed. The World Economic Forum has calculated that it will destroy the jobs of the poorest most, that those jobs done by women will be lost in greater numbers to automation and that more reward will go to the owners of capital than those who work. Rapid technological change is already creating enormous concentrations of power in fewer and fewer global monopolist corporations whose dominance and market power will be huge if left unchecked. These challenges can only be faced by concerted government action at both national and international level to ensure that these huge corporations do not become a law unto themselves.

THE ECONOMIC EFFECTS OF INDUSTRIAL REVOLUTIONS

The past may not be an entirely accurate guide to the future, but it can certainly signpost the likely problems that will confront us. So, what can we deduce from previous experience?

Industrial revolutions are a good thing. They increase economic growth and living standards in the medium to long term. They are highly desirable at a macroeconomic level, though it is becoming clearer as the world continues to industrialise that this has to be done in an environmentally sustainable way if we are to safeguard the future of our planet. Industrial revolutions increase growth and change the way that we live our lives. They transform the way our society is organised almost always for the better in the end. Industrial revolutions change the sectoral balance of the economy, too. For example, in 1700, the agricultural sector comprised over 50 per cent of the UK economy; this has now fallen to 1 per cent. During the same period, manufacturing increased from a very low base to 45 per cent and then fell back to 10 per cent. Now it is services that dominate the UK economy, with 80 per cent of current economic activity falling into this category.[17] Services as a percentage of the whole UK economy have doubled roughly every 100 years.

The new goods and services which have been created by this process of innovation and its application have enhanced our enjoyment of life and dramatically reduced the average weekly hours worked from fifty a century ago to thirty today. Life expectancy and levels of education have both risen dramatically in the last 300 years as scientific and technological progress has enhanced economic performance, transforming our lives out of all recognition.

While desirable, industrial revolutions are also extremely disruptive. Initially, they cause massive job displacement and huge, unanticipated increases in personal hardship for those people who see their livelihoods destroyed by more efficient production processes or new technology. In economic parlance, this is called the substitution effect. As cheaper technology replaces more expensive labour, many are left without any means of making their living. New, more efficient production methods cause the cost of goods and services to fall and this means that real incomes (what can be purchased for a set amount of money minus inflation) rise. This increases the demand for now-cheaper goods and services, thereby creating new jobs to provide for that newly released demand. This is called the compensation effect. Economic theory, and, indeed, observation of previous industrial revolutions in the UK, has demonstrated that these predictions are accurate empirically as well as theoretically. However, the compensation effect rarely happens at the same time as the substitution effect. Nor does it necessarily completely compensate those who find themselves 'substituted'. The time lags separating the bad effects from the beneficial effects can be significant. There is likely to be a great deal of human suffering in the absence of state action to alleviate the problems caused by this transition through a period of great change.

We would argue that the Labour Party's creation was a symptom of the hardship and social disruption caused by the First Industrial Revolution which had begun 100 years earlier. As the prevailing *laissez-faire* economic philosophy of both the Conservatives and the Liberals ruled out *a priori* state action to mitigate such suffering, the Labour Party was created to deliver it. The 'free market' cannot and never has provided the solution to the enormous price paid by those who lose out to 'progress' in times of rapid economic change. Social action and politics have to provide these solutions and society collectively has to wish these answers into being through the political choices it makes. If it can do so successfully, then the benefits of great economic change can indeed be spread more equitably, ensuring the creation of more socially and environmentally sustainable societies.

IDEOLOGY AND ECONOMIC OUTCOMES

Different industrial revolutions do demonstrate differences in outcome, too. Technological change increases the productivity of the economy and as a result both economic theory and empirical experience suggest that wages should rise. This positive relationship between productivity and wage levels has been empirically observed in the UK, but often with a time lag. However, in the case of the Third Industrial Revolution, which developed in the second half of the twentieth century, the increases in productivity were not fully reflected in rising wages either in the US or the UK.[18] Why might this be? And will it be repeated in the future?

The Third Industrial Revolution took place in the era of market fundamentalism, ushered in by the 1980s Thatcher–Reagan consensus. This destroyed the balance between capital and labour which had been established in the post-war period. The weakness of organised labour following the introduction of anti-union laws allowed the owners of capital to reap much higher rewards from innovations than economic theory suggests they should. As we have seen, the theoretical assumption is that productivity increases should be reflected finally in increasing real wage levels. But, in the UK, real wages have fallen short of productivity gains by 0.3 per cent. Had real wages tracked productivity since 1990, the median worker would be 20 per cent better off.[19] In the USA, that figure is a massive 40 per cent. So, the prevailing ideological assumptions and political choices which are made during times of rapid change have a significant material effect on the outcome for society. There are political and economic choices that can and do change the outcome to make it more or less fair.

The predicted interplay between the substitution effect and the compensation effect in economic theory looks very neat on paper. The reality is much messier.

In the First Industrial Revolution, it wasn't much 'compensation' if you were an artisan spinner working from home when the advent of the spinning jenny rendered you destitute, with no chance of feeding yourself or your children and nothing but the workhouse to fall back on. If you were lucky, you could go and work in one of the new mills – forced to accept the loss of all dignity and independence, and for a far lower wage. If you were unlucky, you starved. A similar choice is facing those displaced today, though they are more likely to face food poverty rather than starvation. Being forced to move from a unionised job in manufacturing to a minimum-wage job in non-unionised Starbucks is unlikely to foster happiness and contentment. (Or, in the case of Angela's dad – a highly skilled print-worker, seven years apprenticed at the top of the labour hierarchy – watching his skills made redundant, going on to work in a supermarket earning the minimum wage.) Many who suffer this loss of status and have their place in society wrenched away from them often blame globalisation, trade or immigrants. They feel neglected and left behind and they are right to, but this breach of the un-written contract of status and place in society has been exploited by right-wing populists in America (Trump election) and the UK (Brexit). And, in the absence of any realistic help to retrain and a punitive social security system amplifying nasty ministeri-al rhetoric about scroungers, this should not be a surprise. That is why it is so important to ensure that this loss of prosperity and status for communities most disadvantaged by change is active-ly mitigated by the state. We would advocate a Marshall Plan for working-class communities who have been victims of this wanton neglect by market fundamentalists and the Conservative governments that have adhered to this doctrine.

THE CHALLENGES AHEAD

As democratic socialists, we believe that the state has a vital role to play in ensuring that progress in society is harnessed for the benefit of all. This is especially important in these times of rapid and profound change. It is only by involving the state that 'inclusive growth', which ensures that the benefits are spread widely and felt by all, can be achieved. As we have seen, wealth is already concentrating in fewer and fewer hands. When the richest 1 per cent of people in the world own half the world's wealth and just three Americans own as much as the bottom 50 per cent of American citizens, inclusive growth seems a very distant dream. It will not arise spontaneously, and can only be achieved by deliberate government policy and international co-operation. Not even all of those lucky enough to be counted among the richest 1 per cent who benefit would argue that the current distribution of wealth is desirable or sustainable. As we stand on the cusp of the Fourth Industrial Revolution, achieving inclusive growth is a more crucial requirement than ever.

As always, change is complex, and the devil is in the detail. So, how does the transition from the old system to the new happen? How long does it take? Who does it affect the most and who benefits from it more? Economic historians can answer these questions for us as they survey the nature of the first three industrial revolutions. But are the first three industrial revolutions likely to be good predictors of the path of the fourth, or are we really in uncharted waters? The Bank of England seems to think the latter:

There is growing concern in the global tech community that developed economies are poorly prepared for the next industrial revolution. That might herald the displacement of millions of predominantly lesser-skilled jobs, the failure of many longstanding businesses which are slow to adapt, a large increase in income inequality in society, and growing industrial concentration associated with the rapid growth of a relatively small number of multi-national technology corporations. Economists looking at previous industrial revolutions observe that none of these risks have transpired.

However, this possibly underestimates the very different nature of the technological advances currently in progress, in terms of their much broader industrial and occupational applications and their speed of diffusion. It would be a mistake, therefore, to dismiss the risks associated with these new technologies too lightly.[20]

FOUR CHALLENGES OF THE FOURTH INDUSTRIAL REVOLUTION

AUTOMATION

The Fourth Industrial Revolution is likely to be felt first and foremost in the labour market. It will change the type and nature of work. Without mitigation, it is likely also to skew the rewards to capital still further at the expense of labour. This means that those who own capital will continue to get richer while many of those who work for a wage will get poorer. As levels of global disparity between the richest 1 per cent and the rest have already reached grotesque levels of inequality, there must be agreed global action to address this imbalance.

Estimates of job losses to automation in the Fourth Industrial Revolution vary, but they are all dramatic. The Oxford University Citi study predicted that 35 per cent of workers in the UK could find their jobs at risk from automation in the next twenty years. This figure rises to 47 per cent in the USA and 57 per cent in the OECD as a whole. They predict that these percentages will be even higher for developing countries; thus, for India, the figure is 69 per cent and for China, 77 per cent. The Bank of England has used the methodology developed to produce this report by Frey and Osborne to estimate that, in the UK, that amounts to 15 million jobs at risk in the next twenty years. Those who do routine processing of information, administrative or production jobs are most at risk, but rapid technological advance may put even more occupations in the frame for automation.

Those who used to work in bookshops, travel agents, journalism or the music industry have already experienced what many more will soon discover. The wholesale change in the way that these services are accessed has destroyed existing jobs, replacing them with poorer-remunerated alternatives. But there are limits to this process, in the short term at least. The Citi report identifies what it calls three bottlenecks to automation: perception and manipulation; creative intelligence; and social intelligence. Jobs that rely on the use of these skills are more protected from automation than the rest, at least for now.

A HOLLOWED-OUT AND INCREASINGLY UNFAIR LABOUR MARKET

The disruption to economic life caused by accelerating automation will not affect all equally. The World Economic Forum calculated at its meeting in 2017 that those most impacted will be at the lower end of the earnings scale because their jobs are more at risk from automation. There is also expected to be a differential gender effect too. The WEF estimated that, for women, five jobs will be lost for every one created. For men, three jobs will be lost for every new job created. There will be a polarisation of the labour market, with a premium on the high-skilled, adaptable worker at the expense of those whose skills are low or have – through no fault of their own – become redundant.

Without active intervention to mitigate the effects on the labour market, there will be a proliferation of low-paid precarious work and a shifting of the costs and risks of employment onto individuals from companies. We have already witnessed this with the rise of tech platforms, such as Uber and Deliveroo, which make up the rapidly expanding 'gig' economy. These companies claim to put suppliers in touch with demand, be it for taxis or pizzas, and deny that there is any employment relationship between them and those who offer to deliver the service which is booked on their platform. They are unwilling to take on any responsibility for the duties of an employer, and they operate globally, paying minimal tax. Ensuring that the proper protection of employment rights extends to all employees, offering them the same protection and benefits as others who work in more traditional employment settings, is an important challenge which must be met.

INDUSTRIAL CONCENTRATION AND MARKET POWER

Even in its early stages, the Fourth Industrial Revolution has created corporate behemoths more rapidly than ever seen before. Their presence creates an industrial concentration not seen since the end of the nineteenth century, prior to the introduction of the anti-trust laws in the USA. Unsurprisingly, such companies behave in a monopolistic and proprietorial way to maintain their dominant market position, and minimising their exposure to tax liabilities is one example of this. Billions of pounds of turnover have gone untaxed as every loophole caused by the disparity between regulations written for 'bricks-and-mortar companies' has been ruthlessly exploited.

It was recently estimated that Amazon pays eleven times less tax than traditional booksellers in the UK,[21] and Facebook recently paid corporation tax of just £5.1 million on its UK operations, despite having revenues of £842 million and profits of £58.4 million.[22] As well as exploiting tax loopholes, market power is being abused in other ways, too. The EU Commission, for example, recently fined Google €2.4 billion for privileging its own shopping services with its online search engine. More investigations into a breach of the EU's anti-trust regulations are ongoing.

Much more will need to be done to ensure that the huge global tech companies are not unfairly abusing the dominant market power they have acquired so rapidly in recent years and to ensure that they are paying their fair share of tax in all the jurisdictions in which they operate.

TAX REVENUES AND GOVERNMENT EXPENDITURE

The rapid economic change now upon us creates a paradox for governments that wish to be active in mitigating the increases in inequality and guaranteeing future prosperity. Just as the need for increased investment becomes necessary, for example in education for those workers of the future as well as retraining those with now-obsolete skills, the tax revenues to pay for it begin to melt away. Much as the invention of the printing press put a high premium on literacy and access to books, so the Fourth Industrial Revolution puts a premium on computer literacy and access to the World Wide Web. In these circumstances, therefore, universal and affordable 5G coverage is a critically important investment which the government should be facilitating.

Yet, without internationally co-ordinated action and major reform, the tax base available to pay for these desirable investments is coming under extreme pressure. So too is the concept of social security, as the models of work are transformed out of all recognition. The Beveridge assumption of one single male wage-earner who had a job for life has long since ceased to be an accurate reflection of the realities in the UK labour market. This 1940s model is plainly no longer fit for purpose as a basis on which to organise a system of social security. For one, women have moved into the labour market, and prevalence of part-time work has increased too. As the 'platform economy' advances, the concept of 'employee' itself is in danger of becoming meaningless. Self-employment, whether apparent or real, now comprises 15 per cent of those in employment and its increasing growth demands a substantial redesign of our tax and social security structures.

CONCLUSION

These are formidable challenges and they require the re-engineering of many state systems if they are to be met adequately. To cope with the changes to come, the share of GDP growth accruing to labour must be increased so that the undoubted benefits of technological innovation can be shared more fairly. We must not repeat the mistakes of the Third Industrial Revolution, when the rewards went overwhelmingly to those at the very top. This is not the kind of society we want to live in. We must ensure that opportunity and prosperity is available to all the population of these islands.

CHAPTER FOURTEEN

AN ETHICAL ECONOMY

On 15 January 2018, the construction giant Carillion collapsed, sending shockwaves through the British business and political establishments. Carillion had been the country's second largest construction company and a major government contractor. It was involved in building and running schools, prisons, hospitals, railways and military bases. At the moment of its collapse, Carillion was reported to have financial liabilities, including a pension deficit, amounting to £5 billion. It had just £29 million in the bank. So large was the gap between what it owed and its assets that it had to go into immediate liquidation not bankruptcy. The grotesque mismanagement of this former-FTSE 250 company destroyed 20,000 UK jobs and left thousands of retired employees with reduced pensions and the country with half-built projects including hospitals. There had been three profit warnings and rumours swirling about its parlous financial position the previous year, but this hadn't stopped the government awarding it three new contracts worth £2 billion. And it hadn't stopped the board paying out £400 million in dividends to shareholders since 2012 or handing out obscene levels of boardroom pay to senior managers, despite the fact that they had run the company into a brick wall. Indeed, at the time of the collapse, the *previous* chief executive was still enjoying a salary of £55,000 a month: part of the £6 million in pay and perks he'd guzzled in his five years at the firm. There is no clearer example of the perversities of how our businesses operate and the piratical nature of too many of our self-proclaimed captains of industry.

After near enough a decade of austerity and nigh-on forty years of a market fundamentalist economy, people are crying out for an assertion of ethics and real integrity in the way in which our economy is run. They are fed up of soaring executive rewards juxtaposed with indifference to the living standards of the workforce or mis-selling to customers. They are fed up of the systematic sharp practice engaged in to evade tax liabilities, obeying the letter but not the spirit of the mutual obligation that paying a fair share of tax implies. In short, they want a more ethical economy.

The bank bailouts following the global financial crash in 2008 caused huge and understandable public anger. Matters were made infinitely worse by the fact that the colossal short-term gains resulting from this orgy of greed were pocketed by banking insiders for themselves. Those who drove the bubble and caused the subsequent near collapse of the entire global banking system in 2008 thus paid themselves huge rewards for creating a mirage of success even as they drove their banks into near-insolvency. When the banking system was revealed to be teetering on the brink of annihilation, the costs of the rescue were dumped onto the blameless public in the form of cuts to living standards and public services. The rescue was essential, but no one has ever been held to account in the criminal courts for these acts of greed and vandalism, which have caused living standards in the UK to stagnate for ten years. With the prospect looming of a further ten years of stagnation, the sense of anger is growing. No wonder there is popular resentment. When she was Exchequer Secretary to the Treasury, Angela argued strong-ly in a ministerial meeting that the bonuses which had fallen due in the suddenly nationalised banks for the previous year's 'performance' should not be paid, since it was now clear that the 'value added' which was to be so lavishly rewarded was in fact a mirage. Angela was of the opinion that the executives should be made to go to court to claim them rather than simply have their remuneration agreements honoured by the government. Her suggestion was treated with horror by senior Treasury civil servants, who argued that the bonuses were contractually due: the government must not do anything that might be seen as illegal. The Chancellor sided with the senior civil servants and she lost the argument, but Angela is still of the opinion that the courts should have been asked to decide. It would have been better to test the ethics of the contract and the nature of the 'value' which was really added in court in the light of the near-collapse of these institutions, their need to be nationalised and the huge cost of rescuing them. This would have forced very senior managers to account publicly for their actions in the run-up to the crisis. Public accountability was sorely needed, yet instead the government meekly paid up.

The anger has been made worse and more corrosive by the latest in a string of revelations in the Paradise Papers, on the industrial-scale tax avoidance practised by the privileged and extremely wealthy through a network of UK Crown Dependencies and tax havens. This followed similar leaks from the Panama Papers. The government's obvious lack of shock or disapproval over this behaviour fuels the already widely held view that there is one law for those who can avoid their financial obligations and shelter great wealth offshore and another for the rest of us, who are chased down by HMRC for every last penny of tax due or are obligated to pay it automatically as PAYE. The promises made after the Luxembourg leaks and the Panama Papers, to lift the veil on such practices and collect the tax due, remain unfulfilled. A succession of Conservative Treasury ministers have wrung their hands on *Newsnight* and in the House of Commons, but the government has made no meaningful progress in advancing the transparency needed to put an end to this abuse once and for all.

Market mechanisms do not have ethics or morals, but people do. Society can only be properly and legitimately run in a moral and ethical framework set by law and democratic decision-making. In a democratic socialist society, the law and the practice of enforcing the rules should reflect a healthy ethics which reward genuine excellence but crack down hard on benefits for failure, cheating and free-riding. This is what people still expect, despite the obvious decline in public integrity that has accompanied the dominance of the market fundamentalist ideology over the past forty years. The anger that people feel when they see cheaters prosper may yet illuminate the road to a more ethical future. But we certainly aren't there yet.

We see the indifference of market-delivered outcomes to ethics and fairness manifested all around us. It is present in the soaring levels of executive pay – all of it self-justified and ratified by a very self-interested clique who sit on each other's remuneration committees and appear to have lost all sense of shame. This has now extended to the nominally public university sector, even as students are forced into ever more debt by the tripling of tuition fees. Since the coalition government then cut public funding allocations to universities, it is clear that it is the students who are paying for the huge increases in management remuneration at their institutions, and they are right to question the high level of vice chancellor remuneration which has suddenly arisen in this newly created market of higher education. We see government indifference to discouraging bad behaviour in reports of widespread market abuse in City dealing rooms, when the Financial Conduct Authority has only launched eight prosecutions in the past five years,[23] yet there have been 10,000 DWP prosecutions for benefit fraud in the same period.

The danger, of course, is that we will reach a tipping point of cynicism, where more people decide that the rewards of cheating outweigh the risks of being caught and simply join in to try to grab a share of those ill-gotten rewards. If the risks are minimal and the rewards potentially huge, the temptation grows.

We see the ethical blindness of market outcomes in the indifference with which some business owners treat their workforce. As we have seen, by using insecure forms of employment contract or forcing them to become apparently 'self-employed', they shift all risk onto the employee and short-change the tax authorities in the process.

We also see ethical blindness in the government's nasty and divisive rhetoric about benefit 'scroungers' and 'shirkers', used to demonise and shame those forced to rely on benefits and to justify huge and continuing cuts in levels of benefit, which is causing real hardship for the most vulnerable.

The time has come to create an economy with democratic socialist ethics at its centre, where cheating by insider trading or tax evasion and avoidance will be tackled with determination, not moral reticence and practical indifference – an economy in which enforcement will matter. The days of lavish remuneration packages would be numbered, since they incentivise short-term rises in share values while minimising the scope for real value creation in business by investment and organic growth. It is this value extraction by a 'rentier class' that has so disfigured corporate life in the UK, making it far harder to grow a business and create real value from scratch. Financial crime should be punished and attract the same disapproval as that meted out for any other crime. Until this happens, the view will persist that there are a privileged few who are allowed to buy their way out of their responsibilities to society at large by using their wealth to bypass the rules and shelter increasingly large amounts of capital and income from the taxman. This is unsustainable both financially and morally.

Hayekian theory has lionised what it calls 'self-interested individualism' as the ultimate virtue, yet this is really another way of saying 'unconscionable greed'. If the only real measure of success is income and accrued wealth, then the matter of how it was acquired takes on a secondary importance. In what author Will Hutton has aptly described as a 'mercenary society', the business ethics and subsequent behaviour of the people who benefit cease to matter.

We urgently need to see a shift away from the current ethics of the spiv, which condones any behaviour as morally acceptable so long as it makes a profit. Acting within the letter, though not the spirit, of the law by appointing clever accountants to subvert the tax laws or ransacking a business by temporary inflating the share price, acting on inside information and abusing the market, should be a cause for shame, not an approving slap on the back.

A DEMOCRATIC SOCIALIST ALTERNATIVE – THE FRAMEWORK FOR AN ETHICAL ECONOMY

We need to develop an explicit framework for an ethical economy that will set out the rules by which our system will be run, and we must also put in place mechanisms which embed the social solidarity that is essential to the operation of a good and just society, including a renewal of our public services. Enforcement of the law is currently a major weakness; fraud, market abuse and tax evasion must all become far riskier than they are now.

REASSERTING OUR DEMOCRATIC VALUES

We are living in a new age of populism, in which authoritarian voices sowing the politics of blame and division are getting louder and more insistent. There is widespread and understandable cynicism about politics in the UK because it has failed to deliver inclusive growth and social justice; only hardship and insecurity. The malaise is complex, but we believe at its heart lies a lack of optimism that economic prospects will improve. Here in the UK, our parliamentary system seems quaint and old-fashioned to some, and many are put off by the way our elections are conducted and how our Parliament operates. The adversarial nature of the chamber is anachronistic and alienating; it seems noisy and full of dispute and yet nothing really ever seems to change.

However, despite what many think, politics is not a spectator sport. Neither is it simply a tussle between competing brands. In truth, if you don't *do* politics, you get it done *to* you by the forces which already wield power and influence in our society. The more involvement there is from the population, the more effective and genuine our representative democracy becomes. Achieving profound change to a status quo run by the already privileged can only be done from below. That can only be legitimately achieved by more, not less, democratic involvement – even if our democracy needs to be reformed and renewed to encourage greater participation.

CHANGING COMPANIES

Company law sets out the legal framework within which firms in our economy must be created and the purposes for which they will be run. The values and behaviour of those companies are influenced by these laws, as well as any taxation, regulation and institutional structures that surround them. The UK has a problem of endemic short-termism and low productivity which is well recognised. All too often company growth is through mergers and acquisitions rather than building value over time. Executive remuneration has soared to absurdly high levels and is now completely out of kilter with average rates of pay, which breaks down social solidarity and mutual understanding.

In the UK, company law emphasises maximising shareholder value above all other considerations, using this as a proxy for the highest level of economic utility. Experience has shown, however, that doing so leads to lower levels of investment; managers hoard money for dividend payments to keep the share price high in the short term, reducing productivity and economic value in the long term.

There are other corporate models we should consider. The stakeholder model, championed by Will Hutton, recognises that shareholders are not the only people in a company who bear the risk should that company fail. The workforce, the supply chain, the customers and often the taxpayer have a stake, and they should therefore have their interest in its future recognised and properly represented. This can best be accounted for in decision-making and accountability systems that give this wider group of stakeholders influence and a voice. Similarly, the Japanese concept of *sampo yoshi* (triple satisfaction) asserts that the company should pursue decision-making that is good for the buyer, good for the seller, and good for society. How different might our corporate culture be if it was based on this more holistic concept, rather than the market fundamentalist myth of 'self-interested individualism' (that is, unconscionable greed)?

Different models of company ownership and structure should also be encouraged to develop. Market fundamentalism destroyed most of the building societies, which were demutualised and turned into PLCs – much to the detriment of the housing market and the banking system they became a part of. The establishment of new co-operatives and mutuals should be actively encouraged by government policy and they should be protected from the corporate raiders who destroyed their predecessors. There are other, newer forms of company which should also be experimented with. Foundation companies, which have an explicit social purpose to pursue rather than profit maximisation or increasing shareholder value, are an example of the attempt to diversify the type of firms doing business in the UK. All should be encouraged to establish. The concept of patient capital – investment that doesn't seek immediate return but supports a business venture while it grows – is also an important feature of ensuring a different economic model can be built and succeed in the UK.

TAX

An ethical economy would not allow the huge disparities between the average pay and those at the top to continue to grow. The tax system has a vital role to play in achieving a more equal, ethical economy, as we shall consider in a later chapter.

CHAPTER FIFTEEN

AN ACTIVE,
EMPOWERING STATE

Marx predicted that, if left unchallenged, capital would accumulate and lead to the rise of companies that would exploit their monopoly power for their own interests. In this sense, he foresaw the rise of the global multinational corporations which dominate the economic landscape today. In 2016, the Global Justice Network measured and compared the size of the largest countries by their revenues and the largest corporations by their size in the Fortune 500. The comparison revealed that, of the top 100 entities in the world, sixty-nine are corporations and only thirty-one are countries. While not wishing to trespass on debates about the relative power of some global multinationals and the majority of the countries in which they operate, their sheer size and the fact that they can choose where to register and operate from gives them a power to dictate terms that has not been seen since the heyday of the colonial British East India Company. The global nature of companies, operating across borders in multiple jurisdictions, and their capacity to shift to places where they will be least regulated and taxed can only be controlled by international agreements that close off this damaging race to the bottom. It has never been more important, therefore, to develop a nimble and confident state that can take on and regulate the most excessive self-interested behaviour of the big corporates.

Market fundamentalism has always ridiculed the capacity of the state to achieve anything good or worthwhile outside of its duty to ensure that market mechanisms are protected in law. But the ideological attack on the very concept of government or the state having a legitimate role has prevented its obvious potential for good from being fully explored. Tyrannical authoritarian states were deliberately used to caricature and condemn all state intervention by Hayek and his acolytes. Their argument fails because ensuring the effective operation of a just and decent society, where everyone has access to opportunity and protection, cannot sensibly be compared to operating a tyranny. That the democratic and accountable state must have a wider role in ensuring the continued development of a good society cannot be denied. Moreover, as many of the most pressing problems facing us in the twenty-first century can only be solved by international co-operation and agreement, the case for an empowering and effective state has never been more obvious.

THE ROLE OF THE STATE

If we are to renew democratic socialism and begin to solve the real imbalances of power in our society, as well as the pressing global challenges we now face, we will need to rehabilitate the very idea of the state. After forty years of the state being deliberately delegitimised, defunded, demoralised and discouraged from engaging in active stewardship of our society, that task is not going to be easy. But the turmoil caused by Brexit makes it even more essential that we succeed. If we are to remake our place in a fast-changing world, if we are to guarantee our continued prosperity long into the twenty-first century, we must begin to rebuild our society with a reinvigorated sense of social solidarity, community and national purpose. This will be a formidable undertaking which cannot 'just happen' by leaving everything to the 'free market'. To be successful, those who work in government need to recover their sense of confidence and belief that the state can deliver big strategic change and a new national mission effectively. The size of this task should not be underestimated in the aftermath of Thatcherism and of the deliberate strategy pursued by the post-2010 governments of using the excuse of austerity to shrink the size of the state for purely ideological reasons.

So withered and shrunken are crucial parts of the state machinery now that they are not fit for purpose. If we are to meet the challenges posed by the Fourth Industrial Revolution and our ageing population, outlined earlier, the state has to change – and quickly.

THE MYTH OF THE MINIMAL STATE

Forty years of economic and political hegemony for the forces of market fundamentalism have made it difficult even to imagine the potential offered by an empowering and strategic state. Much less have they prepared us to organise and deliver it. There has been a deliberate, none-too-subtle attempt to wipe the very idea out of our imaginations. So all-pervasive is this dogma in popular discourse that the very idea of an active, dynamic state seems in its own terms absurd. Before we can even imagine the possibilities presented to us by an active, engaged and strategic state, we have first to rescue the concept. We have to challenge directly the dismal, myth-ridden market fundamentalist ideology, which proclaims that the state is always and everywhere useless and doomed to failure – even if it acts with good intentions.

Look at the language market fundamentalists use to describe the state and think about how the political possibilities inherent in its capacity to act in the economic sphere have been systematically narrowed down or eliminated entirely from public discourse. Orwell would have certainly recognised the technique. Market fundamentalists claim that the 'dead hand of the state' stifles individual initiative and discourages 'enterprise'. They assert that the only thing the state should do is 'get out of the way' and 'leave everything to the free market'. However well-meaning intervention may be, they claim, it will be self-defeating in the end because the state is 'bureaucratic' and 'meddling' whereas the market is 'dynamic' and 'entrepreneurial'. In reality, none of these assertions are true, but why let the facts get in the way of a monolithic and hegemonic false narrative which just so happens to benefit those who are already privileged?

This view of the minimal state is libertarian in origin. It allows for the possibility of the state providing only the barest of necessities for the orderly functioning of the market, which must then be allowed to organise as much of life as possible. So, the state's responsibility is to protect market mechanisms by enforcing property rights and the legal system, to ensure military defence and provide the infrastructure needed for the market to operate efficiently – it must on no account be allowed to do more. It means, in effect, that those who already enjoy privilege continue to benefit from it while the majority is distracted with talk of the 'natural law' which keeps their opportunities restricted and the privileged status quo intact.

That most diligent of market fundamentalists Mrs Thatcher famously said: 'There is no such thing as society, there are only individuals and families.' But she needed and ruthlessly used the power of the state to defeat the miners.

In order to imagine a different range of political choices and possibilities for the future, the myth of a minimal state must finally be jettisoned from our own and then from the popular imagination. To do that, we have to recover our intellectual confidence and assert the truth, which is that market fundamentalism has created a New Serfdom, in which an increasing number of workers are treated as 'factors of production', rather than human beings. Lack of robust employment protection and the deliberate weakening of trade union capacity has left one in ten of the UK workforce – that is, 3.2 million people – languishing in insecure work, with few guarantees and even fewer rights. Globally, it has created a polarised world in which the FTSE 100 CEOs are paid an average of £4.5 million in annual salaries – 160 times the average wage – which means that by the first Wednesday of 2017, they had already earned more than the average worker would earn all year. In the UK, 'leaving things to the market' and shrinking state expenditure has created a society in which wages are low and stagnating, where children will do worse than their parents, where few can aspire to get on the housing ladder and where the social safety net for the most vulnerable has been shredded by benefits cuts and pay freezes.

This may be the best that market fundamentalism has to offer, but is this really the best we can do?

MYTH BUSTING

The myth of what economist John Kay has aptly labelled the 'American Business Model'[24] made its global debut after the collapse of Soviet Communism and the fall of the Berlin Wall in 1989. Examining what it asserts as undeniable economic law or doctrine demonstrates just how self-regarding and absurd it really is, and yet it is the cornerstone of the still ruinously persistent market fundamentalist dogma which has driven the creation of the New Serfdom.

The American Business Model has as its predictable starting point that the government should do the very minimum in the economy, confining itself only to protecting property rights and enforcing contracts. Government interference with the work-ings of the 'free market' are almost never justifiable. Because markets work and self-regarding materialism ('personal greed' to you and me) is the dominant form of human motivation, redistributive taxation is undesirable because it blunts 'market incentives'. On the other hand, massive disparities in income are completely justifiable. Conventional morality is thus turned on its head – personal greed is virtuous, while redistributive taxation is evil. In this topsy-turvy, immoral world, 'worth' – even 'moral worth' – is measurable by the size of your personal remuneration package and your property portfolio, which must make it much easier to sleep at night if you have made your money exploiting your workforce or mis-selling useless pension products to your customers. Since market forces have invaded religion, there is even a theology to help ease your conscience (if it was beginning to twitch at all). It's called the prosperi-ty gospel. This asserts that Jesus rewards those who are good Christians with economic success – a hideous perversion of our humanist understanding of the lessons in the Bible, but nevertheless very comforting for the moneylenders who have bought the privatised temple on the cheap and are converting it to luxury apartments to sell off-plan to foreign investors.

The fact is that the elements of market exchange and the boundaries of the market itself do not exist 'naturally' like the laws of physics or mathematics. The scope and extent of markets are obviously decided by politics and subject to decision-making processes which ought to be accountable to the people in a properly democratic system. The market does not operate in a vacuum, therefore, but is shaped by the political, cultural and historical context in which it operates. In some countries, like the USA, healthcare is provided by the market; in others, like Britain, a democratic decision has been taken to move the majority of healthcare provision out of the market because not everyone can afford access to the treatment they need if they have to pay for it. Those who assert that the market must be 'free' are actually asserting a political belief, intended to narrow the scope of political possibility and close down debate about a different vision, though they often hide their own political preference by pretending it is a natural and immutable 'law'. Unfortunately, as the market is allowed to invade yet more walks of life, the possibility of meaningful change narrows still further, even as the results of market outcomes and their indifference to morality or social justice causes inequality to soar.

The fact is that the American Business Model is a self-serving lie. As John Kay masterfully details in his book, *The Truth About Markets*, this myth-laden description of the workings of American capitalism is not even close to an accurate picture of how the economy actually works in the USA itself, let alone elsewhere in the world. He concludes: 'Effective market economies are embedded in an elaborate social, political and cultural context, and could not function outside that context.'

The economist Mariana Mazzucato has likewise chronicled in unanswerable detail a similar analysis in her book, *The Entrepreneurial State: Debunking Public vs. Private Sector Myths*. She shows that, even in the USA, it is the state, not private entrepreneurs, which made the initial risky investments that have powered the internet and the iPhone, thus paving the way for huge tech companies such as Apple and Google to become the corporate behemoths they are today. The state, then, not the private sector, is the market maker, the real entrepreneur. Her analysis and insight point the way clearly to the necessity of a new era of state action to foster and nurture innovation and to help remake our economy so that it is fit for purpose in the twenty-first century. We also need a new social settlement to enable us to achieve inclusive growth, where the proceeds of success are shared by all, not salted away offshore by a few. This vision of an empowering state, which exists to help create and maintain a healthy economy and caring society, is long overdue a revival.

THE CONFIDENT, STRATEGIC, ENABLING STATE

The British civil service has long since lost its institutional memory of the myriad possibilities inherent in an active state. More often than not, since the Thatcher era, central government has concerned itself with privatisation and the constant out-sourcing of public services rather than the innovative management or direct provision of them. As a minister serving in four different governmental departments during her eight years in government, it often struck Angela how reluctant and unconfident members of the civil service generally were to assert themselves strategically. Their lack of confidence usually manifested itself in a reluctance to take decisions without the comfort blanket of a host of eye-wateringly expensive management consultants to validate their choices. Often, responsibility for major strategic decisions was devolved down too low, leaving individuals exposed without sufficient authority or training to problem-solve effectively. And the capacity to manage change, rather than merely run a process, was in short supply. Rarely did departments even maintain an 'intelligent customer capacity' so that they could negotiate with insight and knowledge when outsourcing complex IT projects to suppliers who had far more expertise than they did. They were also overly defensive about the creative use of the financial leverage inherent in large procurement projects to get extra benefits and value for the use of some £200 billion a year of public expenditure which is spent annually by government procuring services.

This is not to be critical of any individual civil servant. This lack of capacity and confidence is not surprising given the ideological predominance of Hayekian ideas, which proclaim that the public service is always bad and the private sector is always good. It is certainly a far cry from the confidence inherent in the service after the war against Hitler had been won, partly by the active delivery of central planning, which co-ordinated a national effort organised by the organs of the state. In the years ahead, it is vital that this strategic confidence is recovered and extended throughout the entire civil service, and in the wider public service, in a conscious and systematic way to make civil servants fully capable of delivering the challenging agenda ahead. Delivering profound change and switching from the self-defeating market fundamentalist mindset is going to be a huge culture shock and, aptly, it will need to be planned.

CHAPTER SIXTEEN

TAXATION IN AN
ETHICAL ECONOMY

The question of why, how and by how much we tax people and redistribute that income is at the centre of all political debate and choice. A state can do nothing without the revenue it collects and uses to create and sustain order and social justice in the society it is charged with maintaining. In the UK, total public revenue from central government and local authorities in the last financial year (2016/17) was £730.2 billion, which is about 37 per cent of GDP. While it might sound like a lot, that's far lower than many European countries, such as Germany, France, Italy and the Netherlands spend (something worth keeping in mind the next time someone tells you that a small increase in tax would cause all UK-based bankers to flee to Germany... where they would pay even more tax).

Three taxes currently comprise 60 per cent of the entire tax take in the UK: income tax (which accounts for 25.4 per cent of the whole); national insurance (17.7 per cent); and VAT (16.8 per cent). Company taxes, which mainly consist of corporation tax and business rates, make up only 10 per cent of the total, though businesses clearly also pay other taxes in the course of their activities. Duties and indirect taxes, of which fuel duty is by far the largest component, also bring in just 10 per cent of the overall receipts from tax. Council tax makes up 4.2 per cent of the total, though this is likely to increase as the current government withdraws more central support for local services and devolves down the 'responsibility' – though not the funding – for services such as social care.

Since Margaret Thatcher came to power, there has been a shift away in the tax receipt mix from direct to indirect taxation. VAT, which was introduced originally at 8 per cent as a prerequisite for joining the Common Market, has been steadily increased to 20 per cent by successive Conservative governments. It is now the third most important UK tax in terms of receipts. At the same time, top rates of income tax were cut from 83 per cent to 40 per cent by Thatcher's Chancellor, Nigel Lawson, while the base rate has fallen from 33 per cent to 20 per cent. Income tax is still the largest revenue-raiser despite these cuts, but changes to the thresholds at which income tax begins to be paid since 2010 have taken many people out of its scope. Corporation tax was reduced from 52 per cent in 1984 to 35 per cent. It has continued on its downward trajectory and is due to have been cut by 11 per cent in this decade alone if the Conservative manifesto pledge to reduce it to 17 per cent by 2021 is met. Little surprise, then, that business taxes account for only 10 per cent of overall revenue.

Because of the changes to income tax thresholds, Treasury analysis shows that 90 per cent of income tax receipts are paid by the top 50 per cent of taxpayers, and over a quarter by the top 1 per cent. However, this highly skewed distribution does not take into account other taxes. While richer households pay more in indirect taxation in absolute terms because they consume more, analysis shows that they pay less *as a percentage of their income*, making indirect taxes, such as VAT, regressive. In 2016, the top 20 per cent of households by income distribution paid 14.4 per cent of their disposable income in indirect taxes, while the bottom 20 per cent paid the equivalent of over a quarter of their disposable income on these taxes. Indirect taxes, therefore, impact most on the poorest. If we wish to reduce inequality, we have to consider whether the current mix of taxes in the UK is fit for purpose.

Our ageing population and the changing ratio between those of working age and those who have retired and rely on pensions, too, requires attention. How can we ensure that there is no return to the real pensioner poverty that marred the 1980s, while at the same time being fair to the current generations of people at work? Their prospects of owning property and building up a pension over their working lives are currently far bleaker than they were for previous generations, and many have also incurred huge debts in university fees for access to higher education that was free in the past. As the ratio of retired people to working-age people continues to rise, the basis on which our pensions system was designed comes under enormous pressure. These structural changes and social challenges all point to the need for a major rethink of our tax and social security systems to make them fit for the changing realities of the twenty-first century.

And yet, within most countries, the main political parties compete on a narrow strip of political ground when it comes to how high they assert that overall tax revenue should be. There are many serious political constraints to bold thinking in this area. Prior to winning its landslide election victory in 1997, for example, Labour agreed to stick to already announced Conservative tax and spending plans. The Liberal Democrats suggested an extra penny on income tax for education. In 2017, Labour suggested raising taxes on people with over £80,000 in income by an undefined but relatively small amount, whereas the Liberal Democrats suggested increasing income tax by 1 per cent, this time to pay for the NHS. The Conservatives suggested raising the limit below which you pay no tax slightly. Part of the reason for this is that it is considered deeply unpopular and therefore very politically risky to suggest raising taxes. However, even now, there is an active debate in all parties on whether to increase taxes for a range of purposes. Conservatives like Nick Boles, who has proven to be relatively unencumbered by the rest of his party's Thatcherite economic orthodoxies, has suggested a specific new tax to pay for the NHS. At the last election, the Conservatives suggested taxing people's wealth – in this case their houses – to pay for their social care. This was the 'dementia tax' policy that probably did most to annoy their existing voters. It was widely dubbed a disaster and helped to cause Theresa May to squander a Conservative majority in Parliament. The irony of this is that the Conservatives themselves cannot escape from their own Thatcherite legacy of prioritising tax cuts above all else. As we saw in the 2010–15 parliament, the Conservatives preferred to make £40 billion in tax cuts rather than using that money to eliminate the deficit, so powerful is the attractiveness of tax cuts to voters calculated to be. Eight years of austerity policies have left the public realm weakened and crying out for major investment, but the great high-tax taboo still survives.

Behind the current orthodoxy of keeping tax levels as low as possible has been the belief that higher taxes disincentivise hard work, especially for the rich. Hayek was, of course, right at the heart of propagating these beliefs. In a televised interview with the Conservative commentator William Buckley, he demonstrated his contempt for the state's involvement in tax and redistribution to reduce inequalities and enact social justice.

BUCKLEY: 'Why couldn't the role of the justice-maker come at the end of a process by taking [money from] someone who has more than he needs for the purpose of satisfying someone who has less than he needs?'

HAYEK: 'Because if he knows that part of his income is going to be taken from him there is no inducement for him to do that particular thing. If I know that if I do a thing that will fetch a very high price, two thirds of it are being taken from me, and I can do something much more pleasant for a third of the income without paying any income tax, I'm going to do that and not … what's beneficial to society.'

BUCKLEY: 'But, in point of fact, a great many people who are taxed at the two thirds rate continue to be very productive.'

HAYEK: 'Well I doubt they are as productive as they could be.'

BUCKLEY: 'All right, let's say they are less productive than they could be, but how do you answer the question that the demands of justice are perhaps approached after you have permitted a natural distribution of the proceeds through the market mechanism?'

HAYEK: 'There are no possible rules for a just distribution in a system where the distribution is not deliberately the result of people bringing it about.'

In one respect, Hayek was absolutely right: the only way to create a just distribution of income and wealth is for people to bring it about. That is one of the core beliefs of democratic socialists, who see the state and the tax and redistribution system as core mechanisms for creating a fairer, more equal society and achieving a greater measure of social justice. The myth of a 'natural' market distribution, however, is false. As we have shown, markets operate in a social context and are not independent of the society they exist in, so there is nothing innate or natural about the distribution they deliver.

For Hayek, a pivotal doctrine is that tax is a bad thing and therefore tax rates must always be kept as low as possible, especially for the very rich. His argument that people are motivated solely by financial reward and not 'what is beneficial to society' has become a central doctrine of Conservative politics. Right-wing politicians all over the world argue that allowing people to keep more of what is erroneously termed 'their own money' (as if it wasn't earned with the collaboration and solidarity of both other people and a state that creates the conditions for their success, whether in terms of infrastructure, education or the other myriad support mechanisms) will increase incentives and guarantee that the market will deliver the most efficient and desirable result. For Hayek and people like him, therefore, reducing rewards by redistributing resources via taxes blunts incentives and is therefore undesirable.

The problem is, as William Buckley hinted at in the interview above, there is no evidence for these assertions. We have dealt with the fallacies of this argument already, but suffice it to say that the market fundamentalist false narrative, which regards taxation as a form of grand larceny by the state, is overcome by the assertion that taxation is in fact the membership subscription for a decent and civilised society. Democratic socialists believe, therefore, that so long as there is democratic accountability (we get to influence how the revenues are spent), taxation is something we should all be proud to pay. It is our individual investment in our own future security and in the wellbeing of our society. It is a part of the social contract. As such, there should be no opt-outs, no avoiding the obligation for each individual to pay their dues, no free-riders and no cheating. If cheating, avoidance and evasion are rife, this only creates cynicism and understandable resentment, which in turn undermines the implicit contract that all should pay their fair share.

Without tax revenues, a state can do very little in the way of improving the lot of human beings and supporting the society in which they live to flourish. Tax can be used to provide transfer payments from those who have to those have-nots who would otherwise be destitute, to fund essential public services like health, education and retirement or to invest in infrastructure such as telecommunications or roads, which in turn facilitate the efficient running of the economy. This creates a virtuous cycle.

Without tax revenues, the state can do nothing whatsoever to combat the social injustice, poverty and inequality which untrammelled and morally blind market forces invariably deliver. And it can do little to uphold human rights and dignity, which are the essence of a civilised society. It cannot organise the effective defence of that society from attack, nor can it project its values abroad. Without tax revenues, the collective will of those who constitute society cannot be expressed in a practical way. Thus, over time, the state in most industrialised societies has tended to take an increasing level of national income in taxation to finance social provision and ensure political and social stability and human progress. As the industrialised societies that have introduced healthcare systems have aged, there is even larger demand for expenditure, since they now have to look after older people for longer too. There is clearly a limit to how much income should be taken in this way, but deciding on what that limit should be is a political decision, which can only be legitimised by being taken democratically and endorsed through the ballot box.

In the twentieth century, the advanced industrialised nations all developed collective social provision, which was made available to all their citizens by increasing the taxes on income. Typically, this provision consisted of access to some form of education, health and retirement arrangement, and it often included a form of employment insurance too. Following the cataclysm of the First World War, a form of income tax was introduced by all the major nations of Europe to pay for reconstructing the huge levels of damage which had resulted from the conflagration. The ever-present threat of revolution symbolised by the Bolshevik uprising in Russia reminded those in power that the patience of the poor and exploited was not endless, and it helped change the minds of those who wished to retain a nineteenth-century minimal state (which had spent around 10 per cent of national income, mainly on defence, prisons and protecting property rights). After the Second World War, the amount taken stabilised at between 40 and 50 per cent of national income, depending on whether you lived in more socially equal Sweden or less equal America. However, since the 1980s and the dominance of market fundamentalism, this assumption that social provision is an essential part of the role of the state has been challenged as Hayek's extreme libertarian ideas have asserted themselves ever more boldly and in more extreme forms. The very notion that collective provision is desirable has been replaced by an ideological assertion on the political right that only 'losers' and 'shirkers' rely on public services, and that all tax is theft. It is time this nonsense was challenged. And it is time the globalised tax-avoidance game was closed down for good.

LETTING THE RICH RUN RIOT

Market fundamentalists conveniently assert that the ownership of great wealth is a sign of merit in itself. Actually, it is not. Thomas Piketty, in his magisterial book, *Capital in the*

Twenty-First Century, explains how the modern dynamics of our globalised economy has meant that in the absence of determined public policy, wealth actually accumulates 'explosively' over time. This is because the returns to capital are now routinely exceeding the levels of economic growth, something that is even more apparent in the low-growth era which has characterised European economies and especially Britain since the 2008 global financial crash. Piketty predicts that, left unchecked, this phenomenon will generate even more extreme inequalities, which will in turn fuel popular anger and undermine faith in the democratic values that are at the core of our political system and that many of us have taken for granted all our lives. He points out that the concentration of wealth generated by the market fundamentalist era has returned Western industrialised countries to levels of inequality that have not been seen since the Belle Époque in France, the nineteenth-century pre-trust-busting days of America's industrial monopolists and, in the UK, the Victorian times so evocatively captured by Dickens in some of his darkest fiction.

Piketty's analysis shows that, in the current climate of *laissez-faire* globalised capital markets, fortunes can grow and perpetuate beyond all reasonable limits and beyond any rational justification in terms of economic or social utility. They grow whether the owners are working or not; they are unrelated to merit, effort or value added in any meaningful way. Such fortunes can also be conveniently sheltered offshore in opaque and secretive tax havens, so that it is actually now very hard to know the ownership of the world's assets with absolute accuracy. But, if returns to capital are routinely outstripping economic growth, as Piketty demonstrates is currently the case, then we need determined international action to counter the resulting concentration of wealth in fewer and fewer hands.

Despite the clearly co-ordinated attempts to discredit his data (which he helpfully and transparently made easily available to all) on the publication of his book, we believe Piketty's warnings must be heeded – and fast. There is already evidence of a ratchet towards his dystopian vision of ever-more-concentrated private wealth amidst rising anti-democratic anger and populism. Unchecked, as he says, this will threaten democracy itself.

A glance at the Bloomberg Billionaires Index indicates that Piketty is on to something. It shows that, in 2017, the top 500 richest individuals in the world became a staggering $1 trillion (£750 billion) richer than they had been only a year earlier, thanks in part to a soaring stock market. That is an increase four times that of the previous year. By December 2017, they controlled $5.3 trillion of assets, which roughly equates to a quarter of the value of the whole US economy. Jeff Bezos, the founder of Amazon, topped the list and saw his personal fortune increase from $34.2 billion to $100 billion in one year – a gain that is roughly the same size as the whole of the GDP of Bolivia.[25] Surely we cannot be content that some individuals are now as wealthy as entire countries, their fortune and power set to continue accumulating simply because of its sheer size and the favourable tax treatment that money can buy and that assets currently enjoy? It is true, some rich individuals give generously to charity. But others use the proceeds to fund the plethora of think tanks and political action committees that focus on maintaining their fortunes, ensuring that they are left unscathed by the tax authorities. The whims of rich men, be they good or bad, should not be the foundation on which our world is constructed. It does not take a mathematical genius to work out that this level of wealth accumulation is unsustainable, even in the medium term. Any merit which might be implicit in controlling wealth or being remunerated on this colossal scale is out of all proportion to the economic or social utility of any initiative to create a business which any one individual might be personally responsible for. Its persistence is then unjustifiable and undesirable – ethically, economically, socially and politically.

Market fundamentalists have sustained their damaging global edifice which lauds low taxes and lionises the 'entrepreneurial rich' by claiming that it is only by incentivising their effort with personal remuneration on this obscene scale that economic progress and growth can be achieved. In fact, there is no empirical evidence for this self-serving claim – a truth which was recently reinforced by a very surprising source. In its dry-sounding Half Yearly Fiscal Monitor, the IMF confirmed the singular lack of evidence for the connection between the remuneration of the super-rich and economic growth. When even the promulgators of the notorious 'Washington Consensus' join the forces of the reformation, we can sense a profound change in the air. Indeed, the IMF even went further and agreed with the democratic socialist 'heresy' that progressive taxation is a good way of controlling the excesses of wealth accumulation by the few that we are now witnessing. They therefore advocated levying higher taxes on the super-rich. It also observed that excessive inequality erodes social cohesion and can actually *reduce* economic growth if it is allowed to become too excessive. This admission alone is potentially transformational, because it flatly contradicts the market fundamentalist dogma that has been dominant for so long in our political and economic discourse. The fundamentalists, from Mrs Thatcher on down, have always maintained that taxing the super-rich is self-defeating as it weakens their incentive to make money and lowers economic growth. Now we see an admission by the IMF that this is a false statement and it is an assumption which must now be disregarded by policy-makers. The IMF go on to argue that achieving (socially) inclusive growth will require a more progressive tax system overall, especially in the developed countries, where both income and wealth inequality have worsened because of the rising income and wealth accumulations of the people in the top 1 per cent of the population. They see scope for increases in taxes on the super-rich and suggest that different types of wealth tax also be considered. They point out that to achieve a properly progressive tax system, income from capital (payments from profits, interest and capital gains, which is often taxed at a lower level or attracts other tax advantages) should be included and taxed at a level which ensures that progressivity is protected. This is because income from capital is distributed far more unequally that that from labour and must therefore be taxed accordingly.

The IMF's disavowal of Thatcherite economic orthodoxy and advocation of the traditional democratic socialist ideas about increasing taxation of the super-rich represents a key moment in the fight for a more equal distribution of income and wealth. But it is only the beginning of the battle.

History shows us how this global domination of wealth by a few individuals has been dismantled in the past, and it offers some guidance, though not a perfect road map, as to how we might do so again. Political will as well as international co-ordination and co-operation will be crucial if we are to restore some balance to the deeply polarised ownership and control of wealth and power in our globalised world. We will have to confront the powerful vested interests which are currently enriching themselves beyond the dreams of avarice. It will not be easy, but it has been done before and it must now be done again. A more progressive tax rate – that levies more from the richer who can afford to pay more – is certainly part of the answer, both for income and – we would argue – also for wealth. This is democratic socialism in action – the return of social solidarity and the values which advocate that the subscription rate for a civilised society should be set at a level which seeks to take from each according to their means in order to provide for each according to their needs.

A further market fundamentalist argument against levying very high levels of marginal tax on large incomes has always been that it yields very little in the way of revenue. It would, however, raise substantial revenue if it was comprehensive and the global tax loopholes were closed. And even if it does not, high marginal tax rates have other uses apart from yield. Some are designed to make the accumulation of high concentrations of income and wealth much harder, because of its unacceptable social effects for society and because it is unproductive economically and most likely lowers growth rates.

Experience demonstrates that high marginal tax rates on wealth or income work to modify inequality between and across generations. They also maintain the entrepreneurial activity which is necessary to generate economic growth in the private sector of a mixed economy. Of course, there will be the usual threats of a 'brain drain' – but it's time to call their bluff. In 1919, economist Irving Fisher called for high marginal rates to achieve the democratisation of the economic system and prevent the rise of a European-esque oligarchical society in the USA.[26] He wished to use high tax rates to tackle the 'undemocratic distribution of wealth', which was in his opinion held in too few hands in the USA. He was right then, and he is even more correct today in Trump's America.

Following the aftermath of the 1929 Wall Street Crash, which nearly destroyed American capitalism and left a quarter of the workforce destitute, high rates of personal income tax were indeed levied by President Roosevelt to stabilise the teetering capitalist system and help pay for the New Deal. He also wished to respond to the rising popular anger at the financial elites whose speculation had caused the crisis in the first place. His predecessor, President Hoover, had set rates at a derisory 25 per cent; Roosevelt put them up first to 63 per cent and then to 79 per cent. During the Second World War, they went up as high as 94 per cent. Between 1932 and 1980, they averaged 81 per cent in the USA, while in the UK they were similarly high, reaching 98 per cent during the Second World War and varying between 80 per cent and 90 per cent between the 1930s to 1980. In the USA, President Reagan reduced income tax rates to 28 per cent in 1986 and a significant reduction was also introduced during the Thatcher years by Chancellor Nigel Lawson in the UK. What happened next proves just how effective progressive taxation is at curbing the rising tide of inequality, which has been experienced since the triumph of the market fundamentalists. Both levels of top remuneration and the accumulating income and wealth of the top 1 per cent soared after their taxes were cut. Since the tax disincentive to bargain for huge increases in executive remuneration had gone, all previous restraint went too, and executive remuneration soared. This trend is now spreading to the public sector and it is causing deep resentment.

The evidence is clear. The size of the decrease in the top marginal income tax rate exactly correlates with increases in the amounts of national income taken by the top 1 per cent. This causes the increasing levels of inequality in society, which have been a feature since top levels were cut in the 1980s. It follows from this that reversing the huge cuts in top rates and restoring progressive tax rates will reverse this trend to unequal distribution of wealth and income.

However, the world has changed since the days when high marginal tax rates were the norm. Capital has globalised, and this means that high marginal rates can only work if they are accompanied by the end of banking secrecy and transparency rules to prevent money being hidden away in secretive offshore financial centres. Bringing the activities of such institutions into the light and ensuring that they operate within the law is also essential. To achieve this openness and transparency, international co-operation and the creation of global enforcement institutions to strengthen tax oversight and enforcement internationally will be needed. No such institutions currently exist, but the gains from forging an international agreement to create them would be very substantial. If the Bretton Woods Conference could bring new institutions for orderly global governance into being in the aftermath of the Second World War, it is not beyond the bounds of human ingenuity or political possibility that new structures could be agreed upon internationally, designed and then introduced. This would enable more progressive systems to be introduced at both the national and international level because dirty money, be it the proceeds of crime or terrorism, would have nowhere to hide and the capacity of individuals and corporations to avoid taxes would be much reduced. It would also significantly improve financial stability and reduce the risk of another global financial crisis occurring.

GLOBALISED FINANCIAL MARKETS

The global financial crisis of 2008 demonstrated just how interconnected and interdependent all parts of the world financial system have become in the past thirty years. The 1986 'Big Bang' in the city was just the beginning of a growing global integration of capital and the financial markets that speculate with and distribute it. According to economic theory, and most policy-makers, globalised financial markets were supposed to spread and therefore minimise risk. At the same time, market mechanisms were meant to provide for the most efficient use of capital by connecting the money people save with the projects that need investment. In reality, neither prediction has proved to be remotely accurate. Far from the efficient distribution of capital, globalised financial markets have succumbed to massive amounts of speculative activity – otherwise known as 'gambling'. At the beginning of 2017, the world's biggest market, that for foreign exchange, had a turnover of $5.3 trillion in trades every single day. This was up from $1.2 trillion twenty years ago but down from its peak of $6 trillion in 2014. Much of the activity in the globalised markets consists of such speculation and clearly has nothing whatsoever to do with the most efficient allocation of capital and much more to do with making a killing betting on movements in prices from one jurisdiction to another (arbitrage). This is neither economically or socially useful, but it can be personally either very profitable or ruinous – as can most gambling. That is why demands for a globalised 'Tobin tax' on market turnover designed to dampen down the very high levels of speculative flows has been growing stronger year by year. And these demands have much merit. As is the case with the suggestion of introducing a global wealth tax, this highly desirable aim has been thwarted so far by the lack of political will and the absence of the global infrastructure which would be needed to introduce it. It is, however, something that would immeasurably improve global economic conditions if it could be agreed and enforced internationally, and the revenue raised could be used to support the global fight against climate change or ensure the achievement of the UN development goals.

TACKLING TAX AVOIDANCE,
EVASION AND SECRECY

The sheer scale of lost revenue caused by the existence of a sophisticated network of offshore financial centres (OFCs), more colloquially referred to as tax havens, can never be known with any certainty until the secrecy which is currently being maintained is finally blown away. These OFCs make a living by obscuring the true owners of wealth via secrecy and a network of obtuse shell companies, which can be used to manage money while hiding their customers from the gaze of the tax authorities. Tax havens also operate within very low- or zero-tax environments, with little or no regulatory supervision, effectively helping to siphon off what would be the tax revenues of other countries for their own benefit. Much of the money which finances right-wing and libertarian think tanks, from Breitbart to the Heritage Foundation, is held offshore in this way.

The leaks contained in both the Panama Papers[27] (11 million documents leaked in 2016) and the Paradise Papers[28] (13 million documents leaked in 2017) reveal these offshore tax havens facilitating financial secrecy, money laundering, sanctions busting and tax evasion on a colossal scale. This activity involves both rich individuals and multinational companies, and is shocking in its scale. Aggressive tax avoidance, it seems, is now the norm, and tax havens are revealed as the key enablers in the rise of global inequality.

The leaks also reveal that the leaching of tax revenues is a serious and growing problem, depriving countries of much-needed revenue that should have been collected and used to finance public services or for development purposes. If this behaviour continues to go unchecked, the scale will only increase. It already presents a growing threat to the rule of law and the integrity of all tax systems across the world, since the legitimacy of any tax system relies on the knowledge that paying tax is the obligation of all citizens and companies, however wealthy and privileged they may be. Paying tax can never become voluntary. The detail contained in the leaks reveal the lengths that companies and individuals will go to in order to avoid their domestic tax authorities' scrutiny of their financial dealings. Both sets of papers reveal the growth of a newly powerful globalised and parasitical web of 'intermediaries' who are responsible for the commoditisation of tax avoidance.[29] Firms of lawyers, accountants and so-called tax specialists are growing brazen in touting their dubious wares to an increasing number of people. Their aim is to make it as easy and convenient as possible for income and wealth to be sheltered from tax offshore. They advertise 'tax packages' as they would holiday packages, equipping individuals with the companies, the bank accounts and the business addresses in different tax havens to facilitate abuse. And this parasitical 'industry' is growing by merger and acquisition; one has offices in forty-six different jurisdictions. Until these facilitators are dealt with, it is hard to see how this global larceny of myriad state tax revenues can be prevented.

While some of this secret activity may be illegal, not all of it is – and tax havens are not the only jurisdictions that facilitate the legal but morally dubious activity of minimising tax liabilities on a huge scale by companies and individuals. In 2014, the so-called Luxembourg leak[30] revealed that an EU member state had created 340 corporate structures designed explicitly to minimise tax liabilities, including for companies such as Dyson from the UK, Disney and the American Koch brothers. The latter have used their wealth to finance a huge network of Conservative and libertarian think tanks and right-wing campaigning organisations which explicitly seek to influence American politics, including the Cato Institute, the Reagan- and Thatcher-worshipping Heritage Foundation and the John Birch Society. They also spend large amounts of money support- ing their favoured Republican candidates in their congressional races. It has recently been reported that the billionaire Koch brothers have pledged to donate $400 million to Republican candidates to defeat the anticipated Democratic surge in the upcoming midterm elections. Thus they seek to buy political influence in a jurisdiction in which they arrange their business affairs to minimise their tax liabilities. This is the very opposite of the 'no taxation without representation' cry which launched the American revolution.

The Luxembourg leaks revealed that there was one modest address in the country which had 1,600 companies registered to it – an absurdity that stretches credulity beyond all limits. This multiple registration of companies at one 'letterbox' address can equally be observed in the offshore financial centres dotted around the world, including many British Overseas Territories. Estimates were that the EU could have lost up to €70 billion in tax revenues as a result of the opportunities for 'profit shifting' and 'base erosion' that Luxembourg facilitated by signing these agreements. In the aftermath of the scandal, no multinational company was ever charged with wrongdoing. Exploiting loop- holes for 'tax minimisation', after all, is not explicitly illegal. The companies concerned seemed to have forgotten that legality is not always synonymous with morality. It appears that the rewards for such immoral behaviour are so large that these companies seem not to care about the reputational damage it may cause them. Every single company involved in this scam evidently had no shame – no sense of loyalty or duty either, to the societies that facilitated and nurtured their existence and development. The Competition Commissioner Margrethe Vestager has used some of the information disclosed to pursue cases of provision of unfair state aid by Luxembourg to individual companies. But this is a very unsatisfactory and indirect way of attempting to call these companies to heel. And it has not worked.

This so-called tax competition, whereby countries compete with one another in the provision of low corporate taxes and tax laws which allow multinationals to shift profits and set up tax-minimising structures, is wholly damaging to the integrity of every national tax system. It facilitates a race to the bottom and the only real beneficiaries are those companies, tax accountants and law firms who create complex structures to avoid paying the taxes which are due. This sets up a dangerous downward ratchet by which, over time, corporate tax receipts will fall again. Yet, following the EU referendum, Eurosceptic government ministers and MPs pursuing a 'hard' Brexit have routinely threatened the rest of Europe with inaugurating a new race to the bottom on taxes, employment and environmental standards, which should make us in Britain very afraid for our future prospects. Furthermore, the devolution of tax powers to Scotland and Northern Ireland creates the potential for a race to the bottom within the UK itself. A downward bidding war on corporate tax rates would only create a situation whereby corporate tax rates fall even further.

The outrage around the Luxembourg leaks was genuine. However, two years later, only the whistle-blowers who had originally leaked the documents had been brought before a court and convicted. And it was revealed that the number of agreements Luxembourg had signed since the revelations had more than doubled.[31] This reveals a truth: outrage is the easy part; effective international action to prevent the abuses has proved to be much harder to deliver.

ACHIEVING TAX JUSTICE

Estimates of tax revenues lost in this benign international environment for the tax cheats vary. The IMF has put it at $600 billion annually. More recently, the Tax Justice Network used the IMF's peer-reviewed study and broke the estimate down country by country. They calculated global losses at $500 billion per annum. The cost of creating new international tax co-ordinating institutions to narrow this gap seems cheap in comparison. Thus far, the G8 and the G20 have taken this forward and tasked the OECD with delivering some of the work on information compliance. As the Tax Justice Network has pointed out, neither of these bodies is designed to tackle this crucial problem. Both the G8 and the G20 meet only intermittently with very crowded agendas, and they have no permanent staffing capacity to pursue these issues effectively in the long term. The OECD is essentially a policy-based organisation which does not command the confidence of the more recently emerging economies. Nor is there any enforcement mechanism available to use to ensure compliance by tax havens with the requirements that have been agreed at the international meetings. The current arrangements are clearly not fit for purpose. Consequentially, while there has been some modest progress, especially on transfer of information, nothing achieved to date is likely to transform the current situation.

In the UK, HMRC calculates the tax gap – the difference between theoretical tax liabilities and tax actually collected – at a much more modest but still substantial £34 billion per annum. This is 6 per cent of theoretical liabilities and, according to the government, this figure has been decreasing. In the latest HMRC report, only £5.2 billion of the UK tax gap was attributed to explicitly illegal evasion, £1.7 billion to avoidance, £5 billion to criminal activity and £3.5 billion to activity in the hidden economy.[32] In an era of seemingly never-ending austerity, it should not be forgotten that this sum is greater than the entire annual transport budget (£29.6 billion), the budget for law and order, the courts, the police and the fire services (£30.2 billion), and the money spent on providing secondary education (£28.4 billion).[33]

The Tax Justice Network proposals for stamping out such routine abuse – which focus on ending secrecy and changing the way multinational corporations are treated for tax purposes – would go a long way to recovering much of the lost revenue if they were accompanied by an international determination to transform the current situation by co-ordination and co-operation.

The introduction of unitary taxation for multinational companies is key to progress. This would end the so-called arm's length principle that has been a feature of international tax law since it was agreed at the League of Nations in the inter-war years. Unitary taxation would stop treating multinational corporations as if they were separate companies in each jurisdiction joined by a head office. Recognising that they actually operate as one global company and assessing their global profits would allow those profits then to be allocated according to the economic activity they are responsible for in each country. This would avoid double taxation of profits but be a much fairer way of assessing their real tax liabilities. Indicators of economic activity could include multinational companies' physical assets, turnover, payroll and sales in each separate jurisdiction. Such a 'unitary' treatment would stop tax avoidance scams such as profit-shifting in their tracks. If this system had been in operation in 2012, Facebook would not have paid only £238,000 in tax on UK sales of £175 million; Starbucks would not have got away with paying only £8.5 million tax in fourteen years on £3 billion of UK sales; and Google would almost certainly have had to pay more than £6 million on its UK revenues of £395 million.[34] This is why both the USA and the EU are now considering introducing a unitary tax for global multinational companies. A requirement for country-by-country reporting by multinational corporations would facilitate more transparency and scrutiny of their accounts to prevent internal accounting tricks which minimise tax liabilities. Publication of the controlling ownership of shell companies and beneficial trusts on a publicly available register would transform levels of transparency, as would the publication and availability of all individual tax returns (as already happens in Norway).

BEEFING UP ENFORCEMENT

It is imperative that we increase the chances of prosecution for those who take part in tax evasion and dubious avoidance. The financial and reputational risks have to be substantially increased in order to discourage it. Globalised capital markets which allow easy transfer of assets across borders and tax jurisdictions imply the need for stronger global co-ordination of enforcement. Building international structures to co-ordinate this will be an investment that will quickly pay for itself in recovered revenue. Other cross-border law enforcement co-ordination structures such as Interpol exist and are used increasingly to strengthen the fight against terrorism and cross-border crime.

We need one for tax enforcement. And we need much closer cross-border co-operation to be routinely practised.

Signalling an intent to crack down on avoidance as well as evasion must be backed up by the provision of the specialist support needed to make it effective. In the UK, we need to invest in HMRC by employing more specialist staff to crack down on avoidance as well as evasion. They must also be properly resourced and incentivised to take on the complex investigations which will yield the most lost revenue. Hearings before the Public Accounts Committee have demonstrated on numerous occasions the cosy relationships that often grow up between powerful large companies and the tax inspectors who are expected to supervise them. This is often in sharp contrast to the service that small businesses receive. In the past, the complexity and cost of pursuing the most powerful companies and the most serious offences has often defeated the tax authorities.

Furthermore, those organisations that opt out of their responsibilities as taxpayers should not expect to have a share in the £200 billion of public contracts which are let in the UK each year. Transparency in tax matters should be a prerequisite in companies that wish to bid for public procurement contracts – a huge new downside to avoidance behaviour. Such a requirement could be introduced in the UK with due warning so that transitional arrangements could be made with minimum disruption to existing contracts.

The greatest victory of Hayek's disciples has been their success in fundamentally changing the way people see tax. Opaque groups like the Taxpayers' Alliance (funded by super-rich donors) use Orwellian phrases like 'tax burden' to reframe the payment of tax as a pernicious thing, rather than an act of social solidarity, mutualism and kindness. We believe that taxes are the subscription fee to belong to a society which will nurture you as it looks out for others. We believe that we do best when we care for each other and care for the kind of society we live in. Before we can make any changes to taxation, however, we need to decide what kind of society we want. Only then can we work out how best to pay for it.

CHAPTER SEVENTEEN

THE LABOUR MARKET AND FAIRNESS AT WORK

The achievement of fair treatment for those at work has always been at the centre of the Labour Party's and the trade union movement's concerns. The nature of those concerns have evolved over the years, but they will never be extinguished. As we have seen, the institutional structures and linkages between those Labour-affiliated trade unions and the constitution and governing structures of the party are unique to Britain. Even though trade union membership has fallen dramatically in the past thirty years, the link between the Labour Party and the millions of people who belong to a trade union is still a potent one. Market fundamentalists know just how powerful it is, which is why they constantly seek to delegitimise it and legislate for its destruction. The latest in a long line of such attacks is the 2016 Trade Union Act, which amended the law yet again to make collective action and freedom of association even harder to organise legally.[35]

Angela led the fight against this attack on collective rights as Labour's shadow Secretary of State for Business, Industry and Skills. While she secured some major concessions during the passage of the Bill through Parliament, the Act as passed by the Conservative majority in Parliament forces each individual trade union member to have to opt in to trade union political funds – an attempt to destroy both the collective political voice of the trade unions in society and the finances of the Labour Party, the likes of which has not seen since the aftermath of the defeat of the General Strike in 1926.

Hayek was unashamed in his hatred of trade unions because he rightly identified collective worker action as a potent countervailing power to capital. Trade unions were highly effective in ensuring that the share of national income that went to those who were employed, as opposed to those who own capital, was more fairly distributed. In a letter to *The Times* on 2 August 1977, Hayek did not mince his words: 'The trade unions being politically sacrosanct have been allowed to destroy the British economy. And it is time that somebody had the courage to eradicate this cancer from the British economy.' In his 1979 publication, *1980s Unemployment and the Unions*, he called trade unions the 'biggest obstacle to raising the living standards of the working classes as a whole, the chief cause of the big differences between the best and the worst paid workers – the prime source of unemployment and the main reason for the decline in the British economy.' He also expressed his opposition to organised labour in his approval of political dictatorship, and was especially supportive of General Pinochet's 1973 military coup, which had overthrown Salvador Allende, the legitimately elected socialist President of Chile. In a 1978 letter to *The Times*, headlined 'The dangers to personal liberty', he opined: 'The marketplace is indispensable to personal liberty whilst the ballot box is not.' We suppose that it never occurred to him to think about the personal liberty of those the Pinochet regime 'disappeared'.

These are the shockingly anti-democratic, authoritarian views of the 'guru' who inspired the rise of market fundamentalism and to whose extreme reactionary views elements of the Conservative Party in the UK has been in thrall since the 1940s. The lack of evidence to substantiate his visceral dislike of trade unions even shocked some of his intellectual supporters,[36] who felt he was propagandising rather than being academically rigorous. Market fundamentalism quickly adopted his techniques and has continued to propagandise regardless of facts or basic truth ever since.

ECONOMIC AND SOCIAL EFFECTS OF THE TETHERING OF ORGANISED LABOUR

If they had access to a time machine, Ned Ludd and Captain Swing would recognise some of the abuses commonplace today in Britain's labour market. But they would also encounter increasing numbers of people who say they are happy and satisfied at work. The explanation for this seeming paradox is that the labour market has never been more 'segmented'. There is an increasing gulf between those who enjoy well-paid, secure, interesting and rewarding jobs (the 'white-collar' workers) and those at the lower end of the income distribution – who tend to be less skilled and more likely to work in 'blue-collar' sectors of the economy – who do not. This phenomenon has been aptly characterised as the split into 'lovely' and 'lousy' jobs,[37] and the lousy jobs comprise the heart of the New Serfdom. Many middle-tier jobs have disappeared and much of the growth of employment recently recorded seems to be taking place at the lower, 'lousy' end. According to the TUC, one in ten of those working today, over 3 million people, are now facing significant insecurity at work.[38] This comprises 900,000 people on zero-hours contracts, 760,000 in temporary agency and casual work and 1.7 million people in 'self-employment' who are paid below the level of the government's so-called living wage.[39]

Figures from the ONS reveal that nine out of ten of the full-time jobs created in the third quarter of 2017 were categorised as 'self-employed'.[40] That would not necessarily be bad in itself, but a closer inspection reveals what is really happening in this sector that now comprises 15.1 per cent of the UK workforce and rising.

THE SELF-EMPLOYMENT SCAM

Hermes is a courier service which is responsible for delivering over a quarter of a billion parcels a year in the UK, and their working practices became the subject of scrutiny and concern in 2016.[41] Hermes insists that all its 10,500 couriers are self-employed. This convenient arrangement transfers 'risks' to their drivers, while cutting Hermes' own costs, including national insurance, and some of the liabilities they would have to face as an employer. Their 'couriers' have to supply, fuel and maintain their own transport at their own expense. They get no sickness benefit, no holiday pay, no pension and no payment for waiting at the depot while their parcels are sorted prior to delivery. If they are absent or wish to take time off, they must find a re-placement courier to cover their workload. It is not unusual for them to work six days a week and have to deliver ninety to a hundred parcels a day, for which they are paid 48 pence a parcel. Because of their 'self-employed' status they are not covered by the minimum wage and can have their work schedule changed arbitrarily if they displease the company. This is called 'with-drawal of your work' and if applied it would further reduce a courier's already meagre earnings. Many couriers are stressed out, driving far longer on the roads out delivering than is safe for them or other road users, and live in fear of their work being arbitrarily 'withdrawn'. There is an employment tribunal claim which has been lodged against Hermes challenging the designation of drivers as self-employed. But as yet no decision has been forthcoming. Other gig economy workers are experiencing similar conditions. There was a recent dispute at delivery company Deliveroo caused by the company's decision to change payments from an hourly amount to a per-delivery rate, which would require the completion of three deliveries every hour to earn the minimum wage.[42] Pimlico Plumbers lost an employment case about the 'self-employed' status of all the plumbers who work for it in February 2017.[43] Taxi app Uber has been in an ongoing dispute with its drivers as well as London's taxi licensing authorities. The company was successfully taken to an employment tribunal by two of its drivers who claimed that they were really Uber employees, and were therefore entitled to some employee benefits, rather than being classed erroneously as 'self-employed'. Having lost at the tribunal and the appeal in November 2017, Uber is seeking permission to go to the Supreme Court to overturn this inconvenient judgment.[44]

Long-established trade unions such as the GMB and newly emerging unions like the Independent Workers Union of Great Britain have been at the forefront of attempts to get existing employment law properly enforced in the emerging 'gig' economy sector. If the self-employment scam is not prevented by modernising employment law to close the loopholes being ruthlessly exploited by employers, then over time lousy jobs will come to predominate. Defenders of this practice claim the rise in self-employment is because of a more 'entrepreneurial' culture. This is nonsense. It is the result of perverse incentives in our tax system and employment law. The financial attractions of transferring all risk to employees by switching to a self-employment model are too lucrative for ruthless employers to ignore. It allows them to compete unfairly with good employers and, over time, the more exploitative model will drive the good employers out of business. This is especially true if company ethics aren't important and the customers don't care to examine too closely how their service is actually being provided.

Self-employment and false 'incorporation' has long been a feature in the UK construction industry; it is not unusual to find that the entire workforce on a large building site is 'self-employed', even though they are clearly working for a larger company which has contracted them to turn up to the same building site until the project is completed, directing them as an employer would. When she was at the Treasury, Angela won the backing of the then Prime Minister Gordon Brown to try to crack down on this longstanding abuse. Working with the construction union UCATT, she developed a proposal for changing the burden of proof on construction sites by 'deeming' that all such workers are employees, not self-employed. It was resisted by the civil service who seemed reluctant to disrupt the established order on construction sites because they believed it would be too difficult to enforce.

Since then, apparent self-employment has spread across the economy, especially in construction, administrative and support activities, transport and storage, professional, scientific and technical and the wholesale and retail trade. This 'free-riding' trend continues to threaten the capacity to collect national insurance contributions and it must be stopped. Left unchecked, apparent self-employment will grow and national insurance revenue will fall. There is also a clear trend away from paying hourly wage rates in these sectors. Increasing numbers of workers are being switched from an hourly rate to being paid per item they pick, produce or deliver (so-called 'piecework'). This is actually a very old and exploitative payment model which predates the emergence of trade unions or employment law protections. We must arrest and reverse the spread of this form of work. Genuine self-employment is a good thing, but fake self-employment is most decidedly not, and it should be reduced by strict enforcement of effective new employment law.

ZERO-HOURS CONTRACTS AND CONSTANT SURVEILLANCE AT WORK

The Labour Force Survey estimates that there are now 900,000 zero-hours contracts currently in force in the UK. As many will know first-hand, the benefits derived from such a contract to employers and employees are wholly asymmetric. Employers gain because they keep wage costs down and reap the benefit of quick, easy access to workers without the costs of having to finance the obligations they might otherwise acquire as employers (such as financing holiday pay, sick pay and redundancy). It is often stated that workers also gain because they prefer the convenience and flexibility of this arrangement, but the reality is that their choice is often a zero-hours contract or no employment at all. Research by the TUC showed that 66 per cent of workers on zero-hours contracts are not there by choice and want a permanent contract. The Resolution Foundation has found that those on zero-hours contracts are more likely to be young, be from a black or ethnic minority background, work in health and social care, work fewer hours and receive lower pay than those who do not.[45] As we have shown, many of those on zero-hours contracts work in the health and domiciliary care sector doing very low-paid jobs in extremely trying circumstances. They routinely suffer from 'fragmented time contracts', where they are only paid for the time that they spend 'face to face' with those they care for and they are expected to 'care' in visits of fifteen minutes' duration. This means they are not paid for the time they must spend travelling from one visit to another. Angela once had to deal with a constituency case in which a domiciliary care worker found her client on the floor after falling from bed overnight. The care worker was not allowed to stay with the patient as she had other visits to do. She alerted the ambulance and the neighbours and then had to go on to her next job. Research into the sector by Manchester University reported by the Institute of Employment Rights demonstrates that 69 per cent of domiciliary care workers were offered a zero-hours contract and given no other choice. Eighty-one per cent of them receive no pay for travelling from one visit to the next and 88 per cent of them get no pay for breaks between visits, when this 'fragmented free time' cannot practically be counted as time off or productively used as personal time. Thus, they often have to work in bits of time across all seven days of the week just to earn a full-time minimum wage. While the vast majority of these domiciliary care services are provided by the private and voluntary sector, the bulk of them are commissioned by local authorities using public money. It is no surprise, therefore, that public-sector unions such as Unison have campaigned loud and long on care work. Unison has particularly focused on securing domiciliary care workers the right to be paid the national minimum wage. The Labour Party has also campaigned against the worst excesses of insecurity highlighted here, and quite right too.

Shocking abuses at the Sports Direct warehouse in Shirebrook, Derbyshire, were documented by *The Guardian* newspaper in December 2015.[46] They sent undercover reporters into the warehouse after hearing about the conditions there and discovered a working environment that William Blake would have recognised from the days of the 'dark satanic mills'. Eighty per cent of the staff working there were on zero-hours contracts. They were harangued by tannoy to work faster, docked fifteen minutes' pay if they clocked on just one minute late, subjected to compulsory body searches on the way in and out of the factory, and subjected to a 'six strikes and you're out' policy. Workers would be summarily sacked if they spent too long talking or going to the toilet, and they were not paid overtime if they clocked off late to finish a job. The local school reported that parents were so frightened they would be sacked if they took any time off to take care of their children that pupils who became ill were routinely kept in school until their parents had finished work and felt able to collect them.

Such a callous approach to the care of workers with family responsibilities is not only confined to those employers who utilise zero-hours contracts. Examples of employers treating their workers as economic factors of production rather than human beings are myriad at the 'lousy' end of the work spectrum. Minimising their cost to the business while maximising their work output appears to be their only concern. And we know that, in the current permissive environment that is the UK labour market, employers can get away with it. Thus, service charges paid using credit cards in restaurants that are meant to go to waiting staff are often taken by the owner. This is why Unite the Union launched its campaign for fair tips as far back as 2008, beginning with Pizza Express. Even if tips are given to employees, there are examples of companies charging an 'administration fee' to distribute them. High-end grocer Fortnum & Mason has attempted to persuade some of its staff to accept a big cut in basic pay in return for a share of tips in a move that will help reduce its own tax bill.[47] Staff at the exclusive Devonshire Club, which is owned by Conservative Party donor Lord Ashcroft, have been asked to take a pay cut, reducing their earnings to the legal minimum wage, in exchange for a share of the service charge. This reduces the club's national insurance bill because tips are not taxed. It also reduces staff entitlements to national insurance-related benefits such as redundancy pay, maternity pay and the state pension.[48] Once more, the risk is passed on to staff, the employer reduces their tax liabilities and the Exchequer loses tax revenue. This may be technically legal behaviour, but it isn't ethical, and it should not be tolerated in law.

Sunday Mirror reporter Alan Selby went undercover at Amazon's creepily named new 'fulfilment centre' in Tilbury, Essex.[49] This is where the UK's largest retailer Amazon dispatches its orders from. The reporter found people working ten-and-a-half-hour shifts chasing impossible targets. They were expected to find 300 items per hour and pack two items a minute or be sacked. He found some workers so exhausted they were asleep on their feet. Staff who earn £8.20 an hour are under constant surveillance and will get a final written warning if they make seven mistakes out of 4,000 items they pick. Staff talked of working though injured, having to do compulsory overtime to take their working hours to fifty-five a week and being under such pressure to meet impossible targets that they could not take time out to go to the toilet. They lived in constant fear of the sack. The undercover journalist, a fit man, reported that he walked ten miles most days fulfilling the orders expected of him and was completely exhausted by the work rate Amazon demanded. Amazon is the UK's biggest online retailer, with an annual turnover of £7.3 billion last year. Its founder, Jeff Bezos, tops the Bloomberg Billionaires Index and earns £2.2 million an hour. The lack of dignity and control at work, fragmented unpredictable hours which deny workers any real time off, the requirement to fulfil almost impossible targets, constant fear and insecurity about the consequences of failing inevitably takes a toll on health and wellbeing. And there is much evidence to suggest that women and ethnic minorities suffer disproportionally in this system because they bear the brunt of discriminatory practices which are rife in the labour market. The situation is made infinitely worse by a benefit system that would sanction anyone who gave up a job such as those we have highlighted here, leaving them without support for weeks as a punishment for leaving their employment voluntarily.

Even the current Conservative government has belatedly become aware of the likely political effects of the spread of this New Serfdom. As a consequence, they have tried to appear as if they are taking action while in reality they are talking, not acting. They banned exclusivity clauses in zero-hours contracts with much fanfare in 2015, leaving many of the other abuses outlined here completely unaddressed. They have even recently appointed a Director of Labour Market Enforcement to try to cut exploitation at work. This appointment is based in the Home Office and BEIS. The scope the director has to tackle the larger issues remains to be seen, especially given his extremely modest budget. His first report was published in July 2017. In addition, the government has changed the name and extended the remit of the Gangmasters Licensing Authority to include 'labour market abuse'. And, in 2016, they asked Matthew Taylor to examine how workers might be protected from exploitation in the so-called gig economy.[50] When it was finally published in July 2017, his report was greeted with widespread dismay by trade unions and those who campaign for fair treatment at work.

Not only were its recommendations modest in the extreme but the government took seven more months to respond to them at all. Finally, in February 2018 they announced a further four 'consultations'. Real action on employment protection for some of the most vulnerable people in the workforce has receded even further into the distance. The government's real attitude to enforcing standards in the labour market can be more easily discerned by ignoring this recent flurry of minor measures and the odd prime ministerial comment about the 'just about managing': they need to be judged by their actions.

Both the coalition government and its Conservative successor have consistently neglected to provide adequate funding for the enforcement of those employment protections which still do exist. As Prime Minister, David Cameron made a habit of ridiculing and attacking health and safety protections, a pastime which was enthusiastically taken up in the Conservative-supporting tabloids. He appointed Adrian Beecroft, a multi-millionaire venture capitalist and Conservative Party donor, to head a review into employment law. First drafts of this report were to outrageously recommend the complete abolition of the concept of unfair dismissal, which would have made summary sackings legal but preserved an employee's right to redundancy pay. Beecroft recommended limiting maternity rights for women of childbearing age at work and proposed a cap on compensation in discrimination cases. The final report was leaked and partially disregarded because of the furore it caused. Some of it, however, was enacted. Consultation periods in mass redundancies were halved from ninety to forty-five days and TUPE rights which protect many low-paid women and BAME workers were also restricted.[51] The full report provides a chilling Conservative blueprint for the future of employment law after Brexit, when EU protections will have been removed and the

Conservative Party and its multimillionaire donors will have 'taken back control'. As we have outlined, the real issue with the labour market is the lack of enforcement of the employment rights that Parliament has legislated for, not that the laws which do exist are cumbersome or unfair to employers.

The current government's record of cuts to and neglect of enforcement is a scandal. It amounts to looking the other way as abusive employers get away with exploiting vulnerable and often powerless workers. Employment rights count for little if they cannot be enforced and the likelihood in the UK in 2018 is that abuses will go unpunished. The deliberately punitive changes to the benefit system also ensure that those who are being exploited have little practical chance of escape by resigning from their job. That is the situation that Hayek would have wanted to bring about and it has been successfully delivered slowly but surely over the past thirty-eight years by successive Conservative administrations. It has systematically lowered the expectations of generations of workers who now accept treatment which would not have been tolerated by the more unionised and more organised workers of the post-war past.

The Conservatives' persistent failure to resource the enforcement of employment rights properly means that Britain has only 0.9 labour inspectors per 100,000 workers – the smallest employment inspectorate in Europe.[52] The aforementioned Gangmasters and Labour Abuse Authority exists to licence and enforce standards in the 'farming, food processing and packaging and shellfish gathering sector'. The sector is worth £109 billion, yet the GLAA operates on a £4 million budget – 0.004 per cent of the turnover of the sector it is supposed to regulate. It employs just sixty-seven staff members.[53] The budget of the Employment Agency Standards Inspectorate, which regulates employment agencies, has been cut by more than half since 2010 as staff numbers fell from thirty to a mere nine – a decline of 70 per cent. Perhaps this is why it failed to bring about a single prosecution in the 2015/16 financial year.[54] Finally, HMRC National Minimum/National Living Wage Inspectorate has recently had its budget increased to £20.0 million, from £9.2 million in 2014/15.[55] This is welcome news, but the introduction of the so-called national living wage means that the inspectorate will have to cover the 2.7 million more workers who will come into its scope on what remains a very modest budget.[56]

The biggest indication of the past two governments' real attitude to enforcement of labour law was its decision to follow the Beecroft recommendation and introduce fees to access employment tribunals in 2013. This sent a powerful signal to employers that the likelihood of their being caught for breaking the law was diminishing rapidly. As we have seen, in the 'lousy' end of the jobs market, it was already vanishingly small. The result of this introduction of fees was a predictably massive 70 per cent fall in applications to the system. Public service union Unison's victory four years later in the Supreme Court, which unanimously ruled the fees were unlawful and must be scrapped, will restore some measure of fairness. But the government fought it all the way to the top court in the land and in the interim the tribunal system has been decimated. Getting it back into reasonable working order in the age of never-ending austerity will be a very difficult task.

ENDING THE NEW SERFDOM

In order to provide the protection from exploitation which workers are entitled to, the balance between employers and the workforce needs fundamental change. And so, at a macroeconomic level, does the balance between the owners of capital and those who work to earn a living. The Hayek-inspired changes to the UK labour market that we have outlined here have helped to decouple earnings from output in the past thirty-eight years. This means that even though the economy and corporate profits have grown, wages have stagnated or gone down in real terms (taking inflation into account). Thus, more of the proceeds of growth in the UK economy was taken by the owners of capital compared to those who rely on wages for their income. The wage share (wages as a percentage of national income) was once erroneously thought to be stable,[57] though while stability has been observed for some periods, Thomas Picketty has shown that the share achieved by capital will rise and become more concentrated over time because, all other things being equal, the returns to capital are higher than rates of economic growth. In keeping with this observation, the wage share in the UK has declined sharply in the UK from 1980, when market fundamentalist ideas were first implemented by the Thatcher government.[58] Mrs Thatcher's reforms weakened the ability of trade unions to bargain for their members while removing most restrictions on capital in the 1986 Big Bang in the City. The aim of securing a more equal society was wrongly decried by market fundamentalist ideologues as a cause of poverty itself. The right-wing theories of the 'trickle down' of wealth have been tested to destruction in this period and found sorely wanting. The result is large and increasing inequalities in wealth and income which disfigure our country. They have added to the economic imbalances which caused the global financial crisis and the austerity-led policies of the government have added insult to injury by hitting wage-earners rather than capital-owners hard. If the economy is to return to healthy growth again and the fruits of that growth are to be shared by all rather than taken by a few, we need fundamental change. We need a new economic model and at its heart must be a new social contract with labour.

This begins with the creation of a powerful new Department for Labour in Whitehall, so that all of these issues can be given the priority and the focus within government that they deserve. Workforce and skills planning would be a priority for this new body – especially important in this era of rapid technological change. It is clear from the persistent failure of the 'free market' to deliver a modern and effective skills and apprenticeship system that government planning is vital if we wish to maximise the prospects of the country and enjoy a prosperous future. Equal access for women and ethnic minorities to the opportunities being created should be an important criterion for success and a way to strengthen the delivery of 'inclusive' growth. The department should also have an important role in ensuring the successful delivery of an industrial strategy which would prioritise development in the regions hardest hit by the deindustrialisation that has taken place since the 1980s. Working-class communities, which have seen their economic prospects blighted by the hands-off approach of successive governments to economic planning and development, need to be prioritised in this new model, so that both disparities in regional and working-class opportunities can be narrowed and the growth of opportunity and economic prosperity made available to all.

Employment rights need to be strengthened and modernised to deal with the abuses we have outlined and to ensure that the most glaring loopholes currently being ruthlessly exploited by amoral employers are closed. Enforcement of labour standards would be a core priority of the Labour Department's work. Enforcement of employment law needs to be less fragmented and much better resourced. A strengthened and centralised Labour inspectorate based in the new department would need much clearer investigatory powers and more resources – enough to initiate criminal proceedings where necessary. Fines for employers breaching the law must be much greater than they are now and should be recycled back into enforcement. Employment tribunal decisions need to be enforced much more effectively, including the collection of the compensation which they award, which is currently haphazard and not effectively enforced.

After thirty years of market fundamentalism and a legal landscape specifically designed to weaken trade unions and collective bargaining, it is time to reverse this damaging trend. Hayek would doubtless celebrate the fact that, in 2018, the majority of wages in the UK are not negotiated but simply handed down by employers to their workers as a *fait accompli*. A recent study by the Greenwich Political Economy Research Centre and the New Economics Foundation has showed that the loss of union density since 1981 has cost a permanent loss of 1.6 per cent of GDP, which will never be recovered.[59] Because growth in the UK economy is wage-led, the suppression of wage levels by weakening trade unions and shrinking the scope of collective bargaining actually costs economic growth. Doubling trade union densities could add £27.3 billion extra to our GDP.

The legal right to trade union recognition and representation, introduced by the last Labour government, was too modest to reverse the baleful effect of Thatcherite anti-union laws aiming to destroy collective bargaining. A return to sectoral bargaining, which became Labour policy in the 2015 manifesto, is much more likely to increase levels of union density and increase trade union effectiveness. Sectoral agreements should be negotiated on wages and conditions, on skills and training requirements, and could be conducted on a tripartite basis by employers, the unions and the government. The Institute of Employment

Rights has set out a compelling case for creating such a structure in its *Manifesto for Labour Law: Towards a Comprehensive Review of Workers' Rights*. Rights to recognition and rights to bargain at company level should also be granted. Trade unions will need to reform themselves to renew their appeal, especially in the private sector, where a majority of the workforce now simply never encounter them. There is innovative work going on within the structures of individual trade unions to accomplish this. Unions 21 are also making a major contribution to this necessary work as is the TUC through such initiatives as the organising academy.

Alongside the institutional reorganisation that will create the framework for our new labour relations, Britain needs to fundamentally rethink its understanding of work. As we argued earlier, work is not just a burden. At its core, it is the means by which we create society and shape our environment to meet the needs and wants of all humankind. Imagine a world in which work was seen as part of the gift that each person gives to others. Everything you are wearing as you read this, everything you consume today, every building you enter and every road you travel on, is the product of other people's labour – perhaps even your own. If we each thought not just of the things we buy but of the people involved in bringing it from raw materials to your hands, then perhaps we would pay a little bit more. The success of fair trade goods indicates that this is true. We might even cherish that object more if we knew that our purchase had put food on a table in a household in which children could admire their parents for having brought enough money home for them to have fulfilling lives and opportunities for their own self-advancement.

This shift in mindset is important, because we will need to change our understanding of work and how we contribute to society in the coming decades. As our population lives for longer, we will need to find ways to contribute for longer, too. Lifelong free education – like the National Education Service proposed by Labour's shadow Education Secretary, Angela Rayner – will allow us to retrain throughout our working lives, to adapt our skills and knowledge to the changing labour needs of society in an age in which automation, artificial intelligence and algorithms will fundamentally reshape our society and completely change work.

We have a serious problem with loneliness in our societies, especially among older people. Our current bizarre solution of warehousing older people in insufficiently funded 'care' homes means we abandon huge amounts of knowledge, experience and wisdom. By re-conceptualising work as a gift to society, we can start to unshackle ourselves from existing approaches that are failing. We might, for example, think about ideas like co-locating adult social care facilities with nurseries. In pilot projects being tried around the world, the results have been dramatic. The kids thrive. And the elderly people thrive too. It has near-miraculous results. *The Atlantic*, reporting on one scheme, described the effects on people who might otherwise be abandoned to a slow, mean decline:

> [A] resident with advanced Alzheimer's whose speech was incomprehensible garble was able to speak in complete, fluid, and appropriate sentences the moment she was wheeled into the baby room. 'You could immediately see that she had accessed some part of her brain that had raised several kids,' [the director] says.

It is that kind of swashbuckling policy-making that will drive the betterment of our society over the coming decades, remoulding our social settlement to meet the demands of the future rather than reflecting the shape of the past. Meeting the challenges posed by demographic change to ensure that we offer all our older citizens the security of a guaranteed high-quality standard of social care means a major change in funding to provide it and a big change in the status of caring jobs. A move away from the low-pay, no-skill model which blights the care sector today is long overdue.

CONCLUSION

A fair and just society pays attention to how those who work are treated. For far too long the weakening of the trade unions has allowed the spread of exploitative jobs and created an economy which is increasingly failing to provide good jobs and secure living standards. Until rights and protections are strengthened, there is little prospect of this improving. The war on trade unions has not helped, but rather hindered societal fairness and even economic progress. That is why regulation of the labour market has to be at the centre of any attempt to create a fairer and more productive society.

CHAPTER EIGHTEEN

A MODERN INDUSTRIAL STRATEGY

For many years, the UK has had no industrial strategy worth the name. Perhaps more so than any other advanced economy, the UK has failed since the 1970s to adopt a coherent approach to the management of this vital part of the economy, preferring, as we have shown, to leave it to the 'free market'. The very notion of having a strategy for building our industries and strengthening the economy was anathema to the Hayekian politicians who came to power in 1979. They would have purred with approval at his words in *The Fatal Conceit: The Errors of Socialism*:

> The curious task of economics is to demonstrate to men how little they really know about what they imagine they can design. To the naive mind that can conceive of order only as the product of deliberate arrangement, it may seem absurd that in complex conditions order, and adaptation to the unknown, can be achieved more effectively by decentralising decisions and that a division of authority will actually extend the possibility of overall order. Yet that decentralisation actually leads to more information being taken into account.

Hayek believed that decisions taken throughout an economy, based on locally held information, would always add up to a better outcome for all than if it was planned centrally. However, as is almost always true in politics, for all the superficial attractiveness of any particular nostrum, the best solution usually lies somewhere in between two ideological poles. If markets are left to their own devices, without any guiding hand to correct their many errors, you end up with the sort of economy we've had in the past few decades.

Once the cradle of the Industrial Revolution and the workshop of the world, UK manufacturing has been allowed to decline so that it now makes up only 10 per cent of Gross Domestic Product, down from 25 per cent in the 1970s. Services – which covers a huge range of activities from logistics, hospitality, communications, government activities including the NHS, and, more obviously, financial services and business services, like consultancy – now accounts for 80 per cent of our economy. Just financial services alone – an industry in which Britain and, in particular, London, is a world-leader, comprises around 12 per cent of GDP and 11 per cent of all taxes paid in the country.

These changes to our economy and the decline of manufacturing has led to profound geographical inequalities. Entire areas of once-proud industrial heartlands have been allowed to go to rack and ruin while those in the cities thrive in the service-based industries that have established themselves in urban centres. The Hayekian belief that leaving free markets to work their magic will inevitably herald a revival of those left-behind regions and local economies, returning prosperity to these areas, was simply not borne out by reality.

Moreover, the UK now runs an ever-widening trade deficit, which means we import more than we export. A surplus on trade in services is outweighed by a deficit on trade in goods. In 2016, the UK's exports of goods and services totalled £555 billion and imports totalled £595 billion, making our overall trade deficit £40.7 billion (2.1 per cent of GDP). It should be noted that the EU accounted for 43 per cent of UK exports of goods and services and 54 per cent of imports, which explains the sheer panic we have been witnessing over post-Brexit trading arrangements. If barriers were erected to that trade, we could find ourselves in real trouble very quickly.

After a long period without anything resembling a cogent UK industrial strategy, rather like buses, three of them suddenly came along at once. The first made an appearance in 2008, when the then Labour Industry Secretary Lord Mandelson re-established an important new framework for active government intervention and involvement in our economy, something he had witnessed working successfully in other EU countries during his time as Trade Commissioner. Quite often, Britain's failure to have an industrial strategy had been blamed by the Conservatives on European Union 'state aid' rules. However, the rules were never as rigid, didactic or far-reaching as the Eurosceptics had claimed. Lord Mandelson rightly believed it was essential that the government become more active in the aftermath of the global financial crash because of the urgent need for economic renewal. And since the bank bailouts, it was now very clear that the dangers of a bloated financial sector posed a larger threat to financial stability than had previously been appreciated by policy-makers and politicians alike. If it is to minimise the chances of a repeat of a catastrophic market event, the UK needs a safer and more sustainable balance between its financial sector and the rest of the economy.

After Labour lost the election in 2010, Lord Mandelson was followed by Vince Cable, who essentially continued what Labour had begun – especially when it came to the system of 'catapults' designed to help innovation in particular chosen sectors where it was thought the UK had a comparative advantage. The prospects for continuity took a turn for the worse, however, when the Conservatives won a majority at the 2015 general election. Sajid Javid, the new Business Minister, was revealed as a man who would not allow himself to utter the words 'industrial' and 'strategy' in the same sentence, and whose ministerial office featured a rather large and forbidding portrait of Margaret Thatcher. Even he – however reluctantly – was persuaded that the government had a role to play during the Tata Steel crisis, when he found himself excoriated on the front pages of the national newspapers for going on holiday instead of attending a crucial board meeting in India just as the UK steel industry teetered on the brink of extinction. As the then shadow Business Secretary, Angela got the chance to see Javid's Thatcher portrait for herself. She found it deeply ironic that it was under Maggie's disapproving gaze that she sat discussing state intervention with a Conservative Secretary of State to save steelmaking capacity in the UK from the utter destruction to which Mrs Thatcher's ideological dogmas had contributed.

Following the shock and upheaval caused by the Brexit vote in 2016, the new Prime Minister Theresa May and her Business Secretary Greg Clark have seemed to embrace more enthusiastically the idea that the UK should have an active industrial strategy. This was something that Mrs May has often mentioned, beginning with the speech she made to launch her bid to be elected Conservative leader. After she became Prime Minister, she merged the Business and Skills Department with the Department for Energy and Climate Change, creating a new platform from which to launch an active industrial strategy. Since then, there has been a transformation in the rhetoric coming from the government – even some reasonable analysis published by the newly renamed Department for Business,

Energy and Industrial Strategy. However, much talk, many press releases and even a modestly received White Paper later, it is clear that there is an embarrassing gap opening up between the rhetorical flourishes and the policies that are actually being contemplated. Instead of a roaring lion, it seems that the government have laboured to bring forth a tiny little mouse of an industrial policy. Modest and worthy it may well be, but it is not nearly radical or transformative enough to deal with the problems the UK must solve, especially against the darkening backdrop of a possible 'hard' Brexit.

THE ROLE OF TRADE UNIONS

Over many years, the Trades Union Congress and those unions who organise in manufacturing and the private sector – including Unite, the GMB, Community and the CWU – have been strong and consistent advocates of a new industrial strategy. As trade unions, they are all at the forefront of the partnership approach at the workplace which is essential to the most efficient functioning of companies and the fair treatment of their workers. The utility of this partnership approach has been proved time and time again in such sectors as automotive and aerospace, in telecommunications and pharmaceuticals. The insights trade unions bring as a result of their direct workplace experience are invaluable. The design of any industrial strategy must therefore include a strong voice for the workforce through their trade unions if it is to maximise the chances of successful implementation and delivery. Yet the government's November 2017 White Paper, entitled 'Industrial Strategy: building a Britain fit for the future', barely mentions employees at all, let alone their trade union organisations.

When the BEIS Select Committee visited Sweden as a part of their inquiry into the government's industrial strategy plans in 2016, this 'social trust' between the government, industry and unions was emphasised to them.[60] Likewise, the TUC made similar points in the evidence it gave to the Select Committee during the course of its enquiries looking at the government's early proposals in the industrial strategy Green Paper of January 2017. The resulting White Paper fails completely to acknowledge that the dogma of market fundamentalism is the real cause of much of the weaknesses it correctly identifies: excessive pay, low and stagnating productivity and flat-lining real wages.

THE ROLE OF AN INDUSTRIAL STRATEGY

The fact that even the UK Conservative Party has finally admitted the need for the UK to develop an activist industrial strategy marks, at the very least, a rhetorical break with their market fundamentalist doctrines. Their heart can never be in it, however, because they don't really believe that strategic interventions by the state can be legitimate or effective, except in those rare areas where the market obviously fails. How then should those who do believe in a role for an activist government shape a successful industrial policy? What would a democratic socialist industrial strategy look like?

OVERARCHING AIMS

Once the decision has been taken to take back control of the direction of economic and industrial policy from the arbitrary chaos of the 'free market', it is essential to define the aims of such a policy. Measurable indicators of success should also be set out so that the efficacy of the strategy can be evaluated and be subject to democratic scrutiny as it develops. There should be a national conversation about it. It should also be considered and discussed by national and local government, companies and their stakeholders, as well as by civil society.

Democratic socialist values offer essential guidelines for the desired outcome of such a strategy. Considerations of fairness and equity would suggest that the rewards of economic activity should be more fairly distributed between women and men, between regions and nations of the country, between social classes and between ethnicities. In other words, the aim of an industrial strategy should be to achieve inclusive growth. This means it should take place first in the regions and the sectors where the poorest live and work. Opportunity should be accessible to all and everyone should have the chance to contribute to the society in which they live and be supported to make a meaningful input. The task of forging a new industrial strategy should be pursued in co-operation with a wide range of economic and political actors. This means that there should be an influential voice for trade unions, local government and industrial sectors at the table where the decisions are being taken. This planning effort should encompass new forms of accountability to a wider group of stakeholders than just those who own shares in companies. Success will require a new settlement at work based on partnership and democratic voice. This will include worker and consumer representation on boards, to break up the male groupthink that all too often predominates in the boardrooms of today. This new inclusive method of building the strategy and the way it is put into effect by the government is an important part of this new approach. Building institutions that encourage co-operation and planning to take root at sectoral, regional and local level will embed the new infrastructure needed to transform the way that our economy works.

In its discussion paper on industrial strategy, the IPPR's Commission on Economic Justice suggested an attractive and timely mission for a transforming industrial strategy. The aim, it said, should be:

> To change the structure of investment and production in the UK economy – its composition, direction and geography. The ultimate goal should be to achieve a more innovative, sustainable and inclusive pattern of economic growth which generates decent jobs and rising incomes for average and below average income households in all parts of the country.

We couldn't have put it better ourselves.

TAKING BACK CONTROL
– THE CHALLENGES WE FACE

Britain is at a crossroads and in need of a radical and fundamental break with the status quo. We do not currently have a society which is economically, socially or environmentally sustainable, and this needs to change. Even without the debilitating effects of forty years of domination by market fundamentalist ideas, we would need fundamental structural reform to cope with the four major challenges which lie ahead.

These challenges are:

- The disruptive nature of the Fourth Industrial Revolution, especially for jobs;

- The challenge of decarbonising our economy to deal with the threat of climate change;
- Coping with our ageing society;
- And now the dangerous and immediate uncertainties and complications of Brexit.

If we are to survive and prosper in this rapidly changing world, we need a radical and profound change from the failing free-market status quo. We have to take back control and stop outsourcing our decisions to the arbitrary and unfair outcomes of 'market forces'. We know that the solutions of the market are neither ethically nor economically superior and they have come at a huge social cost. Our current system is not working for the many. It is unfair and unsustainable and it must be reformed.

Our growth potential as an economy has slowed to historically low levels. We are more unbalanced as an economy by region, by social class and between consumption and production than we have been for a very long time, and these trends are worsening. Despite excellence in higher education and scientific innovation, we have become a low-pay, low-skill economy, with stagnating levels of productivity as our competitors make progress at our expense. We have greater levels of poverty and lower levels of adult skills than many of our competitors and our neglected national infrastructure is creaking at the seams. The prevailing faith in market dogma has delivered the worst of all worlds. We have lost ground, lost growth potential and we are failing to recover quickly enough after the near-collapse of the global financial system.

A look at the current economic forecasts reveals our predicament. At the November 2017 Budget, the Office for Budget Responsibility downgraded its growth forecasts for the UK to under 1.5 per cent for the next five years. This is in the context of a 2 per cent annual growth rate which would have been regarded as very disappointing for most of the post-war period. As a result, the OBR predicted that by 2021/22 we would have an economy in which Gross Domestic Product per person will be 3.5 per cent smaller than they were predicting only a year earlier in March 2016. That is a £65 billion shortfall on the previous year's forecasts.[61] They adjusted downward their forecasts on real annual earnings, too, which they now expect to be £1,400 lower on average than they were expecting last year. They go on to predict nearly two decades of flat-lining real earnings. Meanwhile, inflation is at 3 per cent, which effectively signals a return to falling living standards. And if you were hoping for a pay rise to help plug the gap, you're not in luck. The prospects that Britain will get one any time soon was downgraded from a previous unfulfilled yet modest assumption of 1.7 per cent a year to a mere 1 per cent. And even this is being seen by some analysts as too optimistic given current performance (0.3 per cent in 2017). Thus, Britain has suffered the slowest recovery from recession since the Napoleonic War and the largest squeeze on living standards since Victorian times. Little wonder, then, that unsecured consumer debt is currently at £200 billion and now rising at the fastest rate since the crash. As the Bank of England have noted with some consternation, it is up an alarming 10 per cent in the past year during the time when real wages are falling at 0.4 per cent.[62] As Andrew Bailey, chief executive of the Financial Conduct Authority, has noted, this is not 'irresponsible spending': it is individuals on zero-hours contracts using credit cards to pay essential bills or buy food. Our low-wage economy and insecure labour market are leaving millions of people in work on the edge of catastrophe, fighting to provide necessities, unable to accumulate any savings to fall back on. It has reached a point where one in four of our children are now growing up in poverty. How can this be acceptable in what is still one of the world's largest economies?

THE WEAKNESSES WE MUST ADDRESS

The UK has many deep structural weaknesses in its economy. To overcome these weaknesses we need a radical industrial strategy. It must also be designed to meet the formidable structural challenges that lie ahead.

LOW SKILLS, STAGNATING PRODUCTIVITY AND LIVING STANDARDS

Productivity is one of the most important measures of any economy; it tells us how much we produce per person in a defined period of time. The level of productivity is directly linked to the living standards of the economy and indicates the potential for raising wage levels over time. The capacity for growth in that economy is also directly linked to its productivity levels. If productivity is improving, there will be economic growth. Growth will increase wages and also therefore government tax revenues. To establish a virtuous circle, some of the proceeds of that growth must be used to increase the levels of public investment in skills and infrastructure, which will in turn usually increase productivity levels. Lower productivity levels create the opposite, a vicious cycle of lower growth, lower wages and therefore lower tax revenues and less investment.

Historically, the UK has achieved around 2 per cent growth in productivity a year. However, our performance since the global financial crisis in 2008 has been the worst in the club of G7 nations that make up the largest economies in the world. Productivity growth in the UK has stalled. In the second quarter of

2017, it was still 0.5 per cent below the level it achieved in the second quarter of 2007. This means that, in the interim period, the UK has lost close to 19 per cent of its 'trend productivity growth' – i.e. the amount by which we could have expected to see productivity grow if previous historical trends had been maintained. This stagnation and loss of the potential for economic growth has severe consequences for the UK's economic prospects and for the living standards and prosperity of all our people. (Stagnant productivity was the reason the OBR downgraded its growth forecasts so significantly in the run-up to the November 2017 Budget.)

Even more bad news for the UK is that while our productivity stagnates, our competitors are improving theirs. So the UK is falling further behind in what this government used to refer to as 'the global race'. French and German workers can produce in four days what a British worker produces in five, but this is rarely the fault of our workforce. After all, British workers work the longest hours in Europe, but they are less supported by investment in new technologies, modern management techniques and access to the best education and skills training. Our underfunded national infrastructure also lets them down.

On the supply side of this equation, we have an ineffective skills system and a chronic lack of private sector investment in new plant and machinery. Investment in education, skills and more modern equipment are needed to improve our stagnating levels of productivity and ensure that Britain finally gets the pay rise it deserves.

In its recent survey of adult skills, the OECD revealed that an estimated 9 million adults of working age (16–65) in England have low literacy or numeracy skills.[63] That is over a quarter of the entire workforce. While England was average for literacy, it scored well below average for numeracy. Worryingly, in the UK, young adults performed no better than older workers, which was an unusual pattern not seen in other countries, where general levels of education had improved the prospects of younger cohorts of workers over time. The OECD study found that one third of all 16–19-year-olds have low basic skills, which is three times more than those countries who do best, such as South Korea, Japan, Finland and Holland.

On the demand side, the government has failed on public investment in road networks, super-fast broadband and social infrastructure, such as nurseries, childcare and social care for elderly relatives. This social investment enables those – mainly women – with caring responsibilities to participate fully in working life. Such social investment improves the productive capacity of the economy and the earnings power of individuals, who then become more productive than would otherwise have been the case. A win–win for individuals and society. The OBR has shown that government spending on infrastructure has fallen in real terms by £20 billion since 2010. Meanwhile, the private sector has gone on an investment strike, citing uncertainty over Brexit for its most recent reluctance to invest (though it always seems to use some kind of 'uncertainty' as an excuse for not investing).

For the UK to achieve success in the future, both public and private investment need to rise sharply if we are to kick-start our stalling levels of productivity. No industrial strategy can succeed without tackling this fundamental weakness and the structural reasons for it.

REGIONAL IMBALANCES

The UK is now the most regionally unbalanced economy in Europe. The extent of it is staggering: almost 40 per cent of all output in the UK is generated in London, yet 70 per cent of the population live outside of the London area. As the IPPR noted in its recent discussion paper on industrial strategy:

> Output per head in London is more than twice that of most of the rest of the Country. In no other Nation or Region of the UK is productivity above the national average. Median incomes in the North West, West Midlands, South West and Wales are more than 30 per cent lower than in London and the South East: In Scotland over 20 per cent lower.

In the absence of any government action, this geographical polarisation will become more pronounced over time – as is the case with London and the south-east today. Geographical polarisation starts because growing regions have better infrastructure and so attract more investment and job opportunities. This in turn tempts those who live in poorer regions to migrate to the area where the economy is strong in search of better career prospects. But this outward migration from economically weaker regions impacts detrimentally on the economic potential of the regions they left behind. Success leads to investment, which leads to more success; neglect and decline leads to less investment, which leads to more decline. Public-sector infrastructure investment is a case in point. IPPR analysis in 2014 showed that £5,426 was spent on each resident of London compared to a mere £223 on those in the north-east region. That's over twenty-four times as much. The cost of London's Crossrail project alone is nine times the infrastructure spending the government has planned for the North East, Yorkshire and Humber and the North West put together. The size of such disparities in public infrastructure cannot be justified and can only be explained by the government's abdication of its proper role in planning for fairness and regional development strategies.

There have been longstanding regional disparities in the UK at least since the nineteenth century. The over-centralisation of the UK's political, legal and administrative systems in the capital has made this even worse. However, it was the advent of Thatcherism and the Big Bang in London that caused the gap between London and the rest of the country to begin widening more quickly. The deindustrialisation that was also a feature of Mrs Thatcher's period in office hit the north and the Midlands particularly hard, stalling their economic prosperity. London's dominance of finance, banking and insurance drove its accelerating growth from then until the global crash in 2008, while the north was left suffering relative decline. At the same time, Mrs Thatcher centralised local government finance and even abolished the metropolitan councils in big cities because they tended to be Labour-run and represented alternative centres of power that threatened her hegemony. This exacerbated the problems of the already over-centralised political system, making it far harder for devolved local economic initiatives to succeed. Both for reasons of social equity and economic efficiency, it is now vital that government policy has as a central aim to narrow significantly these large regional disparities in economic performance. To its shame, the coalition government abolished the regional development agencies in what they claimed was a cost-saving exercise in 2010. This set back even further the prospects of strong regionally based economic development, making the geographical imbalances worse and harder to challenge. We still do not have a regional structure that is robust or democratic enough upon which to build regional economic strength. We need to introduce one and quickly.

ECONOMIC IMBALANCES

The UK economy is unbalanced in other ways too. Manufacturing has declined in Britain far faster than it has in other industrialised economies. It suffered greatly during the 1980s when the dominance of the post Big Bang financial sector kept the pound at a level which suited the City but hit manufacturing hard. As a consequence, manufacturing is now too small and too narrowly based on just a few leading sectors. And there is a long-term and growing deficit in the current account (the difference between the value of the goods we import and the goods we export). As we leave the EU it is this deficit which if left unaddressed threatens to be more serious than our borrowing and debt levels for the future wellbeing of the country.

Our economy is now too reliant on consumer spending for growth, and because wages are falling in real terms, this spending is underpinned by rising levels of unsecured household debt. This is an unstable model for growth that cannot be sustained. A successful industrial policy has to change this by ensuring that the economy can grow in more sustainable ways. Removing our reliance as an economy on consumer spending to stimulate future growth requires a positive manufacturing strategy to be a part of the solution.

ENVIRONMENTAL IMBALANCES

The UK economy needs to decarbonise if it is to meet the international obligations it signed up to as part of the Kyoto Protocol in 1997 and the Paris Climate Accord in December 2015. As the first industrialised economy, the UK has recognised that it has a special obligation to lead by example in the battle to avoid the threat to all life on earth posed by 'man-made' global climate change. In recognition of this historic industrial legacy, the last Labour government led the way in seeking to develop an international global response to the challenges currently facing the world's ecosystems. The UK was the first country to pass a Climate Change Act which enshrined our obligations into law, and while this has been watered down since Labour lost office in 2010, the basic framework remains in place. Since 2006, when the Stern Review was published in the UK, there has been widespread acceptance that, if left unchecked, climate change will cause average global temperatures to rise by 5 degrees from their preindustrial levels. The report showed that if this were to happen it would have a profound effect on all life on earth, causing a mass extinction of up to 40 per cent of all current species, rising sea levels, more extreme weather, floods, drought and famine. These phenomena would impact on the world's poorest and most vulnerable the hardest, even though they have benefited least from the economic development which has caused this problem in the first place. The aim of both national and international policy to counter this severe threat must be international collective action to reduce man-made greenhouse gas emissions into the atmosphere. This means decarbonising our economy. There also has to be mitigation to deal with the unavoidable effects which cannot now be stopped. We must also organise for adaptation to the new realities implied by climate change in areas such as flood protection and the creation of food crops which are more adaptable and have higher yields to protect the human food supply.

Decarbonisation requires a major restructuring of our economy and our entire way of life, which cannot simply be left to the market spontaneously to conjure up. Our energy supply and the infrastructure needed both to generate and distribute it require a complete and radical overhaul which only governments can oversee. The Paris Agreement implies similar progress in decarbonising our transport systems, industrial processes and agriculture as well as the systems for heating and cooling our living and working environments. And these obligations provide a major mission which must be at the centre of our industrial strategy in the future. There are great opportunities just waiting to be grasped in this important area. Estimates for the UK Committee on Climate Change, which was created to advise on achieving the goals set out in the Climate Change Act, indicate that the green economy is likely to grow at a far faster rate than the overall growth rate for the economy as a whole. This means that the more clean and green we can make the economy, the faster it is likely to grow. The new industries of the future will be low-carbon technology and the innovation required to make the switch from carbon-based energy sources such as oil and gas to renewable sources such as wind and solar is in the process of being developed now. There will be innovations to help decarbonise the human footprint which we cannot yet anticipate but we should certainly plan to develop and deploy. The rewards for successful innovation in this crucial growth area will be worth pursuing.

Pollution and climate change itself are examples of so-called externalities. Even classical economic theory recognises the presence of such externalities as market failures, which require government intervention and international agreements to fix. This is because the cost of cleaning up the effects of pollution or climate change caused by man-made greenhouse gasses do not fall on those who caused the problem in the first place and so these costs cannot be recognised by the price mechanism. Those suffering from famine due to the failure of the rains were not the ones who benefited from the industrialisation that changed global temperatures and altered the weather patterns. Moreover, we all owe an obligation of good stewardship of our planet to future generations, as well as its current inhabitants. We therefore have obligations which extend outside of the territories of our own countries, across time to future citizens, and to the other species with which we share this planet. Market forces are simply not able to accommodate the requirements necessary to be successful in this multidimensional context. This has to be achieved by political will, international agreement and a recognition that – far from the radical individualism that Hayek asserted – we are actually all interdependent, thus a collective response to challenges is often crucial in overcoming them.

AN OVERLY CENTRALISED STATE

As a prerequisite for a much-needed geographical rebalancing of economic activity in the UK, there needs to be a radical decentralisation of economic and administrative power from national government and from London downward to the regions. This alone will not solve the disparities, but it will be a part of the solution. Such a decentralisation has been called for in the past, but it has never been delivered in an effective way in England. The last Labour government was far too tentative when it sought to balance out devolution settlements for Scotland, Wales and London with a modest programme of devolution to the English regions. Part of the difficulty has been the absence of a powerful regional administrative structure in the UK. And the fact that devolution has worked for Scotland, Wales and London but has failed in the English regions has paradoxically made England's geographical disparities harder to tackle. While devolution has provided Wales and Scotland with some of the policy levers they need to begin tackling the problems caused by the economic dominance of London and the south-east, these imbalances are too stark for any quick or simple solution to be implemented. It will take relentless focus to achieve a geographical rebalancing and it will also require joint working between all levels of government to deliver it. Thus far there's no sign that the Treasury is willing to loosen its vice-like grip on central government expenditure, much less go into a genuine partnership with other tiers of government, be they the devolved administrations or local government.

The Regional Development Agencies which emerged from the last Labour government's modest decentralisation proposals were a mixed bag, with budgets derived from existing funding allocations being devolved down for regional strategic decision-making, which meant they were widely divergent in size and effectiveness. The Regional Development Agencies were based on definitions of English regions which were often more administrative than real, politically, culturally or economically. And it was clear from the beginning that some regions had more of a sense of identity and a willingness to work together than others. When she was a minister in John Prescott's sprawling Department for the Environment, Transport and the Regions, Angela was responsible, with Dick Caborn, for piloting the legislation that set up the Regional Development Agencies through Parliament. It was accepted that some regions would have a stronger sense of identity and a larger budget to work with than others, but it was hoped in time that the administrative devolution could be followed by political powers, too, as well as the creation of democratically elected Regional Assemblies, which would hold the administrative structures to account and allow them to take on wider responsibilities over time. This legislation was designed to be the beginning of a process of rebalancing economic activity out of London. The subsequent loss of the referendum to create an elected assembly in the north-east was catastrophic for the evolution of the RDAs into more democratic structures and this loss was a huge setback for any meaningful form of devolution of real powers to the English regions. In the absence of this progress to a more legitimate democratic oversight of their activities, the RDAs were left with an important administrative role that was still useful in bringing together the regional economic players and created strategic development plans that were far more locally based than anything that would have emerged from Whitehall. Some RDAs were making further progress by combining in order to fulfil wider strategic aims, such as transport. For example, the three northern RDAs – North West RDA, Yorkshire Forward and One North East – had combined to form The Northern Way.

The incoming coalition government, however, decided to abolish RDAs to save money, preferring to dismantle regional structures and begin from scratch at the even more geographically fragmented and confusing sub-regional level. This terrible decision set back the chance of any economic rebalancing for many years. It caused planning blight and a sudden standstill in those regeneration projects which were far advanced in the planning stage. By the time they were abolished, the RDAs had made strategic decisions on the spending of £17 billion over their twelve-year lifetime and still had projects worth £1.86 billion in hand.[64] They owned £512 million of key strategic development sites and property blighted by the sudden uncertainty. Perhaps it gradually dawned on the new government that they had destroyed perfectly viable and useful mechanisms for assisting with regional economic initiatives, meaning that it was nearly impossible for them even to evaluate the bids for their hugely diminished regional funds, let alone distribute the money effectively. It is hard to believe that the Conservatives' inherent belief in the efficacy of the 'free market' did not have a bearing on the decision to abolish the RDAs. What is more surprising, though, is that the Liberal Democrats, who are supposed to believe in devolution, went along with it so readily. Certainly, it was the more free-market-orientated, 'orange book' Liberal Democrats who found themselves in the more powerful economics portfolios making these decisions but that does not excuse their complicity in the setback to genuine political and economic devolution that abolition of the RDAs represented.

In the end, however, the RDA initiative was simply not radical enough to accomplish the geographical rebalancing of economic activity which was a part of the last Labour government's aim. Nor was it radical enough to be an effective counterpoint to the increasing economic pull of London and the south-east, which will continue to get even more out of kilter in the absence of a commitment to meaningful devolution and an inclusive growth strategy. There were other regeneration initiatives both for the coalfield communities and some major UK cities which were very successful in transforming economic opportunity, but this progress could not be sustained when the coalition government drastically cut the funding available for economic regeneration in their ludicrously named 'Emergency Budget' in 2010. The prospects for effective regional economic development went rapidly backwards as a result.

The ad hoc patchwork quilt of thirty-eight Local Enterprise Partnerships (LEPs) which operate at a sub-regional level has proved a feeble replacement for the lost RDAs. And the government's devolution deals are very minor too, offering tiny amounts of funding as an incentive to adopt a combined authority mayoral model. For example, the government boasts about devolving £900 million down to the combined Merseyside Authority over the next thirty years. But, according to the 2017 budgets of the five local authorities, the government have taken £859 million from them in cuts in the past seven years. By the end of the 2017/18 financial year, more than £900 million will have been lost.[65] Without a more robust and independent devolved structure, there will not be a strong enough local framework to build success upon.

FAILING TO USE THE POWER
OF PUBLIC PROCUREMENT

Few government budgets which are available to assist in boosting the 'demand side' of the economy can match the potential of that for public procurement. ONS figures show that currently the UK's public procurement budget stands at £268 billion a year, which is one third of all public expenditure. As democratic socialists, we should remember that this level would be reduced by an incoming Labour government. Labour would cut the levels of outsourcing of public services by returning to direct provision in key areas, because it is more efficient and democratically accountable. This is especially obvious in the aftermath of the collapse into liquidation of outsourcing giant Carillion. However, it remains the case that even a reduced procurement budget offers great opportunities for leveraging more social value, and it therefore must form a key part of any integrated industrial strategy. The era of austerity and cuts to public expenditure has tended to entrench public procurement professionals ever more deeply into the use of low price as the dominant criteria by which to judge those bidding for contracts. As anyone who has worked in public services will tell you, the cost savings are more often than not achieved at the expense of the terms and conditions of employment for the staff currently providing the service. It is not unusual to find public service workers who have been 'TUPEd' over from one employer to another multiple times while doing the same job in the same workplace.

Much anger is expressed when public procurement is seen to benefit non-UK companies, as this is regarded as a lost opportunity to gain added benefits from a specific amount of public expenditure. Likewise, the frequent use of labour from outside the area on development projects in places of high

unemployment is rightly regarded as another missed opportunity. The general response to this criticism by government
procurement officers has been to hide behind EU procurement
rules, which mandate full transparency and non-discrimination
between EU providers as part of the requirements of the single
market. After eight years as a minister, however, Angela believes
that the real reason is that procurement officers tend to be risk
averse and conservative in the way in which they run contracting processes. They simply do not want to mess up so badly
that they cause their Permanent Secretary to have to appear
before the Public Accounts Committee after a procurement
disaster. This might be career-ending for them, so most of them
do not really seek out innovation or creativity since they are not
rewarded for doing so. When Angela was Exchequer Secretary
to the Treasury, she found herself responsible for the Office of
Government Commerce (OGC; now merged into the efficiency and reform group and situated in the Cabinet Office). The
OGC was a novel cross-government agency which sought to
improve value for money in public procurement and improve
the standard of contracts by having the power to approve or
stop the largest procurements from proceeding. It monitored
their progress and mandated the adoption of new and best
practice. Angela was astonished at the unco-ordinated procurement processes she discovered operating both within and across
government departments. It was clear that the largest private
contractors, such as those providing computer services, had a far
more up-to-date picture of the contracts they ran and were bidding for than the departments wishing to contract. Ministerial
responsibility was ad hoc and unco-ordinated too. It took her
months even to establish which government ministers were formally responsible for procurement in each department and even
longer to organise a cross-departmental meeting to attempt

some co-ordination with them. In such circumstances, pursuing a cross-government strategy was nigh-on impossible. The departmental silos were just too entrenched. The OGC was able to change that and put in place a capacity to monitor and improve practice, which was responsible for driving much-needed improvements and savings. Angela was also able to change the procurement guidelines to emphasise that social requirements – such as insisting on local labour – were not illegal under EU rules, thereby challenging procurement professionals to achieve better value for money from their contract deals.

The big general unions – Unite and the GMB – both point out the potential for supporting UK manufacturing and furthering other social and environmental policy aims by innovative use of the UK's massive public procurement budget.[66] Public-sector union Unison notes the potential to use changes to the EU procurement regulations that make it easier for those inviting bids for public contracts to take into account social and environmental aspects in choosing the winning contractors. In theory, this allows for the possibility of requiring 'fair trade' standards of potential contractors, specifying certain levels of local labour be employed, paying the living wage, specifying labour standards and diversity and equality expectations, and requiring skills training and apprenticeships be offered as a legitimate part of the tendering process. While an explicit policy of buying British may not be allowed under EU law (because the tendering documents have to be non-discriminatory), the explicit expansion of allowable social criteria certainly makes it easier to justify such decisions when they are made. In fact, the adoption of such added-value criteria should be encouraged and incentivised as part of best practice for procurement professionals.

There have been positive changes to EU procurement rules

which were agreed in a new directive in 2014. The modest Public Services (Social Value) Act 2012 has also made it more explicit that social criteria can form part of the decision-making processes for procurement. These welcome changes are in the process of being transcribed fully into UK law, something which may be completed in time for the UK to leave the European Union. However, much as Tory Eurosceptics like to claim that 'taking back control' will allow the UK to set its own procurement rules, the reality is that even the WTO has its General Procurement Agreement, which applies to government contracts for certain goods and services. Any future trade negotiations are likely to wish to replicate the rules that the EU has just adopted in its 2014 directive and so the scope for going further than the explicit mention of social and environmental criteria is probably limited. This still leaves substantial scope for achieving extra social and environmental aims as well as value for money, but this will not be achieved without an explicit effort to train those responsible for running public procurement exercises about how they can legitimately seek better value for money – by pursuing local labour requirements or the payment of the living wage or equality and diversity issues – as a part of their procurement exercise.

SUPPLY SIDE WEAKNESSES: INADEQUATE SKILLS TRAINING, EDUCATION AND APPRENTICESHIPS

It is clear that the decision of post-Thatcher governments in the UK to leave our adult skills system to the market has been a terrible failure. This hands-off approach has meant that the infrastructure needed for the strategic co-ordination of a successful approach to adult skills training between government, employers and employees has atrophied. The result has been inadequate skills training, no focus on the geographical areas where economic development is most needed or the industrial sectors where it is most required. Nor has there been any sight of a strategy to help those low-skilled workers who need the most support to improve their job prospects by up-skilling or re-skilling. There are no strong or established levers available to ensure that women have a chance to escape the low-skilled employment sectors, where the jobs they currently work in tend to be clustered. Only very recently has there been any attempt at forward planning by government to provide the skills necessary for the workforce of the future to thrive in the context of the Fourth Industrial Revolution.

Over the years, a great deal of money has been thrown at the supply side on the assumption that the market would miraculously provide the workforce skills that employers needed. It has not, and this lack of workforce skills planning has resulted in suboptimal outcomes for individuals, for employers and for our country. No institutions or sectoral strategies that have a long-term, planned focus on the future have been built. Instead, the assumption has been that employers will simply cause the supply to appear in response to their demands. There has not, however, been a strong employer voice co-ordinating demand beyond a general dissatisfaction with skill standards often accompanied by a search to fill the gap by importing skilled workers from abroad. Meanwhile, training providers have tended to chase centrally set funding allocations and provide easier-to-deliver, lower-level and less economically useful qualifications. Over half the qualifications taken by adults are below NVQ Level 2, which offer poor prospects for individual advancement or promotion but easier pickings for private training providers.

In their 2017 report, the IPPR set out this mismatch and waste of resources in stark terms.[67] They reveal that employer investment in vocational training in the UK is half the EU average and it fell by 13.6 per cent per employee between 2007 and 2017. At the same time, the UK has the highest levels of over-qualification in the EU. This means that the workforce skills that do exist are not being effectively utilised by employers either. Lack of planning has therefore delivered low skills at one end of the spectrum and unutilised skills at the other. A double mismatch of wasted opportunities.

As we enter a period of profound and rapid change in our economy, it is crucial that these weaknesses are not left unaddressed. And it is crucial that the government delivers genuine strategic change.

The introduction of an apprenticeship levy in 2017 should have been a cause for celebration, since it put the standards required to award the qualification on a statutory basis, thereby establishing a definitive quality standard across the country. This came on top of a drive to create 3 million apprenticeship starts by 2020, which was initiated by the coalition government. However, in the first quarter of the operation of the new levy, May–July 2017, apprenticeship starts plummeted by nearly 60 per cent. In the second quarter they fell again by nearly 30 per cent. Some of the decline is being caused by the sheer inability of the government to administer the new scheme in a timely fashion. But more is likely to be a reflection of the low standard of some of the 'training' which was badged as 'apprenticeships' prior to the new quality requirements coming into effect. Many employers are complaining that the levy is simply another tax on business which they feel they are not benefiting from.

The way the government has awarded contracts for delivering training is causing great concern. They have omitted to award contracts to ten tried-and-tested further education colleges, yet some new and untested private providers have been successful in receiving them. This threatens to cause huge disruption among the suppliers for no apparent reason. It is abundantly clear that we are far from creating a coherent, effective and stable structure to deliver vocational education and apprenticeship training in the UK. The steep cuts in funding across the further education sector have further undermined confidence in the government's commitment to deliver such a structure.

No industrial strategy can be taken seriously until these major weaknesses are addressed in a systematic and long-term way which will stand the test of time. Currently, there is no sign that this is about to happen.

CHAPTER NINETEEN

ENLIGHTENMENT 2.0

COMPLETING THE ENLIGHTENMENT

Democratic socialism would have been unable to develop without the tidal wave of ideas that swept across Europe in the seventeenth and eighteenth centuries and which became known as the Enlightenment. The celebration of 'reason' and the view that all people were created equal is the modern foundation of all the concepts of universal human rights, liberty and egalitarianism that have flourished and defined both our philosophy and our politics ever since. It is in the Enlightenment that we find respect for facts and the search for truth – something we all assumed would continue to be an essential part of public discourse until very recently. This European 'Age of Reason' rejected rigid, pre-ordained hierarchies controlled by unquestioned authorities like the monolithic church and absolutist monarchs claiming the divine right to rule. Instead, people came to believe that reason and scientific enquiry would make it possible for humanity to drastically improve its own condition. The flowering of intellectual ideas that followed created a new world view, which in turn nurtured the flourishing of new theories in philosophy, ethics, science and religion.

New political theories suggesting the basis upon which people were to be governed in the future, building on Rousseau's 'social contract' ideas, were developing fast. In the UK,

Hobbes, Hume and Locke in their different ways sought to justify the role, the extent and the legitimacy of the state. They sought to assert the balance that there should be between the state and the individual now that God and the king had been demoted. It was recognised that the pursuit of knowledge, freedom and happiness was a legitimate human endeavour for everyone to pursue. Previously suppressed democratic ideas flourished in this ferment and their strength grew. The Enlightenment era turned from criticising the absolutist and aristocratic status quo to demanding its reform and then on to legitimising the huge revolutionary upheavals in America and France that began to define the modern era. Some, like British Whig politician Edmund Burke, felt it had all gone too far.[68] Others, like Thomas Paine[69] and Mary Wollstonecraft, wanted reform to go further and argued that the inalienable rights of all human beings should be better represented in the political arrangements for governing them. A battle then raged to legitimise new, more democratic forms of political organisation and assembly to provide the underpinnings for this new, more egalitarian world. It was at this time that the contours of the world in which we now live first became visible.

Mary Wollstonecraft, regarded by many as the first British feminist, was an enthusiastic supporter of the Enlightenment and the egalitarian ideals that accompanied it. She was a remarkable, pioneering woman – well ahead of her time. Self-made, she blazed a trail for women everywhere by managing to make an independent living as a writer and educator, becoming, as she put it, part of a 'new genus'. Responding to Burke's coruscating criticism of the situation in France, Wollstonecraft argued, in *A Vindication of the Rights of Men*, in defence of the French Revolution. She wanted parliamentary reform as well as new civil and religious freedoms for all – by which, to the astonishment and disgust of many, she meant women as well as men. As a vocal supporter of the French Revolution, she was enraged when Talleyrand made it clear to the French National Assembly that the revolutionary concepts of *liberté*, *égalité*, and *fraternité* did not apply to women. Women should only have a domestic education and not be afforded access to any real opportunities in his view. This monstrous exclusion of half of the world's population from what were meant to be 'universal' values provoked the publication of Wollstonecraft's best-known work in 1792 – *A Vindication of the Rights of Women* – in which she argued that women should have access to the same education as men because they too were entitled to enjoy the full benefits of reason and the self-fulfilment it brought. She argued for the emancipation and participation of women in civil and political life on equal terms. This simple argument asserting the equality of women with men so outraged Whig politician Horace Walpole (son of Prime Minister Sir Robert Walpole) that in what might be called the second blast against the monstrous regiment of women, he referred to her as 'a hyena in petticoats'. Responding to the predictable outrage her simple call for equality had provoked, Wollstonecraft said: 'I do not wish women to have power over men but over themselves.'

So, 226 years later and in the 100th anniversary year of women first gaining the vote in the UK, an examination of the progress that women have made shows that we still have a long way to go to achieve equality. It shows that we have to complete the Enlightenment by finally including women in our concept of universal rights and fully in economic, political and social life.

We now have a vital opportunity to press ahead with the full equality and liberation of women. Achieving this is necessary if we are to reap the benefits of a properly equal society where the potential of all is nurtured and realised. Disfiguring bigotry and discrimination, with all the waste of social and economic potential it implies for our society, must become a thing of the past. In the twenty-first century, it is also important that we are inclusive of other diversities who similarly find themselves the subject of unacceptable levels of disadvantage and discrimination. Black and ethnic minority communities have long suffered endemic and illegal disadvantage in the UK simply because of the colour of their skin. LGBT people likewise are only just beginning to emerge from centuries of legalised prejudice, oppression and violence. While the UK is a society that recognises many faiths and none, still there is evidence of rising levels of anti-Semitism and Islamophobia, which demonstrate a hatred and intolerance of religious belief and ethnicity that must be challenged and defeated. And we have yet fully to integrate those with disabilities into our political and economic life as a nation. Currently, they are shamefully excluded. We need a new world outlook which continues to be based on reason and respect for facts, but which also accepts difference and pluralism and strives for inclusion.

Just as the beginning of the Enlightenment turned accepted ideas of religion, philosophy and ethics on their head, so in our time there are areas where we need a profoundly new approach. As well as renewing and completing our commitment to achieving genuine equality, two other areas stand out that are relevant to our politics today. In response to the destructive global crisis in our financial system, we need to develop a new, more holistic approach to economics itself. This would integrate the environmental and social effects of human activity rather than ignoring them. Using the price mechanism to exclude these considerations has been disastrous for the fragile ecosystems on our planet and for the prospects of achieving a balanced and sustainable inclusive growth in many communities across

the world. We need to change this by harnessing the undoubted power of markets but integrating them with other equally
vital human considerations rather than merely assuming that
the greed of 'self-interested individualism' is the only acceptable market-based motivation. Finally, as we are on the cusp of
profound and accelerating technological change, we must have
in place systems that ensure the benefits of this digital age go
to society as a whole rather than creating a digital capitalism
as exploitative and rapacious as were some of the older industrial models. This will not happen without a firm and insistent
challenge to the existing status quo and it requires confronting
powerful vested interests. To be successful, however, any new,
more holistic approach in these areas depends on us expanding
our traditional ideas of what human knowledge is and what its
purpose should be.

ENDING THE NARROW UTILITARIAN
APPROACH TO ETHICS AND POLITICS

In his 2007 book *Why We Hate Politics*, the political scientist
Professor Colin Hay rightly identified the 'marketisation' of politics as one of the reasons why many voters feel so alienated and
disengaged. He cites the large-scale contracting out of public
services and the loss of democratically accountable policy-
making by outsourcing it to 'independent' regulators as a cause
of this alienation. As the technocrats take over decision-making, politicians – and therefore voters – have less control over
what is 'supplied' through the political process than ever and
that is regardless of the result of any democratic election. If
the politics is taken out of politics, perhaps we should not be
surprised when voters turn away. The often-unspoken tenets of

market fundamentalism are followed by regulators and experts alike, and voting has not changed the context in which they work or the technocratic decisions they make. Retail politics has pervaded all aspects of our lives, including our method of doing politics itself. Retail politics commodifies even political choice and reduces it to a sterile brand war in which, by analogy, the voters (customers) exercise a passive choice of which brand to buy. In fact, politics is not a spectator sport, nor a retail rivalry. It works best when voters join in and make our democracy more vital and stronger. The retail view of politics and the outsourcing of services, however, has promoted the belief that public and community services are to be provided like any other commodity by the market, outside of real political accountability. Understandably, then, voters formed the view that there was little point in engaging because nothing was really at stake. Retail politics does not look on the voter as a whole person or allow us to consider the kind of society we are trying to achieve by exercising our political choices. Getting these considerations of how society may really be changed off the table at elections was one of the unsung triumphs of the market fundamentalists. This needs to be challenged in politics and in economics. After years of market fundamentalist hegemony, there are finally some indications that this change has at last begun.

In politics, it is only recently that this depressingly narrow range of options has been overthrown. Finally, in the aftermath of the global financial crisis and the long period of austerity that has followed it, people are looking for something different. This presents us with unique opportunities and also unique dangers. The Brexit vote, the rise of the *Alternative für Deutschland* in Germany, the electoral success of Le Pen's *Front National* in France and the election of President Donald Trump show that this is not necessarily a progressive moment, but the changes in the Labour Party and Jeremy Corbyn's rise to the leadership build on a hope among the newly engaged that it might be put to progressive purpose. Our models of retail politics have provided a very narrow range of choice for voters who are looking for something more. Until very recently, this choice had not been questioned. Now it is up to us to shape that change in a democratic socialist direction. It is time to take back control.

INCORPORATING COMPASSION AND HOPE IN OUR POLITICS

Labour Prime Minister Harold Wilson famously said that 'the Labour Party is a moral crusade or it is nothing', by which he meant that campaigning with hope and determination for real change was a central part of the motivation of those who join our party. It was certainly this yearning that Jeremy Corbyn tapped into so effectively in his leadership elections and in the general election which followed in 2017. As we leave the era of New Labour's technocratic managerialism behind, it is important that we rediscover this campaigning tradition and place it in a productive, modern setting. It is also important that politics itself expands to give this tradition the room it needs to flourish, and we can only achieve that by ending the artificial narrowness of our political discourse and the choices that have been on offer to the electorate.

The nature and political significance of compassion has become a focus in current philosophical debate. The influential philosopher Martha Nussbaum[70] suggests that ideals of love and compassion are essential parts of our ethical and political thinking, and that compassion is itself the basic social emotion necessary for the expression of solidarity and the development of social justice.[71] Without this emotion, democratic socialists would have little to say about the world. It is important to note that compassion is the exact opposite of the 'self-regarding materialism' (greed) which animates so much of the creed of market fundamentalism. Nussbaum also strongly articulates the case for feminism as a part of a liberal Enlightenment tradition of what she calls personhood, autonomy, rights, dignity and respect. She argues that the Enlightenment tradition initially excluded the female viewpoint but that it will be transformed for the better by taking on the insights of feminism. She also observes that the radical feminist potential of the Enlightenment tradition is only now beginning to be realised, for example by the recognition of women's rights as central human rights in international law and the empowerment of women in developing countries. She sees the ideals of the Enlightenment as providing us with the justification to strive for a justice and liberty which challenges the power of established hierarchies. She believes this is a vision which can and should lead to social revolution. By its nature, she understands that women's voices and leadership, which has so far been largely absent, can change the world.

The rationalist philosopher Thomas Nagel, like Nussbaum, believes that practical reasoning and compassion are linked and that to achieve progressive political change we need a universalist ethic. The collective improvement of society and respect for others is not inevitable, but the human capacity for objectivity allows for the possibility of moral progress.[72] Imagining the future, he observes: 'I do not think it is utopian to look forward to the gradual development of a greater universality of moral respect, an internalisation of moral objectivity analogous to the gradual internalisation of scientific progress that seems to be a feature of modern culture.'[73]

Nagel suggests that to act ethically we have to transcend our own particular subjective viewpoint to reach a new objective one.[74] Our own interests are therefore just one set of interests among others and this, not a narrow self-interest, is the ethical basis for political action. Egalitarian politics is understanding that we have shared social interests – more in common with each other – than a purely selfish view of the world would imply. Acknowledging our different interests allows us objectively to act for the common good and democracy gives us the framework within which to do so. Our capacity to be objective makes us 'citizens of nowhere' because we understand and empathise with others who may not share our own subjective concerns. In direct contradiction to the current Prime Minister's claims that there are only citizens of somewhere, the truth is that it is only by empathy, objective reasoning and action that we can help to solve the complex problems facing our world. This is so clear when it comes to issues as diverse as climate change, worker exploitation in developing countries and ensuring hyper-mobile multinational corporations pay fair taxes in the jurisdictions in which they operate. Internationalism is an essential Labour value and the means by which we can tackle these problems. Britain has been a leader in the world in soft power. We played a role in founding and engaging with such organisations as the Commonwealth, the United Nations and the European Union. Our public broadcaster, the BBC, has been a voice bringing news not propaganda to the world, and the English language is a global language. However, with both Brexit and Boris doing their best to diminish British credibility, our capacity to lead in the world has been seriously diminished as the post-Brexit referendum shenanigans have made us a global laughing stock. A Labour government will need to re-establish our leadership in international institutions for the betterment of all humanity.

We will also need to lead in achieving the creation of a new generation of international organisations to ensure that the problems which can only be tackled by international co-operation, such as closing down global tax loopholes, fighting money laundering, terrorism and climate change, are achieved.

ENDING DISCRIMINATION – EQUALITY AND LIBERATION FOR WOMEN

Globally, according to the World Economic Forum, it is getting harder to be a woman. The global gender pay gap is widening for the first time since the index was established in 2006, and in their 2017 report, the WEF calculated that at the current rate of progress it will take another 100 years for pay equality to be achieved. They also calculated that it will take women 217 more years to reach economic equality with men.[75] The UK is in fifteenth place in the overall index. Globally, women continue to be discriminated against in law and in access to opportunities, be they economic or educational. They bear the brunt of the health risks of childbirth and the duty to care for the elderly. Violence against women is endemic in many areas of the world, including the threat of rape, honour killing and female genital mutilation. There are some countries where women cannot choose when or who to marry and where they are not allowed to have an existence independent of their husbands or the men in their wider family. Globally, women work two thirds of the world's working hours, produce half of the world's food but only earn 10 per cent of the world's income and own less than 1 per cent of the world's property.

In the UK, there is formal equality in law but, as we outlined in the chapter on bigotry and intolerance, there is still a long way to go until it becomes a reality in practice. Despite forty years of equal pay legislation, the gender pay gap is still 9.1 per cent (for women over fifty it is 18.6 per cent). Perhaps this reflects both the level of discrimination in the workplace and the fact that women end up doing most of the caring for elderly relatives. In 2017, 10 November was the day when women began to work for free because of the still-persisting gender pay gap with men. Female apprentices earn 8 per cent less than their male counterparts at the beginning of their career and they tend to be segregated into sectors of the economy which pay less. We will learn more about the pay gaps when the requirement enshrined in Labour's watered-down 2010 Equality Act for pay transparency in large companies finally comes into force in 2018. We already know from data published early that EasyJet has a 52 per cent gender pay gap; the BBC has a 10.7 per cent gap; and the Bank of England has one of 21 per cent. Since the Home Office has a 10.1 per cent gap, it can hardly be argued that the government is showing the way. A recent report by UK equality campaign the Fawcett Society revealed that violence, abuse and harassment against women and girls is endemic in the UK, with one in five women over sixteen reporting that they had been sexually assaulted. And yet, at the same time, the report discovered that the legal system is routinely failing women who seek redress. As Brexit looms, the fear is that even the existing protections for women in law will be threatened. The backlash against women who demand equality and that their rights be enforced is there for all to see – more crudely and violently over social media and more subtly in the usual dismissive mainstream media coverage.

One hundred years after women first got the vote in the UK, the persistence of this deeply misogynistic culture cries out for remedy by determined political action. If we are to create a more equal and just society, this has to be a priority. One of the most important ways that we will do this is by getting more women involved in political action at all levels – from community organising to Parliament. However, for every bit of progress we make on this, there remain powerful institutional barriers – which we must work to identify and neutralise. There are reactionary opponents who will do their utmost to poison the public sphere and dissuade women from engaging. In particular, the age of social media means that reactionary troglodytes can tweet abuse directly at women and have it turn up as a notification on their personal device. It appears that, at this time, self-regulation by social media channels has failed. If we are to allow the many talented women to take part in politics, we will need to do more to prevent abuse by a minority of hate-filled trolls that are capable of causing huge disruption and hurt.

A NEW, MORE HOLISTIC ECONOMICS

Economics itself must change to be more inclusive and holistic. There have been increasing signs of concern in the economics profession, which was found so badly wanting when it failed to predict the global financial crash. The field of economics has been very effectively colonised for forty years by the market fundamentalist creed, to such an extent that the creation of a viable alternative set of economic assumptions has seemed unimaginable. In the aftermath of this huge crisis, the economics profession wrung its collective hands, tried to resume business as usual and hoped no one had noticed its culpability. But now there are signs of a nascent and long-overdue re-evaluation of the very foundations of economics. If it can be achieved, this will mean the emergence of a new, more holistic and humane world view which will help to change the way economics analyses the world and alter the priorities and decisions that will flow as a result.

Classical economics always relied too much on the figure of 'homo economicus' or rational economic man. The assumptions made about his (and it is always a he) profit-maximising, purely selfish behaviour bear little relationship to reality. Therefore, they render many of the implicit assumptions and predictions of economic theory suspect. Behavioural economists and development economists who work with real people in their communities have unsurprisingly been at the forefront of the work to devise a new, more realistic analytical framework for the profession. The Earth's finite resources and the urgency of dealing with the existential threat of global climate change has meant that incorporating the requirement for sustainability and the best use of scarce resources has been central to the work. So too has trying to recognise that markets are embedded in the wider social and cultural systems in which they operate and that these contexts can often be a better predictor of behaviour and outcome than abstract models of a mythical 'rational economic man'.

In this new work there has been a welcome diversification of the view of what economics looks like in the real world. Some theorists begin by regarding the economic structures as a sub-system of a much higher system, such as society, nature or even the universe, rather than an abstract, all-powerful but separate system. This immediately means that economic activity must be analysed as an integral part of a larger complex system rather than being abstracted from the context it is actually operating within. This more holistic setting is immediately more realistic and predictive, too. Bioeconomics, humanistic economics, socioeconomics and green economics all seek to incorporate the real human context and bring them together with the insights of psychology and observed human behaviour, which is sometimes altruistic and not just narrowly selfish. Concepts such as inclusive growth, which is explicitly designed to benefit the disenfranchised and aim at achieving more equal outcomes, are increasingly making an appearance even in IMF papers. In these new contexts, more generous social protection systems and democratisation can be part of an economic case for a successful inclusive development. In orthodox economics it might be dismissed as irrelevant or, as Hayek notoriously thought, the information delivered by market mechanisms was more important for freedom than democracy itself. Likewise, concepts of emotion, hope, self-esteem and the nature of the social relationships which sustain a community also become a part of the analytical tools an economist can utilise to explain behaviour, predict outcomes and make appropriate policy recommendations. In her recent book, *Doughnut Economics*, Kate Raworth makes a powerful case for a complete rethink of the discipline, including creating an economy which needs to be both redistributive and regenerative by design. She is correct to point out that the world is in need of new thinking on tax, the financial system and what should and should not be left to the market to provide.

There is an urgent need for Treasuries around the world to start putting climate change, public health, sustainable jobs and equality at the heart of their planning. Their models need to be changed to track not just economic output but how different scenarios and approaches affect the future of our country in terms of environment, sustainability and the happiness and wellbeing of our citizens. These models would, for example, show more clearly the case for investing in our green future, in lifelong learning to help those whose jobs disappear due to automation, and in proper childcare and social investment so we can make best use of all our citizens' talents in the workplace. If, at every one of the austerity Budgets laid down by George Osborne and Philip Hammond, they'd had to admit as an integral part of their calculations and presentations how their plans disproportionately harmed women or our environment, the past eight years might have worked out quite differently. Having worked as a Treasury minister, Angela can almost hear the squeals of horror from career Treasury mandarins, but there is no reason beyond inertia for not trying different approaches to economic planning that would benefit us and future generations.

DEMOCRACY AND WOMEN'S VOICES

The Enlightenment cannot be regarded as complete until all of humanity is included in the protection afforded by the concept of universal human rights. This has to apply in theory and also in practice in all societies the world over. But it would be a good start if we could deliver this simple commitment in our own country. It would also be transformative.

No society can be completely fair or equitable without the empowerment and inclusion of the 51 per cent of the population who are female. So, fighting to achieve this is of the utmost importance. The year 2018 marks the 100th anniversary of some women in the UK achieving the vote. (It is ninety years since women won the vote on an equal basis to men in the UK.) Women fought, braved the riot police and were ridiculed and belittled by the entire political establishment. When they stood up for their civil rights they were jailed, tortured and died to win the right to vote. Even a perfunctory glance at the hostile press coverage, the vicious cartoons and the anti-women's suffrage propaganda produced at that time makes it clear how badly they transgressed by daring to campaign for their rights and how heroic and brave they were. They made one error though. They believed with a passion that if they could only win the vote, equality would surely follow as night follows day. They were wrong. The women who followed in their footsteps know better now. Getting the vote was a necessary but by no means sufficient condition for moving towards equality. A century later, there is a great deal still to do. The shocking Fawcett Society report condemning a culture of misogyny in the UK in 2018 is a sign. The necessity for the creation of the #MeToo, #TimesUp or #EverydaySexism hashtags, the sexual harassment crisis engulfing Hollywood and spreading elsewhere (including to our own Parliament), and an occupant of the White House who boasts about assaulting women indicate that we are going backwards. The spectacle of the seedy, men-only Presidents Club dinner, during which captains of industry and the leaders of UK business were provided with young female 'hostesses' earning £175 to amuse and be abused – all these outrages attest to the unfinished nature of the women's revolution and to the necessity for radical change.

Just as we need to move to a more ethical and holistic approach to economics, so the times cry out for a more holistic and ethical approach to our democracy. When Angela was first elected to the House of Commons in 1992, she was only the 163rd woman ever to become a Member of Parliament in its entire history. Only fifty-nine other women were returned to that parliament out of the 650 constituencies contested in that election. And it was clear to Angela from working in Parliament itself that it was created in the image of a Victorian men-only club. It developed many of its odd peccadillos long before women were even allowed to be elected there. Why else would she have to put on a top hat to make a point of order during a division (which she never did as it would have made her look ridiculous!)? Why do government and opposition MPs still face each other while having to remain two sword-lengths apart in the Commons chamber? The adversarial nature of the Commons is widely despised by the electorate, who can barely stand the animal noises and the football terrace nature of Prime Minister's Questions (although Angela relished becoming one of the very few women who have ever been able to take it, against the then Chancellor George Osborne in 2015 and 2016). Reform to our democracy needs to make Parliament and its proceedings less arcane and more understandable to the watching public – in language and in procedure. There has been some progress (and the top hat has thankfully now gone!), but much modernisation remains to be achieved.

The continuing male domination of public and political life skews the nature of the decisions made and that in turn affects the kind of society we create. We doubt very much, for example, that had women gained the vote in 1893 (as they did in New Zealand) or in 1906 (as they did in Finland) that it would have taken women in the UK until 1997 to begin to develop a coherent, if still inadequate, preschool childcare system. Systems of paternity leave move forward at an unpaid snail's pace and yet many men wish to be able to spend time with their very young children without being regarded as strange or not career-minded. Male domination of public and political life causes the separation of what are regarded as 'male' and 'female' characteristics when what we actually need is an integration of them and their free expression in every individual. We need to move away from the idea that women should do all the nurturing and caring while men go out and compete. In reality, every human personality has the potential to be caring and competitive, strong or emotional, and these aspects of being human ought to be allowed to be expressed without the rigid gender stereotyping which so disfigures our society and oppresses men as well as women. Boys don't cry, apparently, but they might grow up to be happier if they were allowed to express emotion without having their masculinity instantly brought into question. And competitive girls should be admired and not just accused of being lesbians.

We need our politics and public life to echo with the voices of women and all other marginalised, rarely heard groups so that we can make our democracy whole and our democratic debate full and more representative than it is now. This needs to be reflected in local as well as national government and in other walks of life too. Democratic engagement will increase if we open up power structures and make them more accountable to all of our communities. That is the way finally to include everyone in the Enlightenment values which made our modern era.

CHAPTER TWENTY

A NEW COLLECTIVE
NATIONAL MISSION

There have been moments in British history where a sense of national mission has crystallised into communal effort for the common good. The fight against fascism in the Second World War was one such example. It was a moment of existential crisis which galvanised the entire country in the battle for survival. Our freedom, our values, our very existence as a nation were at stake. The national mission was the defeat of fascism and all levers of the state and civil society were mobilised successfully to achieve that one purpose.

Britain was determined not to repeat the mistakes made in the aftermath of the First World War, when the British political class's insistence on clinging to pre-war economic and political orthodoxies meant those who fought in the trenches returned to an economic slump and mass unemployment. In 1945, it was imperative that the great sense of national mission persisted after the end of hostilities. The election of a Labour government promised national renewal and a new political settlement based on the same mutualism and state action that had won the war. While the country was grateful to Churchill for his leadership and inspiration in the war, it did not trust the Conservative Party with organising the peace. That post-war Labour settlement was achieved against all the odds by an exhausted and bankrupt nation which defied the odds and rewrote the political terms of trade for the next thirty years.

After forty years in thrall to market fundamentalist small-state dogma, a transformation as dramatic as that required after the devastation of the Second World War is long overdue. We have diagnosed the maladies that ignoring the collective needs of our communities in favour of selfish market fundamentalism has wrought on our wellbeing as a country. We have seen rising levels of inequality juxtaposed with obscene wealth in the shadow of Grenfell. We have highlighted the spiritual damage done to those neglected by society; the scourge of loneliness, mental illness and isolation. The proliferation of foodbanks and rises in homelessness; the neglect of public services; and the spread of exploitative employment practices – all these things tell us we need a fundamental change of direction.

Realising the full extent of the possibilities for action requires us to discard the stifling, withered scope for political action in a Hayekian minimal state. Only then can the world of possibilities for the betterment of society open up. In an era where the potential of the state to deliver change for good has been systematically denigrated, reacquiring the confidence to forge ahead with this vision and deliver on it will be key. And to succeed in this task, market fundamentalist orthodoxies must be directly, specifically and confidently challenged head-on, as we have sought to do.

Creating a better and fairer society despite the formidable challenges we currently face requires nothing less than a new national mission, our goal to ensure that all our citizens have a stake in our country's future, and to develop a more equal society that works for everyone. A society where each can strive to reach their full potential and no one is discarded or left behind. A society where everyone can contribute and expect support when they need it. The uncertainties created by Brexit make this much harder and succeeding becomes even more of an imperative. The relations between labour, capital and the state need to be re-founded on a fairer and more socially sustainable basis.

CIVIC PATRIOTISM – THERE *IS* SUCH A THING AS SOCIETY

Part of our mission is to reclaim patriotism from the nationalists for the progressive cause. We should not just be content for our society to emerge as an incidental by-product of hands-off market mechanisms, where greed is the only accepted motivation. How can we even contemplate being so indifferent to the context in which we must live and thrive? Caring about what kind of society we have created is key to the quality of life experienced by the vast majority of our fellow citizens as well as to our own prospects. That, in turn, as we have seen, is key to their health and wellbeing and as such it is a crucial area of concern in our political endeavours. The super-rich may get to opt out of living among us, but the vast majority have to live in the society that emerges from the context set by our economic and political assumptions and our subsequent political and economic activity. The type of society we live in is therefore directly affected by the choices we make and the interest we take. We should aspire actively to manage and nurture our society like a good gardener improves the soil and plans next year's planting. We need to develop a new 'civic patriotism', which means caring about the collective context in which our own individualism can flourish. Civic patriotism is not jingoistic, nor is it about nationalism or identity politics. It is about developing a collective pride in the kind of society we create, nurture and sustain. It is about developing a holistic rather than simply an individualistic approach to our politics. It is about the context in which we live rather than just focusing on our own concerns.

Civic patriotism asserts first and foremost that there *is* such a thing as society and it is from this assertion that all else follows. After forty years of atavistic, selfish individualism which implicitly judged the vulnerable as losers and measured moral worth in terms of wealth and remuneration, this statement is in itself radical and transformative. Together we want to create a country and a society that works for everyone. And we acknowledge that we have the potential to do so should we choose to see this as a political, social and economic possibility.

We also have a duty to nurture and develop the resilience of our new society. As well as having reasonable expectations of how it can support us in the developments occurring in our own lives, we need to have a view of what we can do to support it. To misquote Kennedy: 'Ask not what your society can do for you, but what you can do for your society.' Within this new vision of society there is an implicit inter-generational contract which will supersede the current breaking down in harmony between generations. As members of that caring collective political entity, we owe duties to others. We need to be able to trust that caring, mutual support is reciprocal and will be there for us in times of need. Intergenerational solidarity is a central part of this new settlement. Collective provision in such a society must include, as a minimum, access to health and social care for those who require it and adequate social security provision too.

The values of democratic socialism, equality, democracy, liberty, co-operation and internationalism all speak to the type of society which should now be forged anew. Individuals should be active participants not passive recipients of any support they may need to access, be it education, lifelong learning, skills training, social care or anything else. Having a say, influencing how provision is organised, listening to all voices, inclusion – all these are principles that must be reflected in the delivery of the services which will make a reality of our new society. Bureaucracy does not have to be bureaucratic; it can be responsive and sensitive if it is properly resourced and valued.

In this way we can reimagine our national purpose and create a new destination to aim for in our political and economic endeavours.

TAXATION – THE MEMBERSHIP SUBSCRIPTION FOR A DECENT SOCIETY

We need to change the debate on tax and the attitude that is taken towards it in current political debate. Without the collection of taxes, governments can have little influence on much of anything and a government wishing to create a fairer society cannot avoid considering reform in this area. Market fundamentalists would like us to believe that taxation is a huge imposition by the state on individuals, which deprives them of 'their' money using coercive power. They then seek to delegitimise taxation as if it were organised larceny, but, as we have argued, it is the membership subscription we all pay to live in a civilised society. Market fundamentalists routinely portray tax as a drag on creativity, innovation and enterprise. In the more extreme versions of market fundamentalism, redistributive taxation is even painted as a morally evil thing which reduces personal remuneration, thereby weakening personal incentives and effort. In such a distorted moral universe it is easy to see why tax avoidance flourishes with the impunity as demonstrated in the leaks of the Paradise Papers. And those who organise it seem to do so without shame.

This corrosive 'everyday libertarian' attitude to taxation has become a well-established narrative, and after years of anti-tax propaganda in the UK it is all-pervasive. But it is wrong. To make the case for redistributive taxation we have to challenge the ludicrous anti-tax narratives that have been allowed to take hold.

The market fundamentalist case against tax is based on assumptions which are simply wrong. The most blatant is that pre-tax market outcomes are somehow 'just'. In reality, they are no such thing. They are actually a function of the political decisions and choices which have been made by the state itself. The market that distributes pre-tax income and wealth between individuals does not exist in a vacuum. It is embedded and regulated by laws the state administers. This web of laws and context directly affects the outcome which is delivered, and the rules often have a direct effect on the rate of profit which is earned itself. The rate of return is, therefore, not some kind of 'natural' return; it is almost always a direct result of the political choices which have been made by the government on behalf of the society it serves and are implicit in the rules it has set. For this reason, it is not legitimate to portray individuals as if they are entitled to money (earned or unearned) which they have acquired before the government 'interferes'.

In *The Myth of Ownership: Taxes and Justice*, philosophers Thomas Nagel and Liam Murphy strongly contest the legitimacy of the neoliberal myth of taxation being the theft by the state of 'my money'. They articulate a social justice model of taxation which is based on an ethical justification. What would actually constitute an entitlement to property and pre-tax income in a complex and interconnected society?

They explain:

If the political debate were not over how much of what is

mine the government should take in taxes, but over how the laws, including the tax system, should determine what is to count as mine, it would not end disagreements over the merits of redistribution and public provision but it would change their form. The question would become what values we want to uphold and reflect in our collectively enacted system of property rights – how much weight should be given to the alleviation of poverty and the provision of equal chances; how much to ensuring that people reap the rewards and penalties for their effort or lack thereof; how much to leaving people free of interference in their voluntary interactions.

In a complex and interconnected society, the equity of distribution of the social product between that which is in private control and that which is controlled by the government – and by analogy subject to the democratic decision-making of law-makers – is a wholly legitimate area for the government to concern itself with. We know that in Scandinavian countries more of this social product is provided collectively than is the case in low-tax Britain or the USA. That is a political choice, pure and simple. After an era in which we have witnessed the remorseless march of greater and greater inequality and the hoarding of vast fortunes in just a few hands, we are long overdue for the revival of a social justice model of taxation.

A HEALTHY ETHICAL SOCIETY

Tax is just one part of the economy. Throughout this book we have argued that the economy as a whole needs to review and renew its ethical base. We are not just individuals. We all have responsibilities to each other; the realm of public ethics cannot stop at the door to the boardroom. Market fundamentalism has erroneously tried to claim that a company's only responsibility is to maximise the profit of its shareholders. This has inculcated a spirit of short-termism and rapaciousness that has itself changed the nature of the private sector. It has seen market sectors consolidate into oligopolies and, in some cases, monopolies of companies that are 'too big to fail'. The world's mega-corporations are now so powerful that they believe they can force governments to kneel before them. It is not too late to change direction. Their arrogant disregard could be challenged by reaching international agreements on tax and enforcing effective regulations for global companies. No longer would they be able to avoid their responsibilities by playing one jurisdiction off against another. Regulating the tech behemoths so that they cannot abstract themselves from responsibility for the content they disseminate is another crucial step. We also agree with the creator of the World Wide Web, Tim Berners-Lee, that we need a Magna Carta for the internet. A digital bill of rights which will support the freedom and privacy of digital citizens worldwide. This will protect us all from the tech giants' commercial inclinations to control the internet and the mass surveillance – be it by companies or governments – which is currently technically possible and proceeding apace.

We are firm believers in the ingenuity and inventiveness of British people. The complaint that Britain invents things and America then 'monetises' them, making them profitable, has more than a little truth to it. Penicillin, the World Wide Web, and countless other technological breakthroughs have been made in British universities and research facilities, but only successfully marketed when in foreign hands. That is in part because Britain has been poor at helping its inventors become entrepreneurs, and so they seek a foreign corporation or foreign capital to get going. A successful knowledge economy needs government to place a defensive fence around its inventors and smooth the transition to market so that our society benefits from its inventiveness. We need to manage our market sectors by challenging uncompetitive and greedy monopolies that take advantage of their workers and customers. We need strong unions and for the voices of workers to be heard in the boardrooms and in Parliament to ensure that the jobs created by the private sector pay well and are fulfilling and rewarding. An indebted, stressed, ill workforce – for that is what Britain is becoming – will not have the confidence or the resources to purchase the goods we produce or to prosper in the modern world. A resurgent, strengthened, emboldened Whitehall, intervening strategically in our economy more actively, nimbly and confidently, can help make our economy more effective and fairer during this time of profound change. Inclusive growth must help those who are currently left out first. It must rebalance our skewed economy and reach beyond the south. Government must leave behind the 'private good/public bad' dogma that has done so much damage. It sought to destroy the public-sector ethos of service and commercialise the provision of everything. Civil servants are urged to think like the private sector, with armies of management consultants bringing their incredibly expensive 'wisdom' into local and central government. In the insatiable search for 'efficiency', the other 'e's' of government – equity and equality – are being abandoned.

Democratic socialists will need to remake the case for these changes in the way we think of tax and the kind of society we wish to create. They are huge and fundamental. It will only happen if we work together to do it. Other European countries, like Germany and the Scandinavian economies, have created models of governance that produce greater harmony between labour and capital, with higher tax bases funding a better quality of life and happier, more productive citizens. In Germany, the trade unions and the private sector form collaborative relationships. Workers have a voice, they sit on company boards. More women need to be in the boardroom where key decisions are made, which fundamentally changes the nature of the debate within the key decision-making bodies of their companies. And governments need to act as confident conductors of the orchestra of modern life. Our behaviour matters. The way we conduct ourselves matters. We need to renew our veneration of knowledge and facts, of the expertise gained through hard work. We need to be motivated by a sense of shared nationhood, of simple love and empathy for all humankind. Competition is an important aspect of human behaviour but left in an ethical vacuum it can become destructive. The greatest societies create the context in which all their members can flourish. And as democratic socialists in the British Labour Party, we are committed to ending the New Serfdom. As our constitution states, we know that

> by the strength of our common endeavour we achieve more than we achieve alone, so as to create for each of us the means to realise our true potential and for all of us a community in which power, wealth and opportunity are in the hands of the many, not the few, where the rights we enjoy reflect the duties we owe, and where we live together, freely, in a spirit of solidarity, tolerance and respect.

In other words, we need to organise our society 'to secure for the workers by hand or by brain the full fruits of their industry and the most equitable distribution thereof'.

Now, that's not a bad place to begin.

ENDNOTES

1   Indeed, homeownership is the primary component of wealth growth in Britain. The Social Market Foundation has found that more than 14 million working-age adults are not saving at all, and more than 26 million adults did not hold rainy-day or pension savings.

2   http://www.endviolenceagainstwomen.org.uk/a-different-world-is-possible/

3   Clause IV until 1995.

4   https://labour.org.uk/about/labours-legacy/

5   That figure rises to twenty-seven years if Labour's participation in the National Government, which guided Britain through the perils of the Second World War, is included in the total.

6   Organization of the Petroleum Exporting Countries.

7   Accelerationist Manifesto: http://criticallegalthinking.com/2013/05/14/accelerate-manifesto-for-an-accelerationist-politics/

8   For a compelling account of the activities of Hayek's Mont Pelerin Society, see Philip Mirowski, *Never Let a Serious Crisis Go to Waste: How Neoliberalism Survived the Financial Meltdown* (London, New York: Verso, 2013).

9   Though revisions to data may change this.

10 The detail of the IFS report can be viewed here: https://www.ifs.org.uk/publications/8706

11 Klaus Schwab, Executive Chair of World Economic Forum, *Foreign Affairs*, 12 December 2015

12 Erik Brynjolfsson and Andrew McAfee, *The Second Machine Age: Work, Progress, and Prosperity in a Time of Brilliant Technologies* (New York: W. W. Norton & Co., 2014)

13 According to Chris Mack, of VLSI Research, 400 billion billion (4×10^{20}) transistors were made in 2015 alone. That is 13 trillion a second.

14 Hermann Hauser, a tech entrepreneur and Fellow of the Royal Society, the Institute of Physics and of the Royal Academy of Engineering and an Honorary Fellow of King's College, Cambridge. Darwin Lecture, 6 March 2015.

15 The Common Era commenced after the birth of Christ.

16 As of 21 February 2018.

17 Andy Haldane, speech to the TUC, 2015.

18 Ibid.

19 Ibid.

20 Bank of England blog, 'Bank Underground', 1 March 2017.

21 *The Guardian*, 12 September 2017. https://www.theguardian.com/books/2017/sep/12/amazon-pays-11-times-less-corporation-tax-than-traditional-booksellers?CMP=share_btn_tw

22 https://www.theguardian.com/technology/2017/oct/04/facebook-uk-corporation-tax-profit?CMP=share_btn_tw

23 This paltry prosecution activity is despite analysis showing suspicious correlations of dealing in the market ahead of the announcements of profit warnings or attempted takeovers which impact the share price. It had to be obtained by a freedom of information request. https://www.thetimes.co.uk/article/city-traders-getting-away-with-abuse-of-markets-3czmo7nkp

24 For a superb discussion of this, see John Kay, *The Truth About Markets: Why Some Nations are Rich But Most Remain Poor* (London: Penguin, 2004).

25 According to Josie Cox in *The Independent*: http://www.independent.co.uk/voices/worlds-richest-are-getting-richer-general-population-stress-bez-os-gates-facebook-zuckerberg-a8129936.html

26 Irving Fisher, 'Economists in Public Service: Annual Address of the President', *American Economic Review*, Vol. 9, No. 1 (March 1919): 5–21. Quoted in Thomas Piketty's *Capital in the Twenty-First Century*.

27 The Panama Papers were leaked to the international consortium of investigative journalists and the German newspaper *Suddeutsche Zeitung* and can be searched here: https://panamapapers.icij.org/

28 The International Consortium of Investigative Journalists has made the Paradise Papers available here: https://www.icij.org/investigations/paradise-papers/paradise-papers-long-twilight-struggle-offshore-secrecy/

29 Deputy Commissioner of the Australian Tax Office, 16 January 2018: https://www.theguardian.com/news/2018/jan/15/paradise-papers-revealed-commoditisation-of-tax-evasion-australia

30 The details of the Luxembourg leak of 28,000 pages of documents involving 1,000 businesses operating in Europe can be seen here: https://www.icij.org/investigations/luxembourg-leaks/

31 Nikolaj Nielsen, *EUObserver*, 7 December 2016: https://euobserver.com/economic/136175

32 https://www.gov.uk/government/uploads/system/uploads/attachment_data/file/655097/HMRC-measuring-tax-gaps-2017.pdf

33 https://www.ukpublicspending.co.uk/uk_budget_detail_17bt12016n_20504070#ukgs303

34 http://www.bbc.co.uk/news/business-19967397

35 http://www.unionhistory.info/timeline/1960_2000_Narr_Display.php?Where=NarTitle+contains+ per cent27Anti-Union+Legislation per cent3A+1980-2000 per cent27

Between 1980 and 2000, the TUC records that there were six hostile Acts of Parliament restricting trade union activity and making it increasingly difficult for unions to strike legally or effectively in defence of their members and smothering them in administrative burdens and red tape which would not be contemplated for any other organisation in society.

36 See a discussion on this: https://link.springer.com/chapter/10.1007/978-1-349-25991-5_12

37 Cameron Tait for the Fabian Society commenting on economists Alan Manning and Maarten Goos's characterisation of the segmented modern labour market: 'What's really happening in the world of work?' http://www.fabians.org.uk/whats-really-happening-in-the-world-of-work/

38 TUC Budget submission 2017.

39 TUC, 'Living on the edge: the rise of job insecurity in modern Britain', 2016: https://www.tuc.org.uk/sites/default/files/Living per cent20on per cent20the per cent20Edge per cent202016.pdf

40 The TUC expresses its unease at the nature of the new 'full-time jobs' being created in 2017. ONS figures show that of the 118,000 new jobs created, 104,000 were categorised as 'self-employed'. https://www.theguardian.com/business/2016/jul/20/jobs-self-employment-workers-rights-tuc-uk-economy

41 As reported in detail here: https://www.theguardian.com/business/2016/jul/18/how-hermes-couriers-shoulder-insecurity-of-internet-shopping-boom

42 Taken aback by the scale of the revolt, Deliveroo has claimed that they will now only *trial* the switch away from an hourly rate to a per-parcel payment. The general view is that the switch will be made, not least by introducing new contracts for new workers.

43 See BBC: http://www.bbc.co.uk/news/business-38931211

A plumber who had worked exclusively for the business for six years was ruled to have employment rights despite his apparent self-employed status. In August 2017, Pimlico Plumbers was given permission to appeal this decision to the Supreme Court. The case has been heard but at the time of writing no decision has been issued.

44 Against this run of favourable judgments for workers, Deliveroo won a case at the Central Arbitration Committee which confirmed that their delivery staff were to be regarded as self-employed. This was because the company has enabled a capacity to swap jobs between staff and the court found evidence that it was used. https://www.theguardian.com/business/2017/nov/14/deliveroo-couriers-minimum-wage-holiday-pay. The IGWG has also submitted a claim for the national minimum wage to an employment tribunal; a decision is awaited.

45 The Resolution Foundation: 'A matter of time – the rise in zero hours contracts' by M. Pennycook, G. Cory and V. Alakerson, June 2013: http://www.resolutionfoundation.org/app/uploads/2014/08/A_Matter_of_Time_-_The_rise_of_zero-hours_contracts_final_1.pdf

46 https://www.theguardian.com/business/2015/dec/09/how-sports-direct-effectively-pays-below-minimum-wage-pay

47 http://economia.icaew.com/en/news/december-2016/fortnum-and-mason-proposes-staff-pay-cut-in-exchange-for-tips

48 https://www.theguardian.com/money/2018/jan/02/members-club-backed-by-lord-ashcroft-seeks-to-cut-staffs-basic-pay

49 *Daily Mirror*, 25 November 2017.

50 The Taylor Report, 'Good work: a review of modern working practices', can be read here: https://www.gov.uk/government/uploads/system/uploads/attachment_data/file/627671/good-work-taylor-review-modern-working-practices-rg.pdf

51 The Transfer of Undertakings (Protection of Employment) Regulations 2006, known as TUPE, is a part of EU employment law which guarantees certain rights to existing workers in the event of a transfer of employment. It ensures that there can be no dismissals and that pay and conditions have to remain substantially the same. It also provides workers with the right to be informed and consulted before, during and after the transfer from one employer to another.

52 http://www.labourexploitation.org/news/uk-falling-behind-labour-inspection-combat-modern-slavery-new-flex-policy-blueprint

53 GLA annual report 2015/16. The latest available: http://www.gla.gov.uk/media/2834/gla-annual-report-and-accounts-2015-16-pdf.pdf

54 Discovered by Labour and reported here: https://www.theguardian.com/business/2016/aug/14/employment-agency-standards-inspectorate-worker-rights-watchdog-labour

55 This NAO report gives a good account of the work of the inspectorate, including its relatively recent naming-and-shaming capacity: NAO: https://www.nao.org.uk/wp-content/uploads/2016/05/Ensuring-employers-comply-National-Minimum-Wage-regulations.pdf

56 This is a TUC estimate.

57 For a superb if somewhat technical discussion of the ratio between capital and labour, see Chapter 6 of *Capital in the Twenty-First Century* by Thomas Picketty, p. 199 (The Belknap Press of Harvard University Press, 2014).

58 See TUC touchstone pamphlet, 'How to boost the wage share', especially Figure 1 on p. 6: https://www.tuc.org.uk/sites/default/files/tucfiles/How per cent2oto per cent2oBoost per cent2othe per cent2oWage per cent2oShare.pdf

59 The economic case for trade unions: http://gala.gre.ac.uk/14102/1/PB052015_Onaran_etal.pdf

60 Annex to 'Industrial Strategy – First Review', the second report of session 2016/17, HC 616.

61 IFS response to the November 2017 Budget, 23 November 2017: https://www.ifs.org.uk/events/1538

OBR: http://budgetresponsibility.org.uk/efo/economic-fiscal-outlook-november-2017/

62 https://www.theguardian.com/business/2017/sep/18/britain-debt-timebomb-fca-chief-crisis?CMP=share_btn_tw

63 The sobering report can be read here: http://www.oecd.org/edu/skills-beyond-school/building-skills-for-all-review-of-england.pdf

64 https://www.gov.uk/government/uploads/system/uploads/attachment_data/file/34749/12-986-closing-rdas-lessons-from-transition-and-closure-pro-gramme.pdf
It is notable that this document concerns itself with the process of closure. Never once does it attempt to assess whether the closure decision was the correct one or attempt to assess its effect on the prospects for regional development.

65 https://www.liverpoollep.org/about-lep/lcr-governance/

66 'Shaping the future of UK Manufacturing – A Unite Strategy', 2016; 'Making it – Campaigning for manufacturing jobs': www.making-it.org.uk

67 J. Dromey and C. McNeil, 'Skills 2030: Why the adult skills system is failing to build an economy that works for everyone,' IPPR, 2017: http://www.ippr.org/publications/skills-2030-why-the-adult-skills-system-is-failing

68 Edmund Burke: *Reflections on the Revolution in France* felt that the French Revolution had thrown off 'the yoke of law and morals' and was close to anarchy. In sometimes lurid terms, he warned the British public against supporting its principles, which he said could only lead to ruin.

69 Thomas Paine, *The Rights of Man*, 1791. Writing two years after the start of the French Revolution, Thomas Paine defended the gains of liberty, equality and fraternity which the revolution had emphasised. He argued that popular revolution was justified if the government did not safeguard the natural rights of the people. His book was written as a riposte to the attack that Edmund Burke had made on the French Revolution a year earlier.

70 Martha Nussbaum, *Political Emotions: Why Love Matters for Justice* (Cambridge, MA: Harvard University Press, 2013). Like Rousseau and others before her, Nussbaum sees emotions as involving thoughts and imagination.

71 Martha Nussbaum, 'Compassion: The Basic Social Emotion', *Social Philosophy and Policy*, Vol. 13, No. 1 (1996): 27–58.

72 *The Possibility of Altruism* was his first major work.

73 Nagel, 'Limits', p. 138. Nagel discusses the 'problem of utopianism' in *Equality and Partiality*, but makes clear that he sees a role for 'imagining the moral future' as a key feature of political philosophy (Nagel, *Equality*, p. 6).

74 Thomas Nagel, *The Possibility of Altruism* (Princeton: Princeton University Press, 1978), p. 14.

75 World Economic Forum Gender Inequality Report 2017. The report, which has been published annually since 2006, benchmarks 144 countries across four areas: health, education, economy and politics. While the picture is mixed, there has been a deterioration for the first time since the index was established. It can be seen here: http://www3.weforum.org/docs/WEF_GGGR_2017.pdf

INDEX

accelerationism 189–93
Accenture Strategy
  UK University
    Graduate Employ-
    ment Study (2017) 52
Age UK 111
Agenda 2030 vii
Allende, Salvador 284
alt right movement 191
Alter, Adam 128
Alternative Economic
  Strategy (AES) 181–4
alternative facts 225
Alternative für
  Deutschland (AfD) 338
Amazon.com 196, 234,
  292–3
Anderson, Benedict
  Imagined Communities
  156
Apple Inc.
  iPhone 223–4, 254
Arab Spring 195
Armstrong, Neil 223
Ashcroft, Lord 292
Assheton, Ralph 6–7
Association of Directors
  of Adult Social
  Services 100–101
Atlantic, The 301
Attlee, Clement xvi, xxi,
  7, 26, 82–3, 89, 182–3,
  187–8, 216

austerity 38, 71, 87, 152,
  166, 188, 195, 208–9,
  211–13, 238, 249
Austria 102
  Vienna 3
Austria-Hungary 3
Aviva
  Health Check UK
    Report (2014) 116

Bailey, Andrew 312
Baker, Prof Maureen
  116–17
Bank of England 231–2
Bannon, Steve 191
bedroom tax 75–6
Beecroft, Adrian 294–5
Bell, Andy 131
Benn, Hilary 76
Benn, Tony 182
Berners-Lee, Sir Tim
  196–7, 358
Bernstein, Eduard
  Evolutionary Socialism
  171
Beveridge Report (1942)
  xxi, 6
Beveridge, William 25–6,
  41, 66, 70, 82, 135, 138,
  202, 216, 235–6
  Full Employment in
    a Free Society
    58–9

Social Insurance and
  Allied Services 57
Bezos, Jeff 266, 292–3
Big Bang (1986) 271–2,
  297, 318
bioscience 220–21
Blair, Tony xii, xxi–xxii,
  83, 93, 170
Bloomberg 293
  Billionaires Index 205
Blue Labour 189, 203–4
BMJ Open 98
Boer War (1899–1902) 211
Boles, Nick 260
Bolivia 266
Boyle, Danny 89
Bradley, Lord 131
Branson, Sir Richard 200
Breitbart 191, 273
Bretton Woods
  Conference 271
Brexit referendum (2016)
  xv, xx, xxii, 22, 225, 230,
  248, 276, 294–5, 307, 311,
  338, 343
Britain First 150–51
British Broadcasting
  Corporation (BBC)
  61, 195, 341, 343
  Newsnight 240
British East India
  Company 247
British Empire 21

British Medical Research Council 91
British Social Attitudes Survey 38, 51
Brown, Gordon 77, 93, 103, 125, 288
Buckley, William 260–62
Burke, Edmund 334
Business Insider 128
Butler, Richard Austen 'Rab' 59

Cable, Vince 305–6
Cacioppo, John 111
Callaghan, James 181, 183, 185
Cambridge Economic Policy Group 182, 184
Cambridge University 66, 98
Cameron, David xvii, 11, 39, 78, 82, 115, 294
  Big Society 108, 200
Campaign to End Loneliness 111, 114
Campbell, Alastair 126
capitalism 30, 170, 172–3, 177, 189–90, 269
  laissez-faire 162, 180, 205, 265
  post- 189, 194
Care Act (2014) 112
Carillion
  collapse of (2018) 237, 325
Carpenter, Edward 161
Castle, Barbara 141
Catholic Church 143
Cato Institute 275
Centre for Mental Health 130–31
Chartered Institute of Personnel and Development xx

Chartists 19
Child and Adolescent Mental Health Services 130
Children Act (1948) 82
Chile
  coup d'état (1973) 284
China, People's Republic of 80–81, 232
  People's Liberation Army 93
Christianity 151, 172, 252
  Bible 252
Church of England 143, 150
Churchill, Winston 6–7, 351
Cisco Systems 221
civil service 288
Clark, Greg 306
Clean200 80–81
Climate Action Network 78
Climate Change Act 187, 318–20
Climate Change Performance Index 78
Clinton, Hillary 140
Clunis, Christopher 124
coalition government (2010–2015) 208, 211, 240, 283–4
cognitive therapy 122
Cold War 188–9
Commission on Social Justice xxi–xxii, 45, 82, 138
common mental disorder (CMD) 127–8
Commonwealth of Nations 341
Communication Workers Union (CWU) 307

communism 188, 193, 251–2
  fully automated luxury 197–9
  luxury 194, 199–200
Communist Party of Great Britain 174
Community 307
Conservative Party (Tories) xi, xvii, 5, 10, 26–7, 38, 50–51, 59, 65, 68–9, 86–7, 97, 105, 112–13, 132–3, 143, 164, 176, 178–9, 182, 184, 212, 240, 260, 262, 274, 283–5, 294–5, 306, 308, 328, 351–2
  electoral victory of (1951) 8–9
  ideology of 41
Copenhagen Agreement 78
Corbyn, Jeremy 339
Cranfield School of Management 142
Credit Suisse
  Global Wealth Report 224
Crime and Disorder Act (1998) 85–6
Criminal Justice Act (1948) 82
Cripps, Francis 182
Cripps, Sir Stafford 174
Crisis 133
Crosland, Anthony 175, 178
  Future of Socialism, The 177, 179–80

Daily Mail 15
D'Ancona, Matthew 13
Davidson, Ruth 13
Deliveroo 234, 287
Denmark 78, 142

Department of Labour
298–9
devolution
taxation powers 276
Devonshire Club 292
Dick, Philip K. 192–3
Dickens, Charles 25,
162, 291
Directory of Social
Change 142
Drucker, Peter
Post-Capitalist Society
194
Dyson 274

Economic and Finance
Council (Ecofin) 139
Economic and Social
Research Council 128
Education Act (1944)
58–9
Educational Maintenance
Allowance (EMA)
86–7
Egypt
Revolution (2011) 196
Employment Agency
Standards Inspectorate
295
End Violence Against
Women Coalition 140
Engels, Friedrich 161
Enlightenment 157,
333–5, 340, 347
Environment Council 139
Environment, Food
and Rural Affairs
Committee 81
Equal Pay Act (1970) 141
Equality Act (2010) 144,
213, 343
Estonia 102
European Common
Market 181

European Union (EU)
27, 31, 68, 82, 91, 275,
279, 294–5, 305, 318,
327–8, 341
Commission 234–5
Council of Ministers
139
Gender Equality
Index 142
member states of 274
Working Time
Directive 53

Fabian Society 161, 164,
172, 175
Facebook 117–18, 150,
156, 224, 279
fascism 193
Fawcett Society 343
Financial Conduct
Authority 241, 312
Financial Times 74
Finland 349
First World War (1914–18)
3, 8, 166, 172, 264, 351
Battle of the Somme
(1917) 172
Fisher, Irving 269
Fortnum & Mason 291–2
Fortune 500 247
France 54, 142
Belle Epoch 265
National Assembly 335
Revolution (1789–99)
161, 334–5
Francis, Pope 36
Friedman, Milton 201
*Capitalism and
Freedom* 200
Front National 338
FTSE100 Stock Index 33
Fukuyama, Francis
'End of History?,
The' 188

Full Fact 77
Further and Higher Edu-
cation Act (1992) 59

Gamergate 140
Gangmasters and Labour
Abuse Authority
(GLAA) 293, 295
general election (2017)
13–14
General Strike (1926) 284
Germany 55, 68, 81, 102,
137, 359
fall of Berlin Wall
(1989) 188–9, 251–2
Germanwatch 78
Giddens, Anthony 185–6
gig economy 286–7
global financial crisis
(2007–9) 206, 271–2,
313–14, 317
US subprime mortgage
crisis xix
Global Justice Network
247
globalisation 114, 176,
185–6
GMB 307
Godley, Wynne 182
Google Inc. 224, 235, 254
Gmail 224
Gore, Al 80
Gorz, André
Paths to Paradise 202
Gove, Michael 62, 65
Grand National
Consolidated Trade
Union (GNCTU) 168
Great Depression 134,
205–6
Greece 195, 208
Greenwich Political
Economy Research
Centre 299

Grenfell Tower disaster
(2017) 71, 352
Griffiths, Peter 145–6
Group of Eight (G8) 277
Group of Seven (G7)
139, 313–14
Group of Twenty (G20)
139, 277
London Summit
(2009) 206
Washington Summit
(2008) 206
Guardian, The 111, 116,
128, 131, 290–91
Gurría, Angel 36

Haldane, Andy 51–2
Hammond, Philip 347
Hardie, Keir 19, 170–71
Hauser, Hermann
concept of 'general
purpose
technologies'
(GPTs) 222
Hay, Prof Colin
Why We Hate Politics
337–8
Hayek, Friedrich xvi–xvii,
xxii, 3–4, 9–12, 15–16,
27, 37, 40, 55, 67–8,
71, 107–8, 119, 134–5,
176, 205, 214, 242, 248,
260–62, 279–80, 299,
303–4, 321, 352
Fatal Conceit: The Errors
of Socialism, The 303
Mont Pelerin Society
192
Road to Serfdom, The
4–6, 12–13, 180
1980s Unemployment
and the Unions 284
Health and Social Care
Act (2012) 125

Health and Social Care
Information Centre 98
Heath, Edward 176, 181–2
Her Majesty's Revenue
and Customs (HMRC)
239, 277–8, 280, 296
Heritage Foundation
273, 275
Hermes 286–7
Herzl, Theodor 3
Hitler, Adolf 3–4
Hobbes, Thomas 334
Hodgskin, Thomas 169
Hoover, Herbert 205, 270
Hopkins, Katie 150
Hume, David 334
Hungary 102
Hunt, Tristram 62
Hurd, Nick 83–4
Hutton, Will 242, 244

Improving Access to
Psychological Therapy
(IAPT) 125
Independent Labour
Party (ILP) 164–5, 174
Independent Workers
Union of Great
Britain 287
India 232
Industrial Relations Act
182
Industrial Revolution
52, 163–4, 226–7, 304
First 217–18, 229–30
Fourth 199, 217–19,
231–2, 234–5, 249,
310–11, 329
Third 228–9, 236
'Industrial Strategy:
building a Britain fit
for the future' (2017)
307–8
Instagram 116, 118, 128

Institute for Fiscal
Studies (IFS) 141, 214
Institute for Jewish Policy
Research 150
Institute for Public Policy
Research (IPPR) 68–9,
316, 329–30
Commission on Eco-
nomic Justice 28, 310
Commission on Social
Justice 124–5
Time for Change: A
New Vision for the
British Economy 28
Institute of Employment
Rights 290, 299–300
Manifesto for Labour
Law: Towards a
Comprehensive
Review of Workers'
Rights 300
Intel Corporation 223
International Journal of
Epidemiology 54
International Labour
Organization (ILO) 205
International Monetary
Fund (IMF) 36, 267–9,
277, 346
Half Yearly Fiscal
Monitor 267
internships 50–51
Interpol 279–80
Islam
persecution of 150, 335
Italy 54, 102, 257

Japan 81, 220, 315
Javid, Sajid 134, 306
John Birch Society 275
Jones, Kevan 126
Joseph Rowntree
Foundation (JRF) 38,
61–2, 114

Judaism 151
persecution of 3, 137,
150, 335

Kay, John
concept of 'American
Business Model'
251–3
*Truth About Markets,
The* 253
Keynes, John Maynard
8, 26, 58, 178, 180, 206
Khan, Sadiq 81
Koch Brothers 274
Kyoto protocol (1997) 318

Labour Force Survey 49,
289–90
Labour Party xi–xiii,
xvii, xxii–xxiii, 8–9, 17,
19–20, 38, 41, 44–5, 76,
87–8, 100, 107, 112–13,
163, 165–6, 169–70, 172,
176–7, 184, 196, 208–10,
228, 259–60, 283–4, 318,
322, 339, 341–2, 360
Clause I 166
Clause IV 20–21, 164
Constituency Labour
Parties 165
Decent Homes
Standard 71–2
electoral victory of
(1997) xxi
healthcare policies of 95
ideology of 17–22, 31,
173–4
National Executive
Committee xi
National Policy Forum
xi
New Labour xxi, 34,
86, 124–5, 143, 153,
177, 187–8, 194, 339

Parliamentary Labour
Party (PLP) xii
Labour Representation
Committee 165
Lafargue, Paul 41
Lawrence, Stephen 146
Lawson, Nigel 258, 270
Layard, Lord Richard 125
Le Pen, Marine 156, 338
League of Nations 278
Lee, Jennie 70
Lehman Brothers
collapse of (2008) 206
Leicester University 127
Lesbians and Gays
Support the Miners
(LGSM) 170
Levellers 19
LGBT equality rights
movement 142–5,
153, 170, 187, 203, 335
Liberal Democrats 59,
82, 209–10, 228, 259,
283–4, 323
Liberal Party 6, 164
libertarianism 197, 207,
250, 264, 274
Lithuania 102
Lloyd George, David 8
Lloyds of London 80
Local Economic
Partnerships (LEPs) 324
Local Government Act
(2003) 143
Local Government
Association 100–101
London Olympics (2012)
89
London School of
Economics (LSE)
4, 49, 58, 125
Lowndes, G. A. N.
*Silent Social Revolution,
The* 57–8

Luxembourg 275
Luxembourg leaks 239–40
Lyons, Sir Michael 76

McDonald's 93
McKinsey 105–6
Macmillan, Harold 204
Macpherson Report 146
Major, John 34, 203
Manchester Cares 113
Manchester University
54, 290
Mandelson, Lord Peter 305
market fundamentalism
14–15, 27, 30–32, 42,
118, 129, 135, 176, 182,
185, 187–90, 192, 196,
200–201, 205, 207–8,
210, 229–30, 238, 240,
245, 248–50, 264–5,
283–5, 355–6
Marmot, Sir Michael 103
Marx, Karl 14, 29, 43–4, 53,
169, 192–3, 247
*Communist Manifesto,
The* 43, 170
Das Kapital 44, 170
Grundrisse 43
Marxism 41, 169, 171
Marxist Social Demo-
cratic Federation 164
Maslow, Abraham 29
hierarchy of needs
29–30
Mason, Paul 196
*PostCapitalism: A Guide
to Our Future* 195
May, Theresa 13, 100, 115,
147, 306
Mazzucato, Mariana
*Entrepreneurial State:
Debunking Public vs.
Private Sector Myths,
The* 253–4

Mental Health Act 123
Mental Health
  Foundation 52–3,
  109–10, 116, 126, 134
Merseyside Authority
  324
Metropolitan Police 146
Microsoft Corporation
  224
Milburn, Alan 48–9, 153
Miliband, Ed 78–9, 125
Militant Shop Stewards'
  Movement 182
Militant Tendency 174
Monbiot, George
  Breaking the Spell of
    Loneliness 111
Moniz, Egas 122
Moore, Gordon
  Moore's Law 223
Morris, William 161
multisystemic therapy
  (MST) 85
Murphy, Liam
  Myth of Ownership:
    Taxes and Justice,
    The 356–7
Musk, Elon
  SpaceX 198–9
Muslim Council of
  Britain 143

Nagel, Thomas 340–41
  Myth of Ownership:
    Taxes and Justice,
    The 356–7
Napoleonic Wars
  (1803–15) 210, 312
NatCen Social Research
  Adult Psychiatric
  Morbidity Study
  127
National Audit Office
  (NAO) 40, 101, 132

National Centre for
  Social Research
  British Social Attitudes
    Survey 46–7, 53–4
National Government 179
National Health Service
  (NHS) xiii, 8, 15, 30, 77,
  92, 96–100, 104, 113, 119,
  121, 123, 126–8, 175, 177,
  187, 211, 259–60, 304
  A&E waiting times
    94–6, 101
  Five Year Forward
    View 101–2
  funding of 102–3, 106
  impact of 89–91
  NHS Direct 95–6
  spending on 91–2, 97
National Institute of
  Education 62
National Living Wage
  296
National Minimum
  Wage 188, 296
national socialism 4
National Union of Mine-
  workers (NUM) 170
National Union of
  Teachers (NUT) 61
Netherlands 257
  Holland 142, 315
New Economics
  Foundation 299
New Statesman 83
New York University 128
New Zealand vii–viii, 349
Niemöller, Martin 137–8
Nietzsche, Friedrich 191
Norris, Stephen 185
North London Cares 113
Norway 102, 279
NRK 190
Nussbaum, Martha
  339–40

Obama, Barack 36
Obesity and Ill-Health
  Industry 105–6
Ofcom 63–4
Office for Budget
  Responsibility (OBR)
  311–12, 314–15
Office for National
  Statistics (ONS) 32, 45,
  48, 54, 73–4, 89, 101, 113,
  286, 325
Office of Government
  Commerce (OGC)
  326–7
offshore financial centres
  (OFCs) 273
O'Grady, Frances 141
Open University 188
  founding of (1969)
  69–70
Operation Black Vote
  147–8
Organisation for
  Economic Co-
  operation and
  Development (OECD)
  36, 61, 93–4, 102, 105,
  141, 232, 277, 314
  Programme for
    International
    Student Assessment
    (PISA) 60, 62
Organization of
  Petroleum Exporting
  Countries (OPEC) 180
Orwell, George 5, 280–81
Osborne, George xviii, 11,
  108, 232, 347, 349
  'Emergency Budget'
    (2010) 188, 208–12,
    324
Owen, Robert 20, 161, 178
  New Lanark model
    community 167

Oxford University xi, 9, 66
 Citi study 232–3
 Conservative Association 9

Paine, Thomas 334
Panama Papers (2016) 239–40, 273
Paradise Papers (2017) 273, 355
Paris Climate Accord (2015) 318–20
Parliament xii–xiii, 151–2, 155, 166, 168, 171, 216, 243, 283, 322, 344, 359
 Equality and Human Rights Commission (EHRC) 143–4, 152, 212–13
 Health Select Committee 96
 House of Commons 77, 167, 348–9
 House of Lords 76, 143–4
 Public Accounts Committee 280, 326
 Women and Equalities Select Committee 140, 155
Parris, Matthew 13
Patients Association 99
patriotism 353
 civic 353–4
Pickett, Kate
 Spirit Level, The 35
Piketty, Thomas 266
 Capital in the Twenty-First Century 264–5
Pimlico Plumbers 287
Pinochet, General Augusto 284
Pinterest 117

Pizza Express 291
Poland 102
Polaris (missile system) 183
populism 3, 14, 16, 138, 230, 243
posttraumatic stress disorder (PTSD) 127
poverty 25–7, 33–4, 38, 188, 215
 pensioner 187
 structural 27
Prescott, John xii, 322
Presidents Club dinner controversy (2018) 348
Prison Reform Trust 131
Prospects 50
Protestantism 137
 Reformation 172
Public Services (Social Value) Act (2012) 328

Race Discrimination Act 149
Race Disparity Audit 147–8
Race Relations Act (1965) 146
Race Relations Act (1976) 146
racism 146–8, 153, 203
Rand, Ayn
 Atlas Shrugged 192
Rational Emotive Behaviour Therapy 122
Raworth, Kate
 Doughnut Economics 346
Rayner, Angela 70
 proposal for National Education Service 70, 301
Reagan, Ronald xvii, 187, 229, 270

Regional Development Agencies (RDAs) 322–4
 North West RDA 323
 One North East 323
 Yorkshire Forward 323
Resolution Foundation 32, 212, 289
 'A steady job?' 51
Rifkin, Jeremy 194
 Zero Marginal Cost Society, The 194–5
Robbins, Tracey 114
Roosevelt, Franklin D. 269–70
 New Deal 205–6, 270
Rousseau, Jean-Jacques
 Discourse on the Origin of Inequality 161–2
 theory of social contract 333–4
Royal College of Emergency Medicine 96
Royal College of General Practitioners 116–17
Royal Society for Public Health
 #StatusOfMind 129–30
Royal Society for the Arts 200
Russian Empire
 October Revolution (1917) 172, 264

Sainsbury, Lord David 67–8
Salisbury Convention 76
Scope 151
Second World War (1939–45) xvi–xvii, xxi, 32, 82, 89, 163, 175, 177, 181, 216, 264, 270–71, 352
 Holocaust 137
Section 28 (1988) 143

Selby, Alan 292
self-employment 28,
    47–8, 236, 286–8
    fake 52
Sex Discrimination Act
    (1975) 141
Shaftesbury Act (1845) 121
Singapore 62
Slovenia 102
Smith, Adam 41–2, 53
    *Theory of Moral
        Sentiments, The* 42–3
    *Wealth of Nations,
        The* 42
Smith, Alex 113
Smith, Andrew 185
Smith Institute 52
Snapchat 128
Social Affairs Council 139
Social Democrat Party
    (Germany)(SPD) 163
Social Democratic Party
    (SDP) 184
Social Market
    Foundation 63
Social Mobility and
    Child Poverty
    Commission 49, 153–4
socialism 4, 13, 20, 161,
    170–72, 216, 284
    corporate 182–3
    democratic xxi, 17, 58,
        103, 167, 172, 176–7,
        187, 230–31, 241–2.
        248–9, 262–3, 269,
        309, 333, 354–5,
        359–60
    utopian 178
Socialist League 174
South Africa
    apartheid 21
South Korea 315
South London Cares 113
Spectator, The 146–7

Sports Direct 290–91
Spread
    Technofarm 220
Srnicek, Nick
    *#Accelerate: Manifesto
        For An Accelerationist
        Politics* 192
Stalin, Joseph 3
Starbucks 230, 279
Stern Review 319
Stone, Oliver
    Wall Street 35
Stonewall 144
Sun, The 145
Sunday Mirror 292
Supreme Court 296
SureStart 15, 65, 85–6
Sutton Trust 64–5
Sweden 102, 142, 264
Switzerland 102

Tan, Clarissa 146–7
Tata Steel 306
tax competition 275–6
tax evasion 278–80
Tax Justice Network 277–8
Taxpayers Alliance 280
Tawney, R. H. 172–3, 186
    Equality 173
Taylor, Matthew 293
Tesco 142
Thatcher, Denis 9
Thatcher, Margaret xiii,
    xvii, 9–11, 14–16, 26–7,
    31, 34, 59, 107, 140, 155,
    176, 180, 182, 184, 187,
    190–91, 229, 250–51,
    275, 297, 306, 317, 328
    economic policies of
        12, 254–5, 268
    Right to Buy 73
Third Reich (1933–45) xvi,
    5, 179
    Gestapo 8

Third Way 176–7, 185–6
Time's Up movement 140
Times Higher Education
    World University
    Rankings 66–7
Times, The 11–12, 147–8, 284
Tobin tax 272
Tolpuddle Martyrs 168
TotallyMoney.com 53
Trade Union Act (2016)
    283
trade unions 11–14, 19, 27,
    32, 40, 51, 168, 174–5,
    307–10
Trades Union Congress
    (TUC) 53, 141, 285, 289,
    300, 307–8
    founding of 169
    'Living on the Margins'
        (2015) 149
    'Shaping Our Digital
        Future' 199
Tribune 174
Trident (missile system)
    183
Trotsky, Leon 3
Trump, Donald xv, xx, 156,
    191, 225, 230, 269, 338
Trussell Trust 213
Twitter 117–18, 156, 224, 348

Uber 234, 287
UCATT 288
UK Committee on
    Climate Change 320
UK Independence Party
    (UKIP) 150, 156
Unions21 300
UNISON 152, 290, 296,
    327
    Confederation of
        Health Service
        Employees
        (COHSE) 122, 124

Unite the Union 291
United Kingdom (UK)
vii, xi, xvii, xx, xxiii,
20, 28–30, 33–4, 37, 49,
52–3, 84–5, 94–5, 104,
106, 109–10, 123, 139,
141–2, 148, 164, 168–9,
178, 183–4, 196, 199, 202,
207, 215, 220, 227–8, 236,
238, 244–5, 251, 253, 257,
270, 285–6, 295–7, 303–5,
313, 315–18, 324–5, 333–4,
342, 357
    City of London 79–80,
        154
    Crown Dependencies
        239
    Department for
        Business, Energy
        and Industrial
        Strategy (BEIS)
        78–9, 81, 293, 306–8
    Department for
        Education 63
    Department for
        International
        Development 91
    Department for the
        Environment,
        Transport and the
        Regions 322
    Department of Energy
        and Climate Change
        (DECC) 78–9
    Department of Health
        91
    Department of Work
        and Pensions
        (DWP) 241
    education system of
        59–61, 66, 68, 314–15,
        329–31
    Home Office 131, 293
    housing market of 74–5

    labour market of 38–9
    London 50, 63, 71, 121,
        126, 155, 304, 315–16,
        321
    Manchester 134
    Milton Keynes 220
    Ministry of Health 123
    Northern Ireland 276
    prison system of 132–3
    Rochdale 168
    rough sleeping
        population of 132–3
    Scotland 276, 321
    Sheffield xi
    social security system
        of 37–8
    taxation system of 6, 10,
        14, 34, 48, 67, 71, 75, 92,
        100, 102, 106, 149, 152,
        181, 197, 200–201, 206,
        209–14, 218, 234–6,
        238–9, 241–5, 247, 252,
        257–9, 263–4, 268–9,
        276–7, 287–8, 355
    Treasury 139, 208, 238,
        321, 326, 347
    unemployment rates in
        45, 47–8, 54
    Wales 321
    welfare state 35
    Westminster 71
    Whitehall 298
United Nations (UN) 80
    Millennium
        Development
        Goals 272
    Universal Declaration
        of Human Rights
        21
United States of America
    (USA) 28–30, 54, 94,
    149–51, 167–8, 205, 229,
    232, 253, 266, 269–70,
    279, 357

    Banking Act (Glass-
        Steagall Act) (1933)
        206
    Congress 201
    Congressional
        Research Service 210
    Department of
        Defense 93
    Family Assistance Plan
        201
    healthcare policy in 31
    Hollywood 348
    House of
        Representatives 201
    Jim Crow laws 146
    Marshall Plan (1948)
        230
    Medicaid 200
    Medicare 200
    Pentagon 220
    Revolution (1765–83)
        275
    Silicon Valley 191, 197,
        200
    US Bureau of Labor
        Statistics 80
    Wall Street 191
    universal basic income
        200–202
    University College
        London 128
    University of Bristol 91
    University of Chicago 111
    University of Liverpool 128
    University of Manchester
        147
    University of Pittsburgh
        117

Vestager, Margrethe 275–6

Walker, Charles 126
Wall Street Crash (1929)
    205, 209, 269–70

Walmart 93

Walpole, Horace 335

Walpole, Sir Robert 335

Walt Disney Company 274

Warwick University Cybernetic Culture Research Unit (CCRU) 191

Washington Consensus 267

Watergate scandal 201

Webb, Beatrice 161

Webb, Sidney 161, 165, 178

Weinstein, Harvey 140

Whigs 334

Wilkinson, Richard
Spirit Level, The 35

Williams, Alex
#Accelerate: Manifesto for an Accelerationist Politics 192

Williams, Baroness Shirley 59

Wilson, Harold 69–70, 175–6, 179, 181, 188, 339

Wittgenstein, Ludwig 3

Wollstonecraft, Mary 334
A Vindication of the Rights of Men 334

Woman's Own 107

women's equality 142, 342, 347–50
pay gap 342–3

Woolley, Simon 147–8

World Economic Forum (WEF) 226, 233–4, 342

World Health Organization (WHO) 117, 129

World Trade Organization (WTO) General Procurement Agreement 328

Wynn's Act (1808) 121

Yom Kippur War (1973) 180

YouGov 144, 150, 156

Youth Justice Board 86

Youth Offending Teams 86–7

YouTube 224–5

zero hour contracts 289

Zito, Jonathan
murder of 124